The Rise of Aggressive Abolitionism

THE RISE OF AGGRESSIVE ABOLITIONISM

ADDRESSES TO THE SLAVES

STANLEY HARROLD

THE UNIVERSITY PRESS OF KENTUCKY

Publication of this volume was made possible in part by a grant
from the National Endowment for the Humanities.

Scholarly publisher for the Commonwealth,
serving Bellarmine University, Berea College, Centre
College of Kentucky, Eastern Kentucky University,
The Filson Historical Society, Georgetown College,
Kentucky Historical Society, Kentucky State University,
Morehead State University, Murray State University,
Northern Kentucky University, Transylvania University,
University of Kentucky, University of Louisville,
and Western Kentucky University.

Editorial and Sales Offices: The University Press of Kentucky
663 South Limestone Street, Lexington, Kentucky 40508-4008
www.kentuckypress.com

04 05 06 07 08 5 4 3 2 1

Library of Congress Cataloging-in-Publication Data
Harrold, Stanley.
The rise of aggressive abolitionism : addresses to the slaves /
Stanley Harrold.
p. cm.
Includes bibliographical references (p.) and index.
ISBN 0-8131-2290-2 (alk. paper)
1. Antislavery movements—United States—History—19th century. 2. Abolitionists—
United States—History—19th century. 3. Slave insurrections—Southern
States—History—19th century. 4. Violence—Southern States—History—19th
century. 5. Antislavery movements—United States—History—19th century—
Sources. 6. Abolitionists—United States—History—19th century—Sources.
7. Slave insurrections—Southern States—History—19th century—Sources.
8. Violence—Southern States—History—19th century—Sources. 9. Speeches,
addresses, etc., American. I. Title.
E449.H299 2004
326'.8'0973—dc21   2003008809

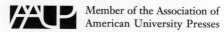

For Merton and Jim

CONTENTS

PREFACE

I think that one of the more fascinating aspects of American history is the interaction between reformers and those they seek to reform. During the decades prior to the Civil War, there were many northern social movements in which reformers attempted to benefit their neighbors by convincing them of the error of their ways. They dealt with such things as health, the consumption of alcoholic beverages, education, the treatment of criminals, the oppression of women, and the enslavement of African Americans. While advocates of temperance, public education, women's rights, and health reform argued that others in the North must change their views, so did those black and white northerners who advocated the abolition of slavery. Unlike other reformers, however, abolitionists could not reach their goal by merely changing opinion in the North. Rather they had to change the South. During the 1830s, they had hoped that their efforts in the North, supplemented by some direct appeals to slaveholders, would lead to peaceful emancipation. But when white southerners staunchly resisted reform and the progress of abolitionism in the North slowed, abolitionists began to consider the radical alternative of working directly with slaves.

Ever since I became aware, during the late 1980s, that abolitionists produced three Addresses to the Slaves during the early 1840s, I have wondered about the Addresses' significance. They seemed to suggest an aspect of the antislavery movement that had not been sufficiently explored, and they seemed to provide a starting point for understanding a reorientation of the antislavery movement toward the South that began during the 1840s. I now believe as well that they provide a means for better understanding the factional, gendered, and racial dynamics of the movement.

This book is the product of my search for the Addresses' significance. It includes an analysis of the Addresses, an investigation of the reaction to them, and an interpretation of what they show about the antislavery movement during the last two antebellum decades. The book also includes complete copies of the Addresses and two related documents.

My approach to the Addresses owes a great deal to Merton L. Dillon, who encouraged me to undertake this project, and to James Brewer Stewart, who suggested that my fascination with aggressive abolitionism might reveal a good deal about the movement's northern factions. I also thank Douglas R. Egerton, William C. Hine, John R. McKivigan, John W. Quist, John F. Zeigler, and the three anonymous readers employed by the University Press of Kentucky, all of whom read my manuscript and provided excellent advice.

INTRODUCTION

On three occasions during the early 1840s an American anti-slavery leader, speaking before a northern audience, claimed to address "the Slaves of the United States." Each did so, however, in a highly tentative manner. On January 19, 1842, Gerrit Smith, the wealthy white philanthropist who led political abolitionists in upstate New York, urged slaves to disregard state and federal law by escaping. But simultaneously he called on them to obey their masters and not use violent means. On May 31, 1843, William Lloyd Garrison, the most famous white abolitionist, proclaimed that in the name of the Declaration of Independence slaves might wade through their masters' blood if necessary to free themselves. But he added that it was too dangerous for northern abolitionists to go south to help them. On August 17, 1843, black abolitionist Henry Highland Garnet, a Presbyterian clergyman, advised faraway slaves that they had better die in confrontations with their oppressors than remain in bondage. But he then warned them against initiating revolt.[1]

The period stretching from before the War for Independence to after the Civil War produced a huge and varied antislavery literature that in turn has attracted the interest of anthropologists, historians, literary scholars, and sociologists. There are essays, letters, slave narratives, novels, plays, poetry, proceedings, and speeches. Much of this material first

1

appeared in antislavery newspapers. Some of it, such as Frederick Douglass's *Narrative* and Harriet Beecher Stowe's *Uncle Tom's Cabin*, still enjoys a wide audience. The words with which Garrison initiated his weekly newspaper, the *Liberator*, in 1831 ("I am in earnest—I will not equivocate—I will not excuse—I will not retreat a single inch—AND I WILL BE HEARD.") are among the more famous in American history. High school and college students still read the American Anti-Slavery Society's 1833 declaration in favor of using exclusively peaceful means to bring about the abolition of slavery and equal rights for African Americans. They also read John Brown's contrasting assertion, which he issued just prior to his execution in 1859, that he was "now quite *certain* that the crimes of this *guilty land* will never be purged away but with *blood*."[2]

Until the 1960s none of the Addresses to the Slaves were prominent within this literature. Since then, Garnet's has gained currency as an illustration of antebellum black militancy. But Smith's and Garrison's, beyond a brief but revealing analysis provided in 1990 by Merton L. Dillon, remain obscure. Some historians assume that Garnet's Address is unique. They contend that it demonstrates dissonance between a black abolitionist demand for action and a white abolitionist tendency toward abstract debate.[3] When the three speeches are grouped together and placed in their physical and cultural contexts, however, a more complex and nuanced situation emerges. The Addresses are products of changing circumstances, emerging perspectives, abolitionist factionalism, romantic masculinity, biracialism, and a growing willingness to acknowledge the role of slaves in the movement. Taken together, they also reflect declining abolitionist commitment to peaceful persuasion directed at whites and expanding abolitionist involvement in slave escapes. They anticipate later examples of abolitionist interaction with slaves and aggressive antislavery action in the South. These include a very significant "Letter to the Slaves" adopted by a biracial antislavery convention in 1850, as well as northern resistance to the Fugitive Slave Law of 1850, John Brown's plan to invade the South, and the Union's recruitment of slaves as soldiers during the Civil War.

Just as important, the impact of the Addresses on the antislavery movement indicates that traditional assumptions concerning the nature and locus of abolitionist radicalism during the period from 1840 to 1860 must be revised. Historians have almost universally viewed the American abolitionists who were active during these decades as agitators who sought directly to influence northern popular opinion and northern politics while only indirectly influencing the South. In this limited context, Garrison and his associates appear to have been radicals while other abolitionist factions, including church-oriented and political abolitionists, appear to have been conservative reformers willing to work within existing institutions. Although church-oriented and political abolitionists opposed slavery in the South, they are often portrayed as less willing than Garrisonians to challenge the status quo in the North, especially in regard to the authority of church and state and the oppression of women.[4] The response to the Addresses to the Slaves indicates that while this assessment is accurate to a degree, it misses the main point. In terms of aggressive action against slavery in the South, of an assertion of black manhood, and of endorsement of violent means, many non-Garrisonian abolitionists and most New York political abolitionists were more practically radical than the Garrisonians. It was New Yorkers, black and white, who during the 1840s carried out the spirit of the Addresses to the Slaves. They supported the notion of a direct assault on slavery in the South rather than an indirect campaign against slavery through northern public opinion. Meanwhile, the very matters that made Garrisonians radical in the North—pacifism, feminism, disunionism, and reliance almost exclusively on agitation to bring about the immediate abolition of slavery—led them to criticize Smith and Garnet's Addresses to the Slaves and to ignore Garrison's. Garrison's closest associates opposed efforts to cooperate with slaves in seeking freedom.

Indeed the Addresses to the Slaves capture an American antislavery movement in tension between its peaceful past and violent future—between agitation and civil war. They are revolutionary, aggressive, and portentous in their consideration of violence. They are determined to embrace slaves as allies. They reflect a major social transformation. But they are also ambiguous and limited by their time and place. When Smith, Garrison, and Garnet prepared their Addresses, they could not fully comprehend the state of the antislavery cause nor that of the slaves, let alone the future courses of their constituents. Each Address's self-contradiction in regard to peaceful versus violent means highlights the volatility of that crucial issue. They also disagree with one another and are unclear concerning the sort of relationship with slaves they advocate. They, nevertheless, provide starting points for understanding the development of antislavery activism in the United States during the last two antebellum decades. They help us to understand which abolitionists pioneered more aggressive action toward the South and how abolitionists fit into the broader sectional struggle that led to the Civil War in 1861.

The origins of the American antislavery movement were biracial. Slave unrest during the early 1700s, Quaker humanitarianism and nonviolence, the black freedom struggle during the era of the American Revolution, and, especially, religious revivalism during the early nineteenth century shaped its character. Black activism and a white foreboding that God would use slave revolt to punish a guilty nation, together with evangelicalism, the principles of the Declaration of Independence, and free labor economics, motivated antislavery action. During the late eighteenth century, these forces led northern states either to ban slavery immediately or to adopt plans for its gradual abolition. In 1787, similar forces produced Congress's prohibition of slavery in the Old Northwest. The end of slavery in the North by no means produced equal rights or opportunities for African Americans in that section. But, particularly in states like Massachusetts and Pennsylvania, where African Americans either petitioned state legislatures or went to court to gain freedom, white abolitionists did not doubt that slaves were active participants in the movement.[5]

Thereafter the geographical and cultural distance increased between northern abolitionists and those they sought to free. By 1800 almost all slaves lived south of the Mason-Dixon Line. Most of them worked on plantations under conditions that diverged radically from those in the North. Abolitionists, like other northerners during the early nineteenth century, regarded their section, with its emerging market economy, commitment to wage labor, vibrant churches, reform movements, and a high literacy rate, as vastly superior to a pre-modern South, committed to slavery, illiteracy, brutal violence, immorality, and distrust of change. By the 1830s, abolitionists portrayed slaves and their masters as inhabitants of a far-off barbarous land, which was nevertheless part of the United States and therefore implicated the North in sin and crime.[6]

At a time when horse-drawn wagons, sailing vessels, steamboats, and trains pulled by wood-burning locomotives were the only means of travel, the idea of a distant South was often correct. Yet the slave South, if not the plantation South, mingled with the North in borderlands stretching from Delaware to Missouri. Philadelphia, for example, was very close to the slaveholding Chesapeake cities of Wilmington, Delaware; Baltimore, Maryland; and Washington and Alexandria in the District of Columbia. From the 1790s through the 1820s, agents of the Pennsylvania Abolition Society not only worked closely with the small gradual abolition societies centered in these southern cities, but they also worked with slaves and free African Americans in the region. During the 1820s, Benjamin Lundy, a northern-born antislavery Quaker, published an antislavery newspaper in Baltimore and interacted with slaves.[7] From its formation in 1816, the American Colonization Society (ACS) also maintained what many regarded as an antislavery presence south of the Mason-Dixon Line. This organization, which dominated antislavery activism during the 1820s, proposed overcoming a major white objection to emancipation—that it would create a large, burdensome, dangerous, and revolutionary class of free blacks—through the transportation of former slaves to Africa. For over a decade, white abolitionists, who still regarded a gradual approach to emancipation to be the most reasonable, and many African Americans, who feared that they would never be accepted as equals in the United States, worked with the ACS. Nevertheless, this organization emphasized cooperation with masters, not slaves. It devoted itself to an extreme version of racial separation rather than to a biracial effort against racial oppression in America.[8]

As the 1820s progressed, increasing numbers of black leaders in the North and in border cities of the South charged that the ACS was a racist scheme designed to remove free African Americans from the land of their birth. It would, they charged, strengthen slavery by getting rid of its most determined opponents.[9] By the end of the decade a new antislavery movement, dedicated to *immediate* emancipation and equal rights for African Americans in the United States, began to emerge. It took form in Baltimore, Boston, New York, and Philadelphia. Briefly it appeared that this new movement would unite slavery's northern opponents with its southern victims. In 1829 Garrison joined Lundy in Baltimore, where the two men worked with free African Americans *and* slaves. That same year, black abolitionist David Walker published in Boston his *Appeal to the Colored Citizens of the World*. Walker denounced colonization and suggested that slaves might justifiably resort to violence to gain freedom. He relied on black and white sailors to distribute his *Appeal* in the South.[10]

For several reasons, immediate abolitionists during the 1830s turned away from these attempts to communicate with slaves. Walker died of tuberculosis shortly after he published his pamphlet. Rising antiabolitionist sentiment forced Garrison and Lundy to retreat northward from the Chesapeake.

After briefly considering Washington, D.C., Garrison in January 1831 began publishing the *Liberator* in Boston, with support from black northerners. In contrast to Walker, Garrison and his associates discussed what slaveholders must do, not what slaves must do. The immediatists of the 1830s also rejected violent means.[11] Nat Turner's Southampton County, Virginia, slave revolt in August 1831 reinforced these tendencies. Claims that Garrison and other northerners had encouraged the revolt led abolitionists even more strongly to renounce antislavery violence and communication with slaves. When in December 1833 Garrison and other immediatists met in Philadelphia to organize the American Anti-Slavery Society (AASS), they emphasized both peaceful means and dealing only with masters.[12]

As antiabolitionist violence mounted during the following years, most abolitionists sought to avoid injury by denying that they would have anything to do with slaves. Abolitionists of both races continued to express sympathy for slave rebels and to warn that God would use black revolt to punish a nation that did not free its slaves. But, to avoid charges that they themselves encouraged bloodshed, abolitionists only called on the free to oppose slavery. They rejected direct appeals to slaves, whom they hoped would be passive beneficiaries of a northern campaign on their behalf. An apparent decline in slave unrest after 1833 encouraged this policy.[13]

During the late 1830s and early 1840s, abolitionists once again reevaluated the nature of their movement and the focus of their efforts. The tactics they employed for a decade—concentration on the North, appeals to white morality, to the churches, and to politicians—seemed to be inadequate.[14] This perception contributed—along with disputes over the role of the churches, the participation of women in antislavery meetings, and political organization—to the splintering of the AASS in 1840. A small Garrisonian faction centered in New England kept control of the "Old Organization." Its members rejected direct participation in politics, while they embraced women's rights, denounced the churches as proslavery, and increasingly favored disunion—the total separation of the North from the South. A much larger faction, led by New York City businessman Lewis Tappan, formed the American and Foreign Anti-Slavery Society (AFASS), dedicated to working through the churches for emancipation. Another group—centered in upstate New York, soon led by Smith, and aligned with the AFASS—formed the Liberty Party to use politics as a means of spreading antislavery sentiment. Almost from its beginning this organization divided into two major factions: Smith's radical political abolitionists and a more moderate group centered in Cincinnati. Meanwhile, black abolitionists, most of whom allied with the AFASS and the Liberty Party, revived a national convention movement that had lapsed with the rise of the AASS. The disputes that led to the breakup of the AASS were bitter. Relations between the "Old Organization" on the one side and AFASS and Liberty Party on the other remained acrimonious, with Garrisonians going so far as to characterize "New Organization" members as proslavery.[15]

At the same time, there were indications that each of the abolitionist factions could and should become more aggressive toward the South. Slave unrest seemed to have revived. Antiabolitionist sentiment in the North had weakened. Railroads had begun to speed travel from the Northeast to the Chesapeake. A few abolitionists had gone south to help slaves escape. Abolitionists were also aware that neither their old tactic of moral suasion nor Liberty political strategy had spread much sympathy for suffering African Americans. Garnet in his Address expressed a widespread concern when he sarcastically advised slaves, "Humanity has long since exhausted her tears in weeping on your account."[16] He, Smith, and Garrison were among the first to realize that abolitionists must reorient themselves toward the slaves in order to take advantage of a new reality.

In contrast to the 1830s abolitionist focus on masters and northern public opinion, the Addresses to the Slaves return to Walker's assertion of a right to communicate with those in bonds. The Addresses propose to direct the movement toward the South, they embrace the slaves as allies, and they emphasize the threat of slave violence.[17] They presume to encourage slaves to gain freedom for themselves through illegal and potentially forceful means. Smith's and Garrison's urge slaves to escape. Garnet's calls on slaves to refuse to work. They each glorify slave rebelliousness. Yet the Addresses are irresolute concerning appropriate means to be used against slavery and unclear concerning the abolitionists' relationship to slaves. They call on slaves to act *and* to rely on northerners. They raise the prospect of slave revolt *but* counsel slaves against initiating violence. They embrace slaves as allies while asserting that northern abolitionists must dictate the antislavery agenda. In other words, they insist on the cultural hegemony of northern reform morality. In part the Addresses' condescension and ambiguity stem from their multiple audiences. There were those who heard the Addresses delivered. There were abolitionist and nonabolitionist northerners who read printed versions. There were those formally addressed: the distant slaves. The northern audiences were crucial to the form the Addresses took and the conditions under which the men presented them. But, while there is little evidence that any of the Addresses reached slaves, Smith, Garrison, and Garnet intended that they should. Smith asserted that his would be distributed in the South. Garrison implied the same about his. Garnet later prayed that his would circulate until "every slave in the Union" adopted its principles.[18]

Two other factors contribute to the Addresses' multiple meanings. First, there is their authors' awareness of the complex and contingent nature of the abolitionist task. Second, there is their reluctance to break with long-held assumptions that they must advocate nonviolence and support the existing legal system, even though tactics based on these assumptions had failed to produce the results for which they hoped. By the time they delivered their Addresses, Smith, Garrison, and Garnet realized that they must embrace a violent revolutionary strategy. Simultaneously they recoiled from doing so.

The three men who shared these dilemmas had dissimilar backgrounds. While both Smith and Garrison were white, they came from differing social strata, religious affiliations, and reform traditions. Smith, born at Utica, New York, in 1797, inherited great wealth from his land-speculator father and high social standing from his mother. He graduated with honors from Hamilton College in 1818 and devoted the rest of his life to managing his family's lands, to philanthropy, and to reform. He remained a supporter of the ACS until 1835. Thereafter, influenced by revivalism and Christian perfectionism, he became one of the more thoroughgoing immediatists. Tall and stately, with a sonorous voice and engaging personality, Smith by the early 1840s was the undisputed leader of upstate New York's radical political abolitionist wing of the Liberty Party. He and his associates held that Christians must leave proslavery churches and proslavery parties in order to form new ones opposed to human bondage. They interpreted the United States Constitution as making slavery illegal throughout the country and called for the righteous exercise of government power to destroy that institution. They believed that because slavery was a crime it was legal for slaves to free themselves and for northern abolitionists to help them.[19]

Garrison, born in Newburyport, Massachusetts, in 1805, was raised by a poverty-stricken, deeply religious Baptist mother who had been abandoned by her seafaring husband. Her Christian moralism and Garrison's apprenticeship to a printer in 1818 shaped his life. By the time he joined Lundy in Baltimore, he had become a self-educated reform journalist. The black abolitionists he met in that city and his imprisonment there on charges that he had libeled a slave trader helped inspire his brand of immediatism. His time in Baltimore Jail may also have convinced him that abolitionists had to restrict their direct action to the North. Although Garrison was of average height, his erect posture and intense earnestness gave him a formidable physical presence. As editor of the *Liberator* and the leader of both the Massachusetts Anti-Slavery Society (MASS) and the AASS, he, more than anyone else, shaped American abolitionism during the 1830s. By the latter years of that decade he had come to believe that slavery had corrupted all American institutions. Heavily influenced by *nonresistance*—the rejection of all violence—and distrust of human institutions, he denounced organized religion, political parties, and the United States Constitution as intrinsically sinful and proslavery. During the early 1840s he began to advocate disunion as the only means of withdrawing northern support for slavery and forcing abolition in the South.[20]

In 1815, Garnet was born a slave at New Market, Maryland. When he was eight years old, he and his family escaped to the North and settled in New York City. Poor and threatened with recapture, Garnet nevertheless received an excellent education at New York's African Free School, the city's High School for Colored Youth, Noyes Academy at Canaan, New Hampshire, and Oneida Institute in Whitesboro, New York. He gained ordination as a minister in 1841 and began serving as pastor of the Liberty Street Presbyterian Church in Troy, New York. A founder of the AFASS and a supporter of the Liberty Party, Garnet was one of Gerrit Smith's stronger allies. He was tall in stature, dark in complexion, and reputedly the grandson of a Mandingo chieftain. Brilliant, eloquent, and arrogant, Garnet by 1843 believed more firmly than either of his white counterparts that black men had to fight for freedom. A budding black nationalism, which flowered during the 1850s, marked his rhetoric.[21]

Despite their authors' differences, the three—probably coordinated—Addresses had much in common due to their shared temporal and cultural context (see p. 160).[22] The age of steam and steel had barely begun in the United States. Urban areas, although more common in the North than in the South, were exceptional throughout the overwhelmingly agricultural nation. People knew nothing of the germ theory, of Darwinian evolution, or of media besides print. Wood burned in open hearths provided fuel for heating and cooking. Blatant racism and sexism pervaded the nation. These conditions sustained a romantic, republican, and extremely masculine ideology, rife with contradictions, that burdened public discourse. Rooted in the American Revolution, this ideology held that *men* had a civic duty to guard against aristocratic forces that sought to control their government, violate their natural rights, and enslave them.[23] While this ideology embraced the common man, it also recognized a hierarchical and deferential social order dominated by the wealthy and educated. It reflected an American society in which distinct class lines separated rich from poor, literate from illiterate, native-born from immigrant, black from white, female from male. Patriarchy reigned north and south as Americans shared with other nations a belief that men must dominate women, whom they held as a group to be mentally and physically inferior.[24] Mid-nineteenth-century American ideology also supported racial assumptions concerning who was entitled to manhood—the prerogatives of an adult male. White men demonstrated manhood as heads of households, as businessmen, as politicians, as religious leaders, as intellectuals, as soldiers, and as wage earners. From a white point of view and from the point of view of many African Americans, black men in slavery could be none of these and, therefore, lacked manhood.[25]

Mainstream religion and science buttressed the cultural status quo. Methodist, Baptist, Presbyterian, Episcopalian, Roman Catholic, and Lutheran church organizations refused to condemn slaveholders as sinners. Within the nation's post-Calvinist Christianity, few doubted that God ordained the social order. Natural philosophy contended that a great chain of being, marked by physical and mental gradations, stretched downward from people of northwestern European descent to the simplest animals. Some intellectuals maintained that, in this great chain, people of Sub-Saharan African descent represented a separate species as close to apes as to whites.[26] All of these views conditioned the consciousness of Smith, Garrison, and Garnet—and other black and white abolitionists—even as they struggled against them. As Christian perfectionists who sought sanctification for themselves and their nation, they regarded slaveholding and racial discrimination to be damning sins. But the very things the three men opposed helped to shape their perceptions.[27]

One of these things was patriarchy. Male abolitionists helped launch feminism during the 1830s and 1840s. But they had difficulty accepting women as equals within the antislavery movement. Smith, Garrison, and Garnet realized that the exploitation of black women in slavery undermined the status of all women. But their Addresses to the Slaves mark a time when many abolitionists began to turn away from their endorsement of the feminine virtue of peaceful persuasion. Smith's Address ignores enslaved women. Garnet's mentions black women simply as dependents of black men. Even Garrison, whose faction most strongly embraced women's rights, directed most of his Address to men. Only in one brief passage does it appeal to both sexes of the enslaved: "fathers and mothers," "husbands and wives," "brothers and sisters" (see p. 176). White abolitionist women, such as Lydia Maria Child and Angelina Grimke, wrote addresses to the slaveholders and to the white women of the South. Black abolitionist women, such as Maria W. Stewart and Sojourner Truth, spoke publicly before northern audiences of black and white men. But only male abolitionists wrote addresses to slaves, and they envisioned an essentially masculine audience. No abolitionist, black or white, female or male, ever framed an address to the enslaved women of the South.[28]

Another thing that shaped Smith's, Garrison's, and Garnet's perceptions was the power of slavery as an institution. At the time of the Addresses to the Slaves, fourteen out of the twenty-seven states, as well as the District of Columbia, maintained slave labor systems. When, in these jurisdictions, masters brutally whipped slaves, when they maimed some of those who unsuccessfully attempted to escape, when they sexually abused enslaved women, and when through the domestic slave trade they ripped apart black families, they had the law on their side. It was illegal in most of the southern states to teach slaves to read and write. Southern authorities jailed men and women who attempted to circulate antislavery literature among slaves or otherwise questioned the legitimacy of human bondage. There were laws in nearly all the states, northern as well as southern, against African Americans (and American Indians) enjoying the same rights as whites. Under federal law, it was a crime throughout the country to help slaves escape. Public opinion North and South supported slavery. Proslavery northern mobs were in decline by the early 1840s, but they continued to enforce white supremacy through attacks on blacks and their white allies.[29]

Slavery also enjoyed the support of northern businesses and the major political parties. The ties between New England's textile manufacturers—"the lords of the loom"—and the South's cotton producers—"the lords of the lash"—are well known. The Democratic Party had always been an explicitly proslavery organization. Although the Whig Party embraced antislavery elements in the North, it nominated slaveholders for national office and followed a proslavery leadership in Congress. Slaveholding justices dominated the Supreme Court, usually enjoying the support of their northern colleagues. John Tyler, president of the United States during the early 1840s, owned slaves. So did all but three of his predecessors. Tyler also sought to annex the slaveholding Republic of Texas. Slavery and racial oppression prevailed in spite of a political rhetoric that proclaimed equal rights for all men and universal freedom. Garnet observed of slavery, "Its throne is established, and now it reigns triumphantly."[30]

So Garnet, Smith, and Garrison realized that northern support for proslavery laws, proslavery churches, proslavery business alliances, and demeaning racial discrimination presented major obstacles to general emancipation. Yet none of their insights kept them and other abolitionists from holding enslaved black men responsible for their condition. To a great extent, Smith, Garrison, and Garnet's Addresses came in response to rising numbers of slave escapes and two successful shipboard revolts—on the Spanish *Amistad* in 1839 and the American *Creole* in 1841—that demonstrated the willingness of bondmen to assert their manhood. The three speakers, nevertheless, could not escape the influence of the notion, so ingrained in American thought, that African-American men were too complacent, too gentle, or too cowardly to challenge their oppressors. That this view was not simply racist myth is indicated by leading black abolitionist Frederick Douglass's May 1843 remark that slavery had instilled in him "a disposition I never can quite shake off, to cower before white men."[31] Even if black men did rise up, Smith, Garrison, Garnet, and other abolitionists assumed they would be slaughtered.

In these confusing circumstances, the most determined northern opponents of slavery had difficulty contemplating how slaves might gain freedom. Prevailing American culture encouraged them to stereotype black character, to think in exclusively masculine terms, to be myopic in their perception of racial justice, and to be distracted in their tactical and moral judgments. Pitted against powerful forces, divided among themselves, and biased by an oppressive reality, abolitionists struggled to conceptualize and implement a means of constructing an alternate reality. The Addresses to the Slaves constitute a milestone in this struggle. What they represent, what they call for, and the response to them define American abolitionism during the 1840s. They clarify the significance of its factional divisions and point toward the major sectional struggles of the 1850s and 1860s.

Chapter One

AMBIGUOUS MANIFESTOS

There is no mistaking the urgency with which Gerrit Smith, William Lloyd Garrison, and Henry Highland Garnet frame their Addresses to the Slaves. They perceive the antislavery struggle to be at a turning point that simultaneously promises opportunity and danger. Their message simply put is that the movement can no longer regard slaves to be passive recipients of northern abolitionist benevolence. Instead, to destroy slavery, abolitionists must embrace slaves as partners in the cause of emancipation. They must contemplate a more aggressive and perhaps violent abolitionism. For several reasons all three men worried about these new departures. They did not wish to weaken other antislavery tactics. They did not desire to alienate their northern associates or potential converts. They questioned the manhood of enslaved black men. They were profoundly ambivalent concerning the link between slave action and violence.

Of the three authors, Garrison emerged earliest, had a huge impact on the character of the movement, and is generally regarded as the greatest American abolitionist. Of the three Addresses, Garnet's is the best known and most dramatic. But during the early 1840s Smith led those abolitionists who advocated and carried out interaction with slaves in the South. In addition, Smith's Address, delivered in January 1842, prompted and shaped the other two.

Gerrit Smith (1797–1874) led upstate New York's radical political abolitionists. A wealthy philanthropist who believed slavery could never be legal, Smith presented the first of the Addresses to the Slaves in January 1842. He is shown here as he appeared in 1856. (*The Speeches of Gerrit Smith in Congress* [New York: Mason Brothers, 1856], frontispiece.)

Smith begins his Address by announcing that he is calling for a radical departure from prevailing abolitionist rhetoric and action. Abolitionists, he maintains, had committed a "great and guilty error" when, following Nat Turner's rebellion, they had forsworn an intention to intervene between masters and slaves (see p. 153). In seeking to counter charges that they had conspired with slaves to foment uprisings, they had foolishly pledged to seek emancipation of the slaves only through appeals to the conscience and intellect of the masters. Continued reliance on this tactic, Smith contends,

showed that abolitionists were "not yet entirely disabused of
the fallacy that slavery is a legitimate institution . . . that . . .
creates rights in the slaveholder and destroys rights in the
slave" (see p. 153).

Abolitionists, Smith insists, must never forget that slavery was "sheer usurpation" and that slaveholders had to expect interference on behalf of their "stolen property." Slaves
had the same rights their ancestors had before falling "among
thieves," including the right to "word of consolation, encouragement and advice." The Apostle Paul, Smith reminds his
audiences, communicated with slaves, called on others to do
so, and did not "condition the duty on the consent of the
master" (see p. 154).

Smith realized that this was easier said than done. His
Address acknowledges that the South was far from New York
and that the masters were on guard. Smith also assumed that
slavery had limited the capacity of most of its victims to respond to an abolitionist message. He believed, nevertheless,
that his Address could achieve a great deal against slavery.

Even if no slave read it, Smith thought his Address could
encourage northern abolitionists to take aggressive action
against slavery. The Address does not deny the importance
of religious efforts in the North, and it calls on northern
state legislatures and Congress to use all their "constitutional
power for the overthrow of slavery." But it charges that abolitionists had been too timid and warns that "unless they are
continually rising higher and higher in their bold and righteous claims, all the past attainments of the cause are left
unsure" (see p. 155).[1] Smith believed that abolitionists had
underestimated how bold declarations could prepare the way
for action. The doctrine of communicating with slaves, his
Address predicts, would lead "to the conviction that the abolitionist has a perfect moral right to go into the South and
use his intelligence to promote the escape of ignorant and
imbruted slaves from their prison-house" (see p. 155).

Abolitionist action in the South against slavery, like slave
unrest, had actually preceded and shaped Smith's Address.

In July 1841 three young northern white abolitionists were arrested in Missouri for attempting to help slaves escape. Just two months before Smith spoke, former slave Madison Washington had, with support from New York abolitionists, returned from Canada to Virginia in a similar effort that led to the *Creole* uprising.[2] Smith's Address, therefore, did not lead to such undertakings but furthered them. What Smith *did* originate was the legitimization of contacting slaves. When the following year Garrison and Garnet presented their Addresses, they felt no need to justify themselves. Garrison assumed that the right existed. Garnet admonished earlier black national conventions for not having tried to communicate with the enslaved.

While Smith had come to regard slaves and abolitionists as intimately connected in a single movement, he portrayed the latter as the senior partners. Like those who followed him in addressing slaves, this outlook led him to assume for himself and other abolitionists two interrelated but potentially contradictory roles. The first was that of a wise fatherly northern philanthropist restraining potential slave rebels and instructing them regarding proper nonviolent means of seeking freedom. The second was that of a prophet warning that without immediate emancipation slaves were bound to turn to revolutionary violence. Smith asserts in his Address that, since Nat Turner's revolt in 1831, "philanthropic efforts" on the part of abolitionists had led slaves to practice "forbearance" but that slaves would not forbear much longer (see p. 156).

Were Smith's reservations concerning the use of violence against evil not so well documented, one might assume that he used this dichotomy between what northern abolitionists desired and what slaves might do merely as a rhetorical ploy.[3] Through such a ploy he could exculpate abolitionists from charges that they fomented slave insurrection while simultaneously threatening slaveholders with such an insurrection. In fact, the dichotomy is *both* a ploy and a reflection of an emotional disjuncture in abolitionist thought that extended to Garrison and Garnet as well. All three men were ambivalent regarding slaves resorting to violence in order to free themselves. In his Address Smith urges distant slaves to refrain from forceful action. He "entreat[s]" them "to endure" slavery "rather than take a violent bloody hold of [liberty]" (see p. 156). He advises them, "Cherish no vindictive or unkind feelings toward your oppressors. Early and late, and with all possible cheerfulness, yield them your unrecompensed toil" (see p. 159). Yet Smith says that he and most abolitionists desire slaves to avoid violence "not on the high ground of absolute morality, but on the comparatively low one of expediency" (see p. 156).[4] Smith counsels slaves against revolt not because he regards it to be morally wrong but because he believes they could not win a war for freedom and would be worse off following a failed revolt than they were at present.

Instead of advising revolt, Smith's Address calls "on every slave, who has a reasonable prospect of being able to run away from slavery, to make the experiment." It also urges sympathetic southerners to provide slaves with "pocket compass[es]" (see p. 158). Implicitly acknowledging what had prompted his Address, Smith claims that northward escapes had already increased by five times to about one thousand per year. Portraying these escapes as a nonviolent, if illegal, alternative to revolt, he fails to mention that slave flight often involved violence on the part of pursuing masters, the escapees, and those who aided the escapees. He does, however, confront the issue of theft involved in effecting an escape. In what became the most controversial part of his Address, Smith indicates that he does not believe slaves who took what they needed to escape were guilty of theft. He assures slaves that God permitted them while escaping to "take, all along your route, in the free, as well as the slave State[s], so far as is absolutely essential . . . the horse, the boat, the food, the clothing, which you require" (see p. 158). Part of Smith's radical political abolitionist point of view was that "slaveholders are but pirates; and the laws, which piracy enacts, whether upon land or sea, are not entitled to trammel the conscience of its victims" (see p. 159). But many abolitionists questioned the legitimacy of fugitives expropriating property in the free states where Smith himself assumed that, under abolitionist influence, most inhabitants would voluntarily help them on their way.

Crediting abolitionists rather than slaves with the increase in northward escapes, he claims that "seven years ago a great majority of the people of the border free States were in favor of replunging into slavery their poor, scarred, emaciated, trembling brother, who had fled from its horrors. But now, under the influence of anti-slavery lessons, nineteen-twentieths of them have come to be ashamed of and to revolt at such monstrous inhumanity" (see p. 157). He assures potential escapees that, in spite of the Fugitive Slave Law of 1793, they could safely remain in the North. Or, if the escapees preferred, abolitionists would gladly employ themselves in "carrying" them on to Canada (see p. 157).

Smith concludes his Address with an ambivalent analysis of the forces working for slavery's destruction. Growing European and American hostility, gradual emancipation in the British West Indies, and the prospect of cotton production in India all suggested to him that the South's peculiar institution would soon peacefully expire. But he also asserts that the slave revolts aboard the *Amistad* and the *Creole* were providential events indicating God's determination "that slavery shall continue to be tortured, even unto death" (see p. 161). Smith, in other words, was not sure whether slavery would go out with a whimper or a bang.

The relationship between Smith's Address and Garrison's is clear. The two men led rival abolitionist factions. They often criticized each other. Some of Garrison's closest associates denounced Smith's Address as a dangerous violation of the long-standing abolitionist commitment to nonviolent and legal means.[5] Yet Garrison immediately invited Smith to attend the next meeting of the Massachusetts Anti-Slavery

Society (MASS).[6] A few weeks later in a *Liberator* editorial, Garrison demonstrated that changing circumstances in the South and within the antislavery movement had made him, despite his more rigorous commitment to nonviolence, receptive to Smith's initiative. Garrison welcomed Smith's "novel" Address in a manner that linked it to his own Address to the Slaves and to Garnet's as well.

Garrison's editorial declares that Smith's words would "add to the excitement of the times," especially in the South. "The right to convey to those who are pining in bondage, words of consolation and encouragement, and judicious and reasonable advice," Garrison observes, "will not be controverted by any one who is a friend of liberty." He comments that "if any real friend of human rights can better these instructions, we shall be glad to publish them in our columns." Pointing out that Smith counseled slaves to escape, *not* revolt, Garrison joined Smith in giving abolitionists credit for the lack of slave uprisings during the previous decade. In spite of charges that the abolitionists conspired "to stir up servile insurrection," Garrison asks, "what more quiet period has ever been known among the tortured victims of slaveholding rapacity?"[7]

Smith nevertheless evoked violent imagery in Garrison's mind. In reaction to Smith's Address and in anticipation of his own, Garrison notes that white southerners who charged abolitionists with violent intent conceded that humans had a right to fight for liberty. In fact, they frequently honored "their revolutionary sires, who waded through blood to establish their freedom." Anticipating Garnet, Garrison declares, "If it be right in any case to fight against oppression, the right belongs pre-eminently to those whose burdens are most grievous. . . . These are the American slaves. If the heroic Leonidas, [William] Tell, [William] Wallace, and [George] Washington are worthy of fame, . . . then, should kindred spirits appear among our southern slave population, and strike for liberty or death, their names should be held in equal remembrance, and their deeds exultingly recorded on

that page of history." Garrison's key word was *if.* As a nonresistant, he maintained that these violent heroes were *not* worthy of praise. But the strength of his language suggests that
his commitment to nonviolence vied with an ingrained cultural disposition to glorify resorting to violence in the name
of liberty.[8]

In late May 1843—fifteen months after he published his response to Smith's Address to the Slaves—Garrison presented
his own at a New England antislavery convention. It begins
with a declaration that slaves were men who had a natural
and moral right to "life, liberty, and the pursuit of happiness" (see p. 169). Despite their condition, Garrison's Address maintains, they were "equal members of the great
human family with immortal souls" and not "an inferior race"
created for bondage. God created all nations "of one blood,"
the Address declares, requiring humans not to "defraud, degrade, torment, persecute, or oppress each other—but [in-
stead] to enjoy equal rights and perfect liberty, to love and
do good to each other, to dwell together in unity" (see p.
170).

   In extending sympathy, consolation, encouragement,
and hope to slaves, Garrison's Address is quite similar to
Smith's. Both assert that masters had no legal authority over
slaves and that God sought to weaken slavery. Both Addresses
also favor peaceful means. Like Smith's, Garrison's assures
slaves that abolitionists labored "to effect your emancipation
without delay, in a peaceable manner, without the shedding
of blood" (see p. 174). Abolitionists rejected "deadly implements" and relied exclusively on "appeals, warnings, rebukes,
arguments, and facts, addressed to the understandings, consciences, and hearts of the people" (see p. 176). In a manner
very much like Smith's Address, Garrison's acknowledges that
abolitionists disagreed among themselves concerning why
slaves should not revolt. "Many" of them, it declares, believed "that not even those who are oppressed . . . can shed
the blood of their oppressors in accordance with the will of

William Lloyd Garrison (1805–1879) led the
Garrisonian abolitionists of New England.
The best known of the white abolitionists,
Garrison was a pacifist who nevertheless admired slave rebels. He presented his Address
to the Slaves in May 1843 and is shown here
as he appeared in 1846. (Wendell Phillips
Garrison and Francis Jackson Garrison, *William Lloyd Garrison, 1805–1879: The Story of
His Life Told by His Children* [New York: Century, 1885–1889], 3: frontispiece.)

God." "Many others" believed "that it is right for the oppressed to rise and take their liberty by violence, if they can
secure it in no other manner" but opposed revolt under existing circumstances. This was, Garrison informs his distant
slave audience, because "every attempt at insurrection would

be attended with disaster and defeat, on your part, because you are not strong enough to contend with the military power of the nation" (see p. 176).

Garrison warns slaves that white Americans, who praised those in Poland, Greece, and South America who revolted against oppression, would nevertheless regard black rebels to be "murderers and monsters" and slaughter them "without mercy" (see p. 173). Therefore Garrison, like Smith, advises slaves to rely on northern abolitionists. He asks each of them "to be patient, long-suffering and submissive, yet a while longer, trusting that by the blessings of the Most High on [abolitionist] labors, you will yet be emancipated without shedding a drop of your master's blood, or losing a drop of your own" (see p. 176). Like Smith, Garrison assures slaves that God and northern abolitionists would soon deliver them from their "chains" (see p. 174).

Yet, to a far greater extent than Smith, Garrison employs violent imagery and portrays an alternate, violent route to freedom. He assures slaves that God punished those who "have refused to let the oppressed go free." He skirts sarcasm when he advises slaves regarding masters, "If you submit unresistingly to their commands, do it for Christ's sake (who died for the unjust,) and not because they claim a rightful authority over you—for they have no such authority" (see p. 171). Smith's Address had led Garrison in February 1842 to recall the analogy abolitionists often made between slave rebels and white American leaders in the War for Independence. In his Address Garrison elaborates on that analogy. The masters, he says, were descendants of American revolutionaries who "for seven years waged war against [Great Britain's] despotic power." The masters honored those who in the Declaration of Independence asserted a right to revolt in the name of human equality and inalienable natural rights. Therefore, Garrison tells slaves, "by precept and example, they declare that it is both your right and your duty to wage war against them, and to wade through their blood, if necessary, to secure your own freedom." He reminds his audiences that Patrick Henry had proclaimed, "Give me liberty or give me death" and quotes Lord Byron's famous admonition to the oppressed, "Hereditary bondmen! know ye not, Who would be free, themselves must strike the blow" (see p. 173). While Garrison embraced an extreme form of pacifism, these were far more incendiary words than Smith used and foreshadowed Garnet's more violent passages.

The most significant difference between Smith's Address and Garrison's, however, lies in their conflicting portrayals of the relationship between abolitionists and slaves. The recent upsurge of slave escapes to the North and Canada impressed Garrison nearly as much as it did Smith. Like Smith's Address, Garrison's regards escape to be an alternative both to patient anticipation of emancipation and to revolt. Like Smith's, it credits northern abolitionists, rather than the slaves themselves, for this increase. It asserts that because of the "influence . . . enterprise and determination" of abolitionists there were "now thousands . . . to succor [fugitive slaves], when a few years since, scarcely an individual could be found to hide the outcast" (see p. 177). Garrison praises abolitionists as the "noblest champions of the human race," fearless and willing to suffer beatings, imprisonment, financial loss, and death for the slaves' sake (see p. 175). Abolitionists, he promises, will feed, clothe, doctor, and hide fugitives. Soon, he assures slaves, "the entire North will receive you with open arms, and give you shelter and protection, as fast as you escape from the South" (see p. 177).

But, contrary to Smith's Address, Garrison's rejects physical interference in the South to help slaves escape. Garrison's imprisonment in Baltimore in 1830 on charges that he libeled a slave trader helped shape this point of view, as did his disunionism. For some time he and his associates had maintained that the U.S. Constitution was intrinsically proslavery and by 1843 had concluded that only the Constitution's demand that the North support slavery kept it in existence.[9] According to Garrison, abolitionists would not interfere in the South. To destroy slavery, they only had to convince northerners to leave the Union. He tells his distant slave audience, "It is not yet necessary" for abolitionists to risk their lives in the South "for it is solely by the aid of the people of the North, that you are held in bondage, and, therefore, they find enough to do at home, to make the people here your friends, and to break up all connection with the slave system" (see p. 175).

Once the North had dissolved its union with the South, the slaves themselves could "obtain" their "freedom and independence in a single day." Again anticipating Garnet, Garrison assumes that slaves had to act on their own against their masters. He tells them, "Your masters are only two hundred and fifty thousand in number, you are nearly three million; and what could they do if they should be abandoned to their fate by the North?" (see p. 178). Overlooking the millions of proslavery but nonslaveholding southern whites, who later joined in a war to keep African Americans in bondage, Garrison ends his Address by asserting that "if it were not now for the compact existing between the free and slave States, by which the whole military power of the nation is pledged to suppress all insurrections, you would have long ere this been free" (see p. 178). Like Smith, Garrison was not sure how slavery would end. But to a greater degree than Smith *and* Garnet, he suggested that peaceful means were the province of northern abolitionists alone. If the disunionist tactics he advocated succeeded, he assumed that slaves would initiate a violent revolution in the South.

In contrast to the explicit link between Smith's Address and Garrison's, only circumstantial evidence ties Garnet's to the other two. Much better documented is his Address's relationship to David Walker's *Appeal to the Colored Citizens of the World*, which Garnet republished along with his own Address in 1848. But similarities in subject matter and phraseology, as well as proximity in time, link Garnet's effort to Garrison's. Ties of friendship, finance, and factional affiliation link it to Smith's. Garnet and his family, who lived in

Troy, New York, during the early 1840s, often visited Smith's mansion in Peterboro. Smith provided funds to support Garnet's efforts to publish antislavery newspapers. Smith led the New York Liberty Party of which Garnet was an active member.[10] It is clear in the remarks Garnet made at the Massachusetts Liberty Convention held in Boston's Faneuil Hall on February 16, 1842—within a month of Smith's Address to the Slaves—that the two men exchanged ideas.

While Garnet's speech on this occasion centered on the prospects of the Liberty Party in the North, it also linked abolitionism and the slaves. In it Garnet contends that abolitionist claims to be able to communicate with slaves were not just rhetorical ploys. "The slaves *know* throughout the entire South, of the movement of the abolitionists," he maintains. "They know they have friends in the North in whom they may *confide* in case they are driven to desperation." Like Smith had been a month earlier, Garnet is ambivalent concerning slave revolt. At one point he declares, "I cannot harbor the thought for a moment that their deliverance will be brought about by violence. . . . No, the time for a last stern struggle has not yet come (may it never be necessary)." But he also warns that only faith in the northern antislavery movement "prevent[ed] a general insurrection of the slaves from spreading carnage and devastation throughout the entire South."[11]

Garnet's Address, delivered in Buffalo in August 1843 at the first black national convention since 1835, is by far the most famous of the Addresses to the Slaves. It begins in a manner similar to Smith's as Garnet reproves northerners—in this case black abolitionists—for their past mistakes. He informs his distant slave audience that those who attended previous black conventions had come together "to sympathize with each other," while doing no more than "weep over your unhappy condition." They had never "sent a word of consolation and advice" to slaves and had been content merely to hope for emancipation (see p. 180). Like Smith and Garri-

Henry Highland Garnet (1815–1882) was the leading black political abolitionist of the 1840s. A
former slave and a brilliant orator, he embodied
black militancy. He presented his Address to the
Slaves in August 1843 when he was twenty-seven.
He is shown here as he appeared much later in his
life. (William J. Simmons, ed., *Men of Mark: Eminent, Progressive, and Rising* [1887; repr., Chicago:
Johnson, 1970], 452.)

son, Garnet claims to represent an abolitionist faction and
presumes to tell slaves what to do. But he is far less focused
than either of them on northern abolitionism and the idea
that "the Almighty Father of mercies" was preparing for
peaceful emancipation. He is, though, closer to Garrison than
to his friend Smith in emphasizing that "a deep gulf" prevented northerners from providing "relief and consolation"

to slaves (see p. 180). Instead of discussing what northern abolitionists might do for slaves, Garnet concentrates on the character and duties of enslaved black men. It is up to them, he insists, to free themselves and their families.

This, according to Garnet, would not be an easy task because slavery sapped the spirit of African-American men. Invoking black nationalist—as well as republican—themes, Garnet reminds enslaved men that their ancestors had not come "with their own consent" to a "land of freedom" in America. Rather, they had come "with broken hearts, from their beloved native land." Millions of them had been "cursed, and ruined by American Slavery" (see p. 181). Much more graphically than either Smith or Garrison, Garnet depicts the destruction slavery wrought among southerners, white as well as black. Masters had become "weak, sensual, and rapacious" (see p. 182), and slaves had fared far worse.

Masters, according to Garnet, sought to make black men "as much like brutes as possible" by undermining their natural "love of Liberty," their intellects, and their faith (see pp. 182–83). To a greater degree than Smith and Garrison, he holds black men responsible for this. In a variation on an old abolitionist theme, he declares that neither enslavement nor ignorance absolved them from their "moral obligation" to God and family. "You are not certain of Heaven," he tells them, "because you suffer yourself to remain in a state of slavery where you cannot obey the commandments of the Sovereign of the universe." In Garnet's view, enslaved men defied Jehovah by not raising their "children with respect for his laws, and to worship no other God but him" (see p. 183).

Garnet's Address also casts shame on enslaved men for their inability to protect their loved ones. "Look around you," it demands, "and behold the horrors of your loving wives, heaving with untold agonies! Hear the cries of your poor children! Remember the stripes your fathers bore. Think of the torture and disgrace of your noble mothers. Think of your wretched sisters, loving virtue and purity, as they are driven into concubinage, and are exposed to the unbridled lust of incarnate devils" (see p. 185). Later Garnet adds, "You are a patient people. You act as though your daughters were born to pamper the lust of your masters and overseers. And worse than all, you tamely submit, while your lords tear your wives from your embrace, and defile them before your eyes. In the name of God we ask, are you men? Where is the blood of your fathers? Has it all run out of your veins? Awake, awake; millions of voices are calling you! . . . Heaven, as with a voice of thunder, calls on you to arise from the dust" (see p. 188).

More emphatically than Smith and Garrison, Garnet calls on black men to assert their right to freedom. He advises his distant audience, "IT IS YOUR SOLEMN AND IMPERATIVE DUTY TO USE EVERY MEANS, BOTH MORAL, INTELLECTUAL, AND PHYSICAL, THAT PROMISE SUCCESS" (see pp. 183–84). His rhetoric is especially inflammatory and personal. He is most insistent that "hereditary bondmen . . . must themselves strike the first blow" (see p. 184). He calls on them to "think of the undying glory that hangs around the ancient name of Africa" as well as their rights as "native-born American citizens" (see p. 185). Of the three Addresses, Garnet's goes furthest in offsetting a portrayal of the weakness of black men in slavery with praise for black rebels. He explicitly links Toussaint Louverture, who during the 1790s led a successful slave revolt in Haiti; Denmark Vesey, who in 1822 plotted revolt at Charleston, South Carolina; Nat Turner, who led the Southampton, Virginia, slave revolt of 1831; Cinque of the *Amistad*; and Madison Washington of the *Creole*, with such white freedom fighters as John Hampden, William Tell, Robert the Bruce, William Wallace, Marquis de Lafayette, and George Washington (see pp. 186–87).

At one point Garnet follows Garrison in citing the Founders' embrace of "LIBERTY OR DEATH." Unlike Garrison, he does not equivocate. He notes that "among the diversity of opinions that are entertained in regard to physical resistance, there are but few found to gainsay that stern declaration. We are among those who do not" (see p. 182).

In his last paragraph Garnet declares, "Let your motto be RESISTANCE! RESISTANCE! RESISTANCE!—No oppressed people have ever secured their liberty without resistance" (see p. 188).

On the basis of these exhortations, some scholars have interpreted Garnet's Address to be an unqualified call for slave revolt.[12] The Addresses *had* grown more favorable to violent means—Garrison's more so than Smith's and Garnet's more so than Garrison's. But, like its predecessors, Garnet's Address is self-contradictory on this issue. *Expediency* is a crucial consideration as Garnet, like his predecessors, expresses doubt that slave revolt could achieve its objectives. He also displays a moral bias in favor of peaceful means. Toward the end of the Address, he explicitly rejects rebellion, saying, "We do not advise you to attempt a revolution with the sword, because it would be INEXPEDIENT. Your numbers are too small, and moreover the rising spirit of the age, and spirit of the gospel, are opposed to war and bloodshed" (see pp. 187–88).

There is, however, an additional layer of ambiguity concerning this passage. Historians Jane H. Pease and William H. Pease maintain that Garnet did not include this disavowal of slave revolt in the Address he presented in 1843. It was the only one of the three Addresses to the Slaves that was not published by the group that initially heard it, and, while Garnet promised in November 1843 to publish it himself, he did not do so until 1848. It was at that point, Pease and Pease maintain, that he "toned down" the Address by adding the passage declaring slave revolt inexpedient and immoral. Another possibility is that, while he was still at the Buffalo convention, Garnet added the passage in response to criticism from other delegates. In any case—whether the passage was originally in the Address, whether Garnet added it shortly after he presented the Address, or whether he added it in 1848—it is missing from the only other extant version of the Address. This version is included in an introduction, provided by black leader James McCune Smith, to a sermon

Garnet preached before the House of Representatives in 1865 shortly before the end of the Civil War.[13]

But the passage's absence from the 1865 version of the Address does not mean it was not in the Address as Garnet presented it in 1843. By 1865, the Civil War had contradicted the passage's rejection of "a revolution with the sword" as a means of ending slavery. Internal evidence indicates that, as Union armies were about to overwhelm the Confederacy, Garnet and James McCune Smith simply updated the 1848 version of the Address by deleting its endorsement of a peaceful means. There is no indication that they returned to an earlier version of the Address that had not been "toned down."[14] Instead several things suggest that the passage rejecting slave revolt had been in the Address as Garnet originally presented it in 1843. It is compatible with Garnet's rejection of slave revolt in his ambiguous speech at the 1842 Massachusetts Liberty Convention and with the similar ambiguity on the issue evident in Smith and Garrison's Addresses.[15] Also, neither Garnet nor his critics acknowledged during the 1840s that there had been a major change in his Address. Submitted to committee at the Buffalo convention, it came back to the floor "with some slight alterations" or "about the same thing."[16] In his preface to the 1848 version, Garnet noted that it had been "slightly modified" since 1843, "retaining, however, all of its original doctrine" (see p. 179).

Most important, the passage is compatible with the sophisticated and qualified way in which Garnet, elsewhere in his Address, approaches the question of how slaves could gain freedom. Unlike Gerrit Smith's and Garrison's Addresses to the Slaves, Garnet's rejects massive northward black exodus as a means of weakening slavery. He had gained his own freedom through escape and, like Smith, participated in underground railroading. But, while Smith and Garrison insist in their Addresses that abolitionists had made it easier for slaves who reached the North, Garnet declares escape to be pointless because, "THE PHARAOHS ARE ON BOTH SIDES OF THE BLOOD-RED WATERS" (see p. 186).[17]

Rather than calling on slaves to initiate escape or revolt, Garnet's Address advises them to launch a general strike. It maintains that by this means they could open "a more effectual door" to freedom than northern abolitionism offered (see p. 184).[18] Garnet advises bondmen, "Go to your lordly enslavers and tell them plainly, that YOU ARE DETERMINED TO BE FREE. Appeal to their sense of justice. . . . Entreat them to remove the grievous burdens which they have imposed upon you, and to remunerate you for your labor. . . . Tell them in language which they cannot misunderstand, of the exceeding sinfulness of slavery . . . and of the righteous retributions of an indignant God. . . . Do this, and for ever after cease to toil for the heartless tyrants, who give you no other reward but stripes and abuse" (see p. 185). Later, Garnet declares, "Let every slave throughout the land do this, and the days of slavery are numbered" (see p. 188).

This does not, however, settle the issue of Garnet's views in 1843 concerning violent means. As in the case of Garrison's Address, explicit denials of violent intent and plans for peaceful action counterbalance but do not negate violent imagery. This is especially the case for Garnet. He assumes that a general strike by slaves will very likely lead masters to "commence the work of death" and urges slaves to fight in response. "However much you and all of us may desire it," he proclaims, "there is not much hope of Redemption without the shedding of blood" (see p. 185). Like Smith and Garrison, he believes that slaves would not win in such a violent struggle. More than once he declares that it is better to "*die freemen, than live to be slaves*" (see pp. 185–86, 188). But he also suggests that God would help slaves in battle and that, since "pain, sorrow, and even death . . . are the common lot of slaves," they might prevail (see p. 186).

The central paradox of Garnet's Address—as it is less explicitly of Smith's and Garrison's—is the assumption that enslaved black men were simultaneously degraded and cowardly *and* capable of heroic action. This perplexing outlook transcends the three Addresses, the early 1840s, and the antislavery movement. It reflects a broader, deeper, racialism in American culture that affected both the North and South. Americans commonly assumed that black men were more *feminine* than white men, more sedentary, more inclined to forgive their oppressors than confront them, more inclined to the Christian virtues. Yet Americans also assumed that a capacity for violent action resided not far beneath black men's peaceful demeanor. Garnet traced that capacity to Africa's ancient glory. Racist theoreticians linked it to an African savagery they equated with an essentially bestial nature.[19]

Both abolitionists and slavery's defenders believed that outside intervention was the key to transforming black men to the degree that they would take action to free themselves and their families. On this assumption Smith, Garrison, and Garnet each intended his Address to reach slaves as well as to influence northerners. Yet increasing southern black resistence to slavery was what had encouraged the three men to prepare their Addresses calling on enslaved men to become more assertive. Paradoxically, enslaved men, whom Smith, Garrison, and Garnet regarded as too submissive, had inspired the Addresses. Smith and Garrison hoped to increase the number of northward escapes as a means of weakening slavery. Garnet hoped to promote a general strike that he assumed would lead to violent confrontation. All three raised images of slave revolt while simultaneously favoring peaceful means. Conflicted, contingent, and self-contradictory as they are, the Addresses point toward a future in which underground railroading and violent rhetoric characterized a northern abolitionism that sought contact with slaves.

Chapter Two

CIRCUMSTANCES

Beyond a sense of crisis among abolitionists, which led Smith, Garrison, and Garnet to advocate communicating with enslaved men in order to demand action, several circumstances shaped the Addresses to the Slaves. They were products of an antislavery movement that had for many years contended that the Bible and America's revolutionary heritage justified slave revolt. They were written and endorsed by immediate abolitionists who, despite the breakup of the AASS, continued to have a great deal in common and to communicate with one another. Ideas spread from individual to individual, meeting to meeting, and faction to faction. In particular, the three Addresses to the Slaves emerged from a genre of abolitionist propaganda designed to direct calls for action to specific constituencies. Most important in creating the Addresses, however, were the meetings at which Smith, Garrison, and Garnet presented them. Like other abolitionist gatherings, they followed patterns established over the previous generation by sectarian organizations, political parties, and voluntary associations. To understand the Addresses requires locating the meetings in time and space, establishing their gendered and racialized contexts, portraying their internal dynamics, and noting the events and ideologies that informed their participants.

The slave revolts aboard the *Amistad* in 1839 and the *Creole* in 1841 were central to the sense of crisis among abolitionists. The *Amistad* revolt had by the early 1840s led to sustained cooperation between antislavery leaders and the African rebels who had taken control of a Spanish slave ship, only to be arrested by Americans and jailed in Connecticut. Continuing coverage in the antislavery press of what became a successful effort to gain freedom for the rebels provided examples of black manhood and the ability of abolitionists to work with slaves. Meanwhile, the *Creole* rebels, who sailed to freedom in the British Bahama Islands, demonstrated that American slaves could be brave and successful. A few days before Smith's Address to the Slaves, Liberty abolitionists meeting at the Long Island town of Williamsburg praised the rebels, expressed a hope "that their noble example will be imitated by all in similar circumstances," and pledged not to help put down future slave revolts.[1]

Other dramatic events contributed to a belief among abolitionists that they faced a turning point. Confrontations between the forces of freedom and those of slavery had multiplied during the years prior to 1842. They seemed to offer both dangers and opportunities. In the same year as the *Amistad* mutiny, a dispute began between New York and Virginia concerning three black sailors accused of helping a slave escape. New York Governor William H. Seward's refusal to extradite the men helped publicize the idea that abolitionists had a duty to assist in escapes. The case also highlighted southern interference in a northern state and the willingness of a northern politician to resist. In January 1841 the arrest in Annapolis, Maryland, of Smith's colleague Charles T. Torrey for attempting to report on a slaveholders' convention called attention to abolitionist activity in the border South.[2]

Meanwhile, well-publicized political developments seemed to demonstrate the subservience of the U.S. government to slavery's interests and the need, therefore, for more aggressive action by abolitionists. Since 1836, Massachusetts Congressman John Quincy Adams had led a courageous but unsuccessful struggle against the Gag Rule that banned antislavery petitions from the House of Representatives. Then in March 1842, a few weeks after Smith's Address, three events deepened abolitionist concern. First, the issues of slave revolt and the power of slavery in the national government combined as the House of Representatives censured Congressman Joshua R. Giddings of Ohio for his words in support of the *Creole* rebels. Second, the Supreme Court in *Prigg v. Pennsylvania* declared unconstitutional a Pennsylvania law protecting fugitive slaves from recapture and recognized national authority over the rendition of fugitives. This prompted New England's leading Liberty newspaper to declare that black men had a duty to resist the Fugitive Slave Law of 1793.[3] Third, the slaveholding Republic of Texas renewed its request to be annexed to the United States. The likelihood that Congress would respond positively to this request led Torrey, who was already cooperating with slaves, to call for a biracial military response. He predicted that "50,000 colored troops, including 15,000 *fugitives from slavery*, from every Southern State, with the war cry of freedom for their fellow sufferers on their lips . . . aided by 100 or 200,000 white troops, would sweep over the South, without even the possibility of serious resistance."[4]

As both the Williamsburg resolutions and Torrey's remarks indicate, a willingness to approve a black war against slavery transcended the Addresses to the Slaves. For many years abolitionists had drawn on the Bible to justify slave revolt. Since the 1750s they had warned that God would unleash a black uprising to punish white America for its sinful slaveholding. Repeatedly during the 1830s immediatists contended that emancipation was the only alternative to divine retribution. Shortly after Nat Turner's revolt in August 1831, Garrison linked slave uprisings with the "vengeance of Heaven." Angelina Grimke, in her *Appeal to the Christian Women of the South*, referred to "Divine vengeance." Following the *Amistad* mutiny, Smith declared, "I cannot but look on these remarkable and exciting occurrences in a very cheering light. God has ordered them to hasten the overthrow of slavery."[5]

Years prior to the Addresses to the Slaves, abolitionists had also linked slave revolt to the spirit of the American Revolution. Garrison always insisted that *he* would not advocate violence. But he was the chief proponent during the 1830s of the contention that the Declaration of Independence justified slave revolt. In 1837 he noted that the slaves suffered worse oppression than that which had driven Americans in 1775 to take up arms against Great Britain. If whites claimed they had a right to fight for liberty, he contended, they had to recognize that blacks did too. If whites persisted in oppressing other men, they had to "confess that they deserve[d] to perish."[6] A year later James G. Birney, a former slaveholder turned abolitionist who would in 1840 and 1844 serve as the Liberty presidential candidate, expressed a similar sentiment. He declared that "those who approve of the conduct of our fathers in the American Revolution, must agree that the slaves have at least as good a natural right to vindicate their rights by physical force." Throughout the 1830s and for years thereafter, abolitionists combined their respect for the power of God and their reverence for the Founders by quoting Thomas Jefferson's warning that if the slaves revolted "the Almighty has no attribute which can take sides with us in such a contest."[7]

The American Revolution was also the principal source of abolitionist devotion to a republican morality that contributed to their view of black masculinity. A republican tenet was that a man who submitted to oppression and thereby lost his manhood could regain it by struggling for his rights. Abolitionists had no difficulty applying this notion to white men. In 1843 church-oriented New York abolitionist William Jay called on submissive nonslaveholding southern "WHITE MALES" to abolish slavery in order to gain freedom for themselves. "Up, [ac]quit yourselves like men," he declared, "and may Almighty God direct and bless your efforts."[8] That same year Torrey castigated northern white men for failing to defend their freedom and families from southern aggression.[9] Sometimes, however, racialist notions concerning the intrinsic docility of black men kept abolitionists from applying this view of redeemable manliness to them. "We act for him, who is the most helpless creature in the Universe of God," declared white radical political abolitionist Alvan Stewart in 1839. A few years later Frederick Douglass told a group of Garrisonians that slaves were "goods and chattels, not men." It was, he maintained, up to abolitionists "to save them from all this."[10]

Yet abolitionists knew that black men had fought in the American Revolution, had fought for freedom in Haiti, and had rebelled or plotted rebellion in the South. Following Turner's revolt, a *Liberator* correspondent declared, "Negroes, like other men, have a spirit which rebels against tyranny and oppression."[11] From the late 1820s onward abolitionists assumed that God, Independence Day celebrations, and abolitionist propaganda could inspire enslaved black men to seek freedom. While Garnet harbored doubts about black masculinity, his aim was actually to shame enslaved men into action. His model was David Walker, who in his *Appeal* declared, "The man who would not fight . . . to be delivered from the most wicked, abject and servile slavery . . . ought to be kept with all his children or family, in slavery or in chains to be butchered by his cruel enemies." Well before Garnet, Walker demanded, "Are we MEN? . . . How could we be *so submissive* to a gang of men, whom we cannot tell whether they are *as good as* ourselves or not?"[12]

There were also prior assertions, concentrated in Smith's radical political abolitionist faction, of the right to contact slaves. While almost all abolitionists had, during the 1830s, promised not to intervene between slaves and masters, a few had continued to assert that they had a "*right* to address" black southerners, both slave and free. William Goodell, a white New Yorker who later worked with Smith, declared in October 1835, "Even in respect to the slaves, there is no earthly power that can possibly have a right to forbid our intercourse with them for Christian and moral purposes. . . . Whatever the Bible teaches, respecting oppression, or any other subject, we have a right to teach to every one, and of course to the slave. If *others* may teach him to 'obey his master,' we may teach him the same thing. And we have an equal right to add—'if thou mayest be free, use it rather.'" In June 1839 an abolitionist from Kentucky urged his northern counterparts to go into the South to help African Americans. Later that year Smith advised abolitionists, "Let the slaves of Delaware, Maryland, Virginia, Kentucky, and Missouri know, that, on entering the free States, they shall find friends."[13]

During the 1830s and early 1840s a genre of abolitionist literature followed Walker's *Appeal* in singling out specific groups to receive advice, prophecies, and calls to action. Garrison's *Address Delivered before the Free People of Color, in Philadelphia, New-York, and Other Cities, during the Month of June, 1831* went through three editions that same year. Angelina Grimke wrote her *Appeal to the Christian Women of the South* in 1836. Her *Appeal to the Women of the Nominally Free States* appeared the following year. The AFASS published William Jay's *Address to the Non-Slaveholders of the South* in February 1843, with the stated purpose of arousing southern white men to antislavery action, just as the Addresses to the Slaves claimed to target southern black men.[14]

Regardless of whether they were black or white, Garrisonian or Liberty abolitionists, most of those who heard Smith, Garrison, or Garnet deliver their Addresses to the Slaves shared a perception of crisis, understood the Addresses' conceptual backgrounds, and were familiar with the genre. They also shared an ambivalence concerning peaceful versus violent and legal versus illegal means and understood the relationship between assertions of manhood and freedom. Just as important, they knew the function of antislavery meetings, the purpose of addresses, and their own role. The meetings at which Smith, Garrison, and Garnet spoke followed procedures characteristic of northern reform organizations. They were public gatherings that included attentive audiences of men and women. In each case, a few well-informed and experienced leaders dominated program, resolution, and address committees. They managed delegates—many of whom were self-appointed—and entertained spectators by intertwining emotional fervor with careful stage-managing. The leaders were experts in dramatic factional maneuvering. That expertise together with the meetings' venues invariably influenced the spirit, content, and style of the Addresses, which were designed to bridge, as best they could, the geographical and cultural distances between their auditors and the slaves.

Smith delivered his Address at the January 1842 New York Liberty gubernatorial nominating convention. This impressive gathering convened in a large Presbyterian church near his estate in the tiny, heavily abolitionized, and nearly all-white "lively and cheerful" village of Peterboro located in Smithfield Township. Smith, of course, advocated embracing slaves as allies in a more aggressive effort against the South. Yet physically and culturally the meeting was far removed from the southern black men who comprised his designated audience. In contrast to other New York Liberty meetings and those that Garrison and Garnet addressed, there is no record that former slaves or other African Americans were in attendance and able to symbolize the oppressed.[15] Smith was well aware of these deficiencies and attempted to counteract them. Later Garrison and Garnet used other means to emphasize the spiritual, if not physical, unity of northern abolitionists and southern slaves.

The Peterboro convention came at a time when the New York Liberty abolitionists believed that God looked favorably on their efforts against slavery. Many of them were small-town community leaders representing agricultural regions. Long active in various reform movements, heavily influenced by Christian perfectionism, and willing to work with clergy, they used moral suasion and political action as a means to reach millennial goals. They realized, nevertheless, that they could achieve only so much in the North, and they embraced governmental and nongovernmental strategies by which they could directly influence the South.[16] Therefore, they readily accepted Smith's call for a relationship with slaves, although some quibbled over the details.

Garrisonian journalist Oliver Johnson, a guest at Smith's home, provides an evocative description of the physical setting in Peterboro as the convention got underway that frigid January. Johnson estimates that between one thousand and fifteen hundred men and women attended the meeting. Four hundred men served as delegates, while the rest came to observe. Having arrived "in sleighs from the neighboring towns and counties" and "every part of the state," they found accommodations in one or the other of the village's "two temperance houses" or as guests in private homes.[17] A nonabolitionist correspondent of the *New York Tribune*, who filed a report very similar to Johnson's, notes that those who attended the convention filled the church "almost to suffocation" and that some had to be turned away.[18] This federal-style building had great significance among New York abolitionists because it had been a place of refuge for participants in a 1835 antislavery convention, whom a mob had driven out of nearby Utica. It had particular importance to Smith, because it was there that he responded to the abolitionist refugees from Utica by deciding to become an immediatist.[19]

As those attending the January 1842 convention entered the church, they observed two large paintings suspended above the pulpit. The paintings had been created at Smith's request by Edwin W. Goodwin, a skilled artist, an associate of Torrey, and the editor of the *Tocsin of Liberty*, a weekly newspaper published in Albany in behalf of the Eastern New York Anti-Slavery Society. Designed as backdrops for Smith's Address and as weak substitutes for black participation, Goodwin's paintings sought to enhance empathy for distant slaves. One of the paintings mixed religious and political imagery, just as the New York Liberty Party mixed church and state in its demand for "righteous government." The painting portrayed "a kneeling [male] slave, his body red with the stains caught from a recent scourging, lifting his chained hands on high, and casting his eyes imploringly toward the capitol of the United States." In the background were depictions of the slave trade in the District of Columbia. Entitled *Prayer of the Slave to the People of the United States*, the painting served as a graphic counterpoint to Smith's "Address of the Anti-Slavery Convention of the State of New-York . . . to the Slaves in the U. States of America."[20]

This painting unequivocally presented the view that enslaved black men were passive victims awaiting deliverance from benevolent northerners. It contrasted with the mixed messages in Smith's Address. While Smith asked enslaved men to act on their own *and* to rely on northern benevolence, the slave in the painting is helpless. He cannot act on his own. Instead, in the painting's caption, he implores white northerners to "*Talk* for me—*Write* for me—*Print* for me—*Vote* for me." Goodwin's other painting had a similar theme. It portrayed another kneeling male slave "undergoing flagellation by a savage overseer," raising his eyes to heaven, and praying, "Induce my fellow-men to *feel* for me, and *do* for me."[21] By counteracting Smith's more assertive statements concerning slave agency, the paintings made the statements more palatable to those assembled.

Sixteen months later, the New England Anti-Slavery Convention met in Boston. Those who gathered were socially similar to those who had met in Peterboro, except that a few African-American men and a few white women were active delegates. The New Englanders were also more likely than the evangelical political abolitionists of upstate New York to reject church and governmental institutions. The New Yorkers had left proslavery churches to establish antislavery churches and had left the proslavery major political parties to form the Liberty Party. The New Englanders rejected all religious and formally political organizations as inherently sinful, violent, and proslavery.[22] They were more opposed to patriarchy than were the New Yorkers and more advanced in their conception of women's rights.

The New Englanders, nevertheless, were as aware as their counterparts in Peterboro that they had to use dramatic techniques to promote empathy for slaves. Where Smith had relied on Goodwin's paintings to accomplish this, Garrison relied on George Latimer, who months earlier had been the subject of a fugitive slave controversy, and on four members of the Hutchinson family of white antislavery minstrels. Intended as supplements to Garrison's Address, just as Goodwin's paintings supplemented Smith's, Latimer and the Hutchinsons contradicted Garrison in ways that allowed auditors to hold differing impressions of his point. Latimer, who had been freed in Boston as a result of an interracial petitioning campaign, symbolized the benevolent relationship between northern abolitionists and southern slaves. His light complexion surprised some in the audience, who had assumed that "only a dark black man" could be enslaved, and enhanced their sympathy for those in bonds. In his speech Latimer relied on a northern sentimentalized regard for women as symbols of sacred family ties, which had developed as more men left home each day in an industrializing economy, to strengthen emotional ties to slaves. He stressed that his blind, "aged mother" had no one to help her because all of her children had "been sold under the hammer into different States." One observer declared that as a result of Latimer's story "there were new hearts, great and good hearts too, touched by his wrong, and his wo[e] . . . which will beat for his deliverance till death."[23]

Emotions intensified as, on at least eight occasions during the convention, the Hutchinsons—with Garrison and others joining in—sang about similar tragedies. The minstrels, who were "from the hills of New Hampshire," mixed "thrilling mountain strains" with hymns, accompanied themselves on fiddles, and encouraged audience participation. A few months earlier, Garrison had declared music to be a "natural ally" of abolitionism, and the Hutchinsons' sentimental songs brought "tears . . . which never fell for the slave before." The militantly pacifistic "There's a Good Time Coming" fit in well with Garrison's semi-violent imagery. Among the lyrics was "Cannon balls may aid the truth, but thought's a weapon stronger." But when the Hutchinsons' sang "The Bereaved Mother," which portrayed a slave woman driven to insanity by the sale of her children, they contradicted Garrison's advice that abolitionists concentrate their activities in the North. The song's lyrics implored the audience, "Go! rescue the mothers, the sisters and brothers, from sorrow and woe."[24] They suggested that aggressive actions more in line with Gerrit Smith's Address constituted a proper northern response to the outrages slaveholders perpetrated on black families.

The Boston gathering had an edge in attendance and historical setting over the earlier one in Peterboro. The New England Anti-Slavery Convention, which had been an annual event since 1834, usually met in Boston's Chardin Street Chapel. But, as large numbers of abolitionists arrived in the city during the days preceding the 1843 meeting, Garrisonian leaders determined to hold it instead at the Miller Tabernacle on Howard Street. The Tabernacle, Garrison declared, was a "vast" building that could accommodate a "mighty throng." That is exactly what turned out for the meeting, which had a daily attendance of between two and three thousand. Expecting an even larger crowd for the evening sessions, the local leaders reserved the even more spacious Faneuil Hall, and Garrison delivered his Address to the Slaves in that venerable building.[25]

"The famous old Cradle of Liberty," although poorly maintained during the 1840s, was evocative in its republican simplicity. As Elizabeth Cady Stanton recalled, "This old hall was sacred to so many memories connected with the early days of the Revolution that it was kind of a Mecca for the lovers of liberty visiting Boston."[26] Garrison knew that there could have been no better setting for his comparison of slave rebels and America's revolutionary generation. O. A. Bowe, an observer from Gerrit Smith's upstate New York region, reported that as Garrison stood on the hall's "lofty platform" and "read in clear and glowing tones the Address to the American slaves," he could see "a vast sea of faces, at least five thousand in all." All agreed that the New England convention had been "the largest and most enthusiastic gathering of abolitionists that we have ever witnessed."[27]

Although there are limits to comparing rural Peterboro and urban Boston, the two gatherings, in their historical surroundings, in their great size, in their reliance on emotional paintings or songs, as well as in their diffuse, self-contradictory messages, had much in common. While the meetings represented feuding abolitionist factions that disagreed on fundamental points concerning antislavery ideology and tactics, a Garrisonian could feel at home in Peterboro and a radical political abolitionist in Boston. Each meeting shared a reform culture broad enough—or imprecise enough—to embrace a variety of views. To a degree, the same may be said of the black national convention in Buffalo at which, ten weeks after the Boston meeting, Garnet presented his Address to the Slaves. Neither Smith nor Garrison would have felt out of place at the Buffalo gathering; white abolitionists had been attending black national conventions since their beginning. Like the Peterboro meeting, each session of the National Convention of Colored Citizens opened with a prayer. Like the Boston meeting, those assembled frequently "united in singing" antislavery, or what the convention minutes calls "liberty," songs.[28] As was the case in the other meetings, dramatic debate held the audience's attention.

Yet in its physical, cultural, and factional contexts, the Buffalo meeting diverged more from the other two than they did from each other. Like Smith and Garrison, Garnet spoke before a particular constituency. His was overwhelmingly black, while Smith's was exclusively white, and Garrison's overwhelmingly white. In regard to outcomes, however, a more important difference was that, in contrast to Smith's and Garrison's immediate audiences, Garnet's was neither regionally nor ideologically cohesive. As a result, he faced a more difficult situation than either Smith or Garrison. Also the National Convention of Colored Citizens attracted far fewer participants than the other two meetings. The main reason for this is that, while Peterboro and Boston were major centers respectively for Smith's and Garrison's brand of abolitionism, Buffalo was not for Garnet's. Although there were black and white abolitionists in that city, they were far less numerous than they were in central New York or in New England.[29]

Instead of being an abolitionist center, Buffalo, during the summer of 1843, was a target for abolitionist agitation by Garrisonian and Liberty abolitionists, with each group attempting to expand its influence to a point that linked western New York to the Old Northwest. In July two New York Liberty abolitionists—Torrey early in the month and his colleague Abel Brown shortly thereafter–had held meetings in the city. In early August an interracial band of Garrisonians—including George Bradburn, Frederick Douglass, Sydney Howard Gay, Abby Kelley, and Charles Lennox Remond—had, as part of what the Garrisonians called their "Hundred Conventions" effort, held another series of meetings there. It was no coincidence that Garnet and other black Liberty abolitionists arranged for the black national convention to meet there during the middle of the month, nor that at the end of the month the Liberty Party national convention met there to nominate a presidential ticket for 1844.[30]

The Liberty Party had strength in Ohio, as well as in western New York. Consequently its convention drew a respectable crowd, estimated to have been as high as five thousand. But Buffalo was not only a long way from the eastern cities where most northern African Americans lived—it also had at that time no direct railroad link to those cities.[31] It made sense for black Liberty abolitionists to counter the Garrisonian efforts by holding the convention in that city. But the location significantly limited turnout. Also, when Garnet issued a call for the convention, black Garrisonians in Pennsylvania and Massachusetts discouraged attendance. They maintained that unilateral black action contradicted the biracial character of the AASS, that Liberty and AFASS leaders would control the convention, and that the AASS had already established the best means of achieving abolition. Ironically, considering what Garnet would say in his Address to the Slaves, black Garrisonians also charged that the convention would concentrate on northern black grievances and neglect the plight of the slaves.[32] No delegates from Pennsylvania attended. From Massachusetts there were only Douglass and Remond, who were already in Buffalo.[33]

When the convention convened on the morning of August 15, there were just forty delegates present. By the following morning there were fifty-eight. The audience, composed of men, women, and children, numbered, according to Remond, in the "hundreds" and, according to historian Benjamin Quarles, included "scores" of whites. This was a tiny gathering compared to the ones that Smith and Garrison addressed. It is significant, nevertheless, that, just as having women in the audience modified the all-male character of the Peterboro convention, the presence of white men and women in the audience modified the "exclusive" character of the black convention.[34]

In addition to being distinctly fewer in number than those who heard Smith and Garrison deliver their Addresses to the Slaves, those who audited Garnet's speech did so in less grand physical surroundings. The "large public hall on the corner of Washington and Seneca streets," which the convention was able to use without charge, lacked the historic symbolism of either the Peterboro Presbyterian Church or Faneuil Hall. Frederick Douglass described the Buffalo hall as "an old dilapidated, and deserted room formerly used as a post office." Earlier yet it had been a Baptist church, so there may have been some lingering religious ambiance. But, except for evening sessions held at Park Presbyterian Church, the middle-class respectability and historical continuity of surroundings enjoyed by Smith, Garrison, and their audiences were missing. That many of the black people in Garnet's audience were poor and shabbily dressed—a white

Garrisonian described them as "ragamuffins"—also contrasted with the genteel, overwhelmingly white audiences that heard Smith and Garrison.[35]

Yet, despite the much smaller attendance and less auspicious surroundings, Garnet was as well prepared as Smith and Garrison to place his Address within a dramatic visual and auditory framework. Where Smith had paintings and Garrison had Latimer and the Hutchinsons to engage emotions, Garnet had his own persona. At age twenty-seven he was a striking figure—tall and muscular, with "ebony skin." Although one of his legs had recently been amputated below the knee, he seemed to be a black Apollo, and he already had a reputation as a speaker who could "fire up his auditors." After listening to him, a white correspondent of the *Buffalo Commercial Advertiser* declared, "I have heard some of the first men of our land speak, but they never held their audience under such complete control as Garnet."[36]

Mixing humor and pathos, he made himself the embodiment of black suffering and resolution in slavery. In support of his Address, he noted that "he had been a slave himself when young" and provided a "thrilling portraiture of his own feelings." His gracefully animated presentation moved his auditors, "white and black, woman, and child," to tears. Not even white lawyers could control their emotions. Then when Garnet turned to denounce the "character of slave-holders, all over the house, the tear was instantly dried, the fist involuntarily clenched." An antiabolitionist white clergyman declared "that were he to act from the impulse of the moment, he should shoulder his musket and march South"—a remark that, once again, would have been a more appropriate response to Smith's logic. Garnet was so effective, the correspondent contended, that he did "not believe there was a white man present who was not forced to acknowledge to himself, that for one hour in his life his mind had not been his own, but wholly at the control of the eloquent negro, the gifted man." If anything, Garnet had an even greater emotional impact on the African Americans present. Twenty years later, one delegate recalled that his presentation was "one of the most powerful and eloquent, which ever fell from mortal lips. Stern men were moved by it, and shaked as the wild storm sways the oaks of the forest, every soul was thrilled, every heart melted, every eye was suffused with tears."[37]

Some authorities consider the antebellum period to have been the golden age of American oratory. It provided entertainment to audiences and a "path to honor and fame" for speakers who sought to be persuasive through passion and reason. Of the three who presented Addresses to the Slaves during the early 1840s, Garnet was the most able and dramatic speaker. While his contemporaries regarded Smith to be eloquent, he did not approach Garnet's level, and, aside from a striking earnestness, Garrison was the least impressive orator of the three.[38] He and Smith, however, had the advantage of addressing large antislavery gatherings held in historic venues located at the geographical centers of their respective abolitionist factions. They were also the undisputed, if not unchallenged, leaders of those factions. Garnet's immediate audience was much smaller and his venue much less meaningful. Stirring as his remarks were, he confronted a far more ideologically and geographically, if not racially, diverse group of delegates than either of the others. He also lacked their status as a factional leader. Therefore, he was less effective in Buffalo than were his counterparts in Peterboro and Boston.

Chapter Three

PROCEEDINGS

All three Addresses to the Slaves depart from abolitionist rhetoric of the 1830s by advocating communication with slaves in order to encourage unrest. For years historians have assumed that black abolitionists were more enthusiastic than white abolitionists about such departures. Yet this is not borne out in the immediate reactions to the Addresses, as Smith's and Garrison's respective conventions endorsed theirs and Garnet's refused to endorse his. The reason for this important difference in the fates of the Addresses lies in the proceedings of the three meetings, which reveal a relationship between abolitionist factionalism and widely differing views concerning aggressive antislavery tactics.

The gatherings addressed by Smith, Garrison, and Garnet each represented a distinct antislavery community. Almost all of the white Liberty abolitionists who voted on Smith's Address were evangelical perfectionists from central New York, who denied that slavery could enjoy the protection of church or state. Almost all of those who voted on Garrison's were social perfectionists who embraced nonresistance, opposed the creation of abolitionist third parties, and supported his emerging disunionism. But only most of those who voted on Garnet's Address were evangelical black political abolitionists from Garnet's region of upstate New York. In contrast to the Peterboro and Boston conventions, at Buffalo there were influential minorities who represented other regions and differing points of view.[1]

Conflict between a longstanding commitment to nonviolence and a desire to encourage action on the part of slaves, which could become violent, existed within all three groups. So did an awareness of the struggle between political abolitionists and Garrisonians to define the character of the antislavery movement. But, because of its greater diversity, the black national convention had more pronounced tensions. Garnet and other radical Liberty Party advocates organized the meeting. But Garrisonians and moderate Liberty abolitionists had considerable influence on its proceedings. As a result, the dynamics at Buffalo differed from those at Peterboro and Boston. Smith and Garrison, as the universally respected leaders of their relatively homogeneous gatherings, were, through a variety of means, able to diffuse tensions and limit objections to their Addresses to the Slaves. Garnet, dealing with an ideologically more heterogeneous group and lacking Smith's and Garrison's prestige, could not.

The manuscript "Minutes of the New York Liberty Party Convention" reveals a great deal concerning the religious, intellectual, and factional contexts within which Smith presented his Address. Evangelical Christianity had an especially important role, as clergy were ubiquitous among the four hundred delegates who gathered at Peterboro. For example, the Reverend John Cross of Illinois, one of the five honorary out-of-state delegates, presented an address on "political action."[2] In addition, an experienced group of abolitionists, all of whom were tied to Smith by ideology, friendship, or by a mixture of the two, dominated the convention's leadership. Among them were Alvan Stewart and William Goodell who were in their fifties, Beriah Green who was in his mid-forties, Henry B. Stanton who was thirty-six, and James C. Jackson who was nearly thirty-two.

Stewart, a wealthy lawyer from Utica, had for years predicted that, in lieu of immediate emancipation, slaves would revolt. During the late 1830s, he pioneered the contention that Congress had power to abolish slavery in the southern states. Goodell, who also resided in Utica, had edited reform and antislavery newspapers since 1827. He helped found the AASS and in 1844 published a synopsis of the radical political abolitionists' contention that slavery was unconstitutional throughout the United States. Green had been since 1833 the president of the Oneida Institute, a racially integrated abolitionist manual labor school in Whiteboro, New York. (One of Green's students during the late 1830s was Henry Highland Garnet.) Jackson, who in 1842 resided near Smith's home in Peterboro, was an antislavery journalist who was for a time *both* a Garrisonian and Liberty abolitionist. He worked closely with Torrey and William L. Chaplin, both of whom helped slaves escape from the South.[3] Stanton, who had during the 1830s been a fearless antislavery speaker and a member of the executive committee of the AASS, was a lawyer residing in Johnstown, Fulton County, and the husband of Smith's cousin, the feminist leader Elizabeth Cady Stanton. As the Peterboro convention got under way most of these individuals, as well as Smith's friends Edwin W. Goodwin and New York City resident Limaeus P. Noble, assumed prominent roles. Noble chaired the convention, Goodwin chaired the gubernatorial nominating committee, Stanton chaired the resolutions committee, and Stewart chaired the address committee. Stanton, Goodell, Noble, Stewart, Jackson, and Goodwin engaged in the debate over Smith's Address to the Slaves.

Of these six, Stanton alone was not a radical political abolitionist. He had more in common with Liberty leaders in Massachusetts and Ohio who hoped to turn the third party into a mass political movement.[4] But even Stanton agreed to facilitate a more aggressive abolitionist stance toward the South. Early in the afternoon of the convention's first day, he reported nineteen resolutions that foreshadowed a positive response to Smith's Address. Two resolutions that dealt with the *Creole* revolt demonstrated that abolitionists touched emotionally by Goodwin's paintings of helpless slaves also admired slaves who fought for freedom. One of the resolutions anticipated Garrison by comparing "the insurgents on board of the Creole" with the "heroes of the American Revolution." The other thanked God for the insurgents' heroism. Shortly after Stanton introduced the resolutions, the delegates created a committee to devise "measures to excite a deeper and more efficient interest among the people of this State and nation in the cause of the oppressed and arouse the forces of Freedom and humanity to action for the overthrow of slavery more energetic and determined than hitherto."[5]

Meanwhile the militant abolitionists at Peterboro assured their more moderate associates that they would not abandon less-dangerous activities in the North. On the first evening of the convention—just before Smith presented his Address to the Slaves—Stewart read a draft of the gathering's official "Address of the Liberty State Convention . . . to the Electors of the State of New York." This document indicates that, whatever new measures Smith might propose, the party would continue to pursue electoral politics.[6] Stewart did not avoid issues related to black rights or to violent means. His address declares that the domestic slave trade "vies in cruelty with the blood-stained piracy of the 'middle passage,'" and it denounces the kidnapping of free blacks into slavery. It calls for the enfranchisement of black men, praises the *Creole* rebels for driving "terror through the heart of every oppressor in the nation," and warns that there would be a larger slave revolt if slavery were not immediately abolished. But its main appeal is to the self-image and self-interest of northern white men.

Utilizing rhetorical techniques that Garnet later employed to demand action from enslaved black men, Stewart challenges northern white men to regard slavery as a threat to their masculinity. Invoking memories of the Revolutionary War and claims of southern aggression against northern interests, he declares that a slaveholders' conspiracy threatened the equal rights principles of the Declaration of Independence, which white northern men had fought for against Great Britain. Slaveholders, he charges, had taken control of the United States government, crippled the "prosperity of the free North," annexed slaveholding territories, and limited the spread of free labor. While Stewart confines himself to advocating a peaceful political strategy to counter these aggressions, he, like Smith, Garrison, and Garnet, employs violent imagery. Addressing white northern men, he goes so far as to contend that slaveholders had "assaulted our wives and daughters, burnt down our halls, blown up our churches, broken our presses . . . [and] for nine long years filled our borders with persecution, violence, terror." In response, he warns, Liberty "assaults" on the proslavery Democratic and Whig Parties "shall be incessant and unrelenting" and the antislavery struggle in Congress will "soon burst into a consuming flame."

Despite Stanton's and Stewart's efforts to accommodate different points of view and prepare the way for Smith's call for aggressive action, controversy had a role at Peterboro. Two disputes—one concerning the Liberty gubernatorial nomination and one concerning Smith's Address—provided entertainment for those assembled and revealed controllable tensions within New York's Liberty Party. All abolitionists admired Smith for his generosity, eloquence, warmth, and leadership, and, although he was notoriously reluctant to run for office, those assembled hoped to nominate him for governor. With that aim in mind and well aware of Smith's predilections, Stanton's committee proposed a resolution declaring that no abolitionist should "refuse any position which his station, endowments and resources fit him to honor." When Smith declared "emphatically, that he could not accept the nomination; as he believed it to be the will of God that he should not hold civil office," the delegates spent "nearly the whole evening session . . . in a fruitless effort" to have him change his mind. The convention then passed Stanton's resolution anyway, "large minority voting in the negative," and nominated Stewart in Smith's place.[7] The disagreement neither harmed Smith's standing nor the spirit of the gathering.

The second controversy had more serious implications regarding the relationship of radical political abolitionists to the rest of the antislavery movement. But, like Smith's refusal to be nominated, it served to enliven the gathering at Peterboro and had no impact on the fate of his Address to the Slaves. On the first night of the convention, after Smith had presented his Address, the delegates voted to submit it and Stewart's to committee for revision and publication. The following morning an "informal discussion upon the address to the Slaves" began.[8] Noble, Goodell, Stanton, and others wanted to delete the portion advising fugitive slaves to take in the free states as well as in the slave states what they needed for a successful escape. Stewart, Smith, Jackson, Goodwin, and others wanted to retain it. This debate foreshadowed a broader one among abolitionists and other northerners that began after the Address's publication.[9]

Although the convention minutes do not indicate them, the issues in the debate probably were Christian morality and northern public opinion on the one side versus the slaves' right to self defense and abolitionist solidarity with escapees on the other. In any case, a motion to delete the passage lost by a resounding 127 to 48 vote. Then the delegates agreed by voice vote, with only "several voices being heard in the negative," to adopt and publish the Address. Just before the convention ended, the delegates adopted several more resolutions in accord with it. They expressed support for the three young white men who had been arrested in Missouri for attempting to help slaves escape, vowed not to "take up arms against the slaves, should they use violence in asserting their right to freedom," and pledged to protect from recapture fugitive slaves who reached New York.[10]

Sentimental graphics, verbal ambiguity, celebration of slave rebels as heroes, and a willingness among leading New York Liberty abolitionists to modify their own views helped produce acceptance of Smith's call for a more active involvement with slaves on the part of northern abolitionists. More important, an ideologically coherent group had assembled under Smith's undisputed leadership at Peterboro. When the New England Anti-Slavery Convention met in Boston, similar conditions and strategies produced what at the time appeared to be even more united support for Garrison's Address to the Slaves.

The Garrisonian leaders who managed this meeting were a larger, more varied, and more striking group than the Liberty leaders at Peterboro. They left more extensive records of their doings and have been more closely studied by historians. They were also on average younger, less religiously orthodox, less statist in political orientation, more committed to equality of the sexes, and more urban than Smith and his colleagues. In contrast to the Peterboro gathering, black men and white women actively participated in the Boston convention.

Aside from Garrison himself, the more influential white men attending the New England Anti-Slavery Convention were Charles C. Burleigh, Stephen S. Foster, Samuel J. May, Wendell Phillips, Edmund Quincy, and Nathaniel P. Rogers. Most prominent among black men attending were Douglass and Remond. Among white women, thirty-seven-year-old Maria Weston Chapman, an able antislavery administrator, author, and editor, was most influential. With the exceptions of May who was forty-six and Rogers who was forty-nine, all of the white men were in their thirties. Burleigh was a lawyer, who advocated antisabbatarianism and women's rights, as well as abolitionism. Foster, a former minister, worked full time as an abolitionist agent. May was a Unitarian minister. Phillips and Quincy were Boston aristocrats who had joined the abolitionists during the late 1830s. Of the two black leaders, Remond, who was born free in Massachusetts, was at age thirty-three a veteran antislavery orator. Douglass, who was twenty-six, had in 1838 escaped from slavery in Maryland and was just beginning his career as a professional abolitionist.[11]

The engagement of both blacks and whites, men and women as delegates at the Boston convention set it apart from the Peterboro and Buffalo gatherings. Yet this difference should not be exaggerated. The participation of three black delegates—Douglass, Remond, and George Latimer—at the Boston meeting certainly exceeded the number of black delegates at Peterboro, where there were none, and the number of white delegates at Buffalo, where there were also none. But it is unlikely that black men were excluded from the Peterboro meeting, since Garnet and other black men regularly participated as delegates at other New York Liberty Party conventions, and there were a number of whites in the audience at Buffalo. Also the only white women in addition to Chapman who actively participated at the New England Anti-Slavery Convention were Abigail Folsom—widely regarded as eccentric—and the little-known Sarah C. Redlon of Maine. And there was considerable sexual segregation at the Boston meeting. According to visiting New Yorker O. A. Bowe, when Garrison presented his Address to the Slaves, Faneuil Hall's "broad galleries were filled to overflowing with ladies, and the ample area below was densely crowded with the other sex."[12] Having women in his audience did not lead Garrison to modify the masculinity of his Address any more than it led Smith and Garnet to temper the masculinity of theirs. It was the power of women in Garrison's faction, nevertheless, that made the triumph of his Address at Faneuil Hall more apparent than real.

Rather than in its slightly greater degree of inclusiveness, the Boston meeting's main difference from the one in Peterboro lay in its ideological foundations. Those at Peterboro believed that governmental and religious institutions could be used to abolish slavery and perfect human society. Those at the Boston meeting regarded government and churches to be inherently sinful. Most of those in Peterboro interpreted the United States Constitution to be antislavery to the degree that slavery had no legal existence anywhere in the country. Those in Boston believed the Constitution to be fundamentally proslavery, requiring them not to vote or hold office under it, though not necessarily to violate its provisions. New York Liberty abolitionists supported efforts to go into the South to confront slavery. Most Garrisonians believed the key to abolishing slavery was to separate the North from the "guilt of that great national crime."[13]

Yet during the spring of 1843 Garrisonians, still hoping to win over Liberty abolitionists, avoided offending antislavery voters. They approached Liberty views when they declared that abolitionists should not vote for slaveholders rather than not vote at all. They also asserted that those assembled were "truly faithful to the spirit of that Constitution, and to the great work that our [Revolutionary] fathers began."[14] When Foster offered a resolution contending that no abolitionists could consistently accept office or vote under the Constitution, Quincy, who was presiding, ruled him out of order. In contrast to other Garrisonian proceedings, those of the Boston meeting contain no nonresistant denunciations of violence and of human governments which necessarily rest on violence.

Instead those gathered showed their love of debate by engaging in a long discussion of how harshly to condemn the clergy and churches for hampering the antislavery movement and upholding human bondage. While clergy and prayer were ubiquitous earlier in Peterboro and later in Buffalo, extreme anticlericalism characterized the Boston convention. Although a fair number of ministers attended the Boston meeting, most of them had "no heart to come forward . . . to do battle."[15] Therefore, there was little risk that a discussion of the clergy's character would seriously divide the Garrisonian faction of abolitionists. Shortly after the convention began, the business committee reported a resolution denouncing the churches as corrupt, dangerous, and unworthy of the trust of a "moral and religious people." There followed a running debate over whether resolutions offered by Foster, which condemned organized religion even more harshly, should be adopted. Those who joined with him in seeking to declare the "clerical office" inherently favorable to "despotism and slavery" included, among others, Redlon, Remond, Rogers, and Garrison. Among those opposed were May, Phillips, Douglass, Quincy, and Burleigh. In the end, the convention rejected Foster's resolutions. But the long, entertaining debate served several purposes. It created drama. It demonstrated Garrisonian commitment to freedom of speech on an issue on which there was essential agreement. It helped, along with Latimer and the Hutchinsons, to pre-pare the way for a coming together in unanimous support of Garrison's Address to the Slaves. Considering the violent imagery in this Address, the techniques that led to its adop-tion provide a revealing context for the quite different re-ception Garnet's Address received in Buffalo.

The circumstances could not have appeared more auspi-cious for Garrison's Address when the second evening session of the New England Anti-Slavery Convention began at 7:30 on Wednesday, May 31, in a "crowded to overflowing" Faneuil Hall. The Hutchinsons sang and Quincy introduced Garri-son. As noted in chapter 1, Garrison contended that the Dec-laration of Independence authorized slaves to "wage war" against their masters "and to wade through their blood, if nec-essary" to gain freedom. He also quoted Lord Byron's demand that "hereditary bondmen" must strike the first blow in a war for freedom. Once Garrison finished, Remond and Douglass rose to call on those assembled to adopt the Address. They may have considered themselves to be representatives of Garrison's slave audience, and there is no indication that they objected to his violent language. Then, in anticipation of the arrival in Boston of President John Tyler to attend a June 17 commemoration of the Battle of Bunker Hill, Phillips read an address, also written by Garrison, demanding that Tyler free his slaves. When Phillips finished, the delegates "separately and unanimously adopted" each address. Finally Garrison of-fered a resolution linking the antislavery movement to the War for Independence, the Hutchinsons sang, and the meeting adjourned with three cheers for "the cause of liberty."

Douglass and Remond were the *only* individuals who heard both Garrison's and Garnet's Address to the Slaves—the only ones to witness the initial presentation of more than one of the Addresses. That they reacted very differently to Garnet's than they had to Garrison's is extremely significant. The Boston meeting had formally initiated the "Hundred Conventions" speaking tour that led Douglass and Remond to hear Garnet, whom they had never met. When the two men began the tour they hoped to attract New York's Liberty abolitionists to Garrisonian doctrines. But, by the time they reached Buffalo, they realized that the tour had exacerbated disagreements between the two groups.[16] They had become angry and determined to emphasize differences between the two factions rather than minimize them, even if they had to contradict their earlier support of Garrison's Address. In part because of their ability as debaters, in part because they had the support of a significant minority among the delegates at the Buffalo convention, Douglass and Remond were able to mount an unreconcilable opposition to Garnet. To make matters worse for Garnet, two other groups of delegates had reservations about his Address. The delegates from New York City embraced peace principles similar to those of white AFASS leader Lewis Tappan. Most of the delegates from Ohio had views in accord with the legal positivism of that state's Liberty Party.

Except for their race and average age, the delegates at the black national convention were more similar to those who assembled in Peterboro than those who participated in the Boston meeting. They were of a single race and gender, a large proportion of them were members of the clergy, and they were overwhelmingly political abolitionists. The leaders were young—in their late twenties and early thirties—but exhibited some of the same skill in factional maneuvering as their counterparts in Peterboro and Boston. Aside from Douglass, Garnet, and Remond, the more prominent of them included Rev. Amos G. Beman of New Haven; Rev. Samuel

H. Davis of Buffalo; Rev. James N. Gloucester, Rev. Charles B. Ray , and Rev. Theodore S. Wright, all of New York City; A. M. Sumner of Cincinnati; Rev. William C. Munro of Detroit; and William Wells Brown of Buffalo.

Beman (who served as president of the Buffalo meeting), Wright, and Gloucester were among the black men who helped found the AFASS in 1840. Davis, a skilled craftsman as well as a minister, was a Liberty abolitionist mainly concerned during the early 1840s with the rights of northern African Americans.[17] Ray, an able journalist, was affiliated with the AFASS. Munro later presided at John Brown's antislavery convention at Chatham, Ontario.[18] Sumner, a school master and temperance advocate, was the leader of the Ohio delegation at Buffalo. A recent antiblack and antiabolition riot in Cincinnati, in which a white mob assaulted black-owned shops and houses, had enhanced his distrust of violent rhetoric.[19] Brown was a Garrisonian who is best known for his later achievements as an author. Another black leader, Jermain Wesley Loguen was a fugitive slave living in Bath, New York, in 1843. Loguen had only a minor role at the Buffalo meeting, but Garnet's Address to the Slaves touched him deeply.[20]

The regional and factional diversity of these leaders, combined with the small number of delegates attending the Buffalo meeting, had a crucial impact on how that Address fared. Diversity meant that Garnet could rely on a smaller core of supporters than either Smith or Garrison. The low attendance meant that each of the delegates was more important in deciding issues and more susceptible to the persuasive talents of the leaders. Garnet's Address *did* come closer than Smith's and Garrison's to calling for slave revolt. But it was only marginally closer than Garrison's and had its share of qualifications and contradictions. Similar equivocation helped Smith's and Garrison's Addresses gain the endorsements of their conventions. But Douglass and Remond, who had provided unqualified support for Garrison's Address despite its violent passages, refused to acknowledge more than one way of interpreting Garnet's. They caused the contentiousness, typical of antislavery gatherings, to spiral out of control at Buffalo.

The opening address that Davis presented to those assembled, when compared to his later conduct, demonstrates the volatility of issues and individuals at the National Convention of Colored Citizens. The relationship of Davis's Address to Garnet's is analogous to that of Stewart's to Smith's. Before Smith addressed enslaved black men, Stewart had addressed the white men of New York. Before Garnet addressed enslaved black men, Davis addressed the black men of the North. Just as Stewart anticipated Smith's aggressive language, Davis anticipated Garnet's by declaring that black men would no longer "submit tamely" to oppression. Raising the examples of struggles for freedom in Greece, Poland, Ireland, and revolutionary America, Davis declared that black northerners must seek equal rights for themselves "and the liberty of our brethren in bonds, by every means in our power." He criticized the "Christian community" and the Whig and Democratic Parties. He dismissed peaceful petitioning as a failure. African Americans, he said, could not rely on white abolitionists to do their work for them. Rather, he maintained, "No other hope is left us, but in our own exertions, and an appeal to the God of armies!"[21] Yet Davis voted *against* Garnet's Address!

Davis's inconsistency reflects broader disjunctions among the Liberty and AFASS abolitionist leaders at the Buffalo convention. The black leaders were not as familiar with each other as were those who had gathered at Peterboro and Boston. They distrusted each other and worked at cross-purposes. While the leaders at the two earlier conventions debated relatively minor issues and united on major ones, those at Buffalo repeatedly clashed on major issues with the Garrisonian minority and with each other.

During the morning session of August 15, Ray and Beman, who supported the Liberty Party, sided with Douglass and Remond in calling for seating as delegates sixteen men, most of whom were from western New York, who had arrived without credentials. Garnet, Munro, and Wright, all of whom supported the Liberty Party, succeeded in keeping the men out during that session. Adding local delegates, they maintained, would detract from the convention's national scope. A white Garrisonian observer contended that Garnet, Munro, and Wright's effort was part of a strategy to enhance Liberty strength at the convention. This was not the case, since western New York was a Liberty Party stronghold. Rather, it seems to have been the result of miscommunication, as Garnet soon reversed himself and brought about the seating of the men.[22]

The next day Garnet, Loguen, Munro, Ray, and others joined with Garrisonians Brown, Douglass, and Remond to pass resolutions condemning "the great mass of American sects, falsely called churches, which apologize for slavery and prejudice." They accomplished this over the opposition of ten church-oriented delegates, including Gloucester and Wright, who maintained that it was necessary to stay in the churches in order to reform them. Garnet was himself a minister of the Presbyterian church, which many abolitionists considered to be proslavery. It may be that he hoped to appease the Garrisonians by siding with them on this issue. If so, he did not achieve his objective. He *did* alienate Gloucester, Wright, and the others who opposed the resolutions.[23]

At Peterboro no one raised issues of credentials or churches. In Boston there was no opposition to allowing all in attendance to participate in the convention, and there was no opposition to condemning the churches—the only disagreement involved how harshly to do so. In Buffalo these were contested issues. Garnet had no difficulty garnering, over Douglass's, Remond's, and Brown's protests, large majorities in behalf of resolutions supporting the Liberty Party, including one declaring that "it is possible for human government to be righteous." But he never had the prestige among his constituents that Smith and Garrison had among theirs, and divisive early debates weakened his standing. Still, according to local white Garrisonian E. A. Marsh, Garnet expected the convention to adopt and circulate his Address to the Slaves.[24] It did not because of preexisting divisions among upstate New York, New York City, and Ohio Liberty abolitionists, which the early debates deepened.

Most crucial was a rhetorical error committed by Garnet, following his presentation of his Address during the afternoon session of August 16. Ray had sought to avoid controversy by having the Address referred "to a select committee of five" to be chaired by Garnet. According to Ray this would allow the Address to "pass through a close and critical examination, and perceiving some points in it that might in print appear objectionable, to have it somewhat modified." But Garnet, fearing for "the fate of the address," opposed Ray's motion. It was at this point that Garnet delivered the riveting one and one-half hour speech, which the convention *Minutes* describes as "a masterly effort." The speech brought the assembly to tears and ended "amidst great applause." Yet in his presentation Garnet veered away from the ambiguity of his Address and toward a forthright call for slave revolt. He talked about Denmark Vesey, Nat Turner, Madison Washington, and other black rebels in the South and "asked what more could be done?" He declared "that [northern] abolitionists . . . had done about all that they could do; that non-resistance was ridiculous, and not to be thought of, even for the present, by the slaves. . . . [that] 'Resistance to tyrants is obedience to God.' [that] *the time has come.* He was ready for 'war to the knife, and knife to the hilt.'"[25]

Such statements allowed Douglass, when he rose to support Ray's motion, to present the issue as a clear choice between encouraging slave revolt and continuing to rely exclusively on the orthodox Garrisonian tactic of peaceful moral suasion. The convention minutes report that "Douglass remarked that there was too much physical force, both in the address and the remarks of the speaker last up [Garnet]. He [Douglass] was for trying the moral means a little longer." Were the Address to reach the slaves, he contended, it would "necessarily be the occasion of an insurrection; and that was what he wished in no way to have any agency in bringing about, and what we are called upon to avoid." According to Marsh, Douglass also gave a very optimistic portrayal of the accomplishments of peaceful tactics. He noted "the light shed, the good already accomplished—the example afforded in the abolition of West Indian slavery, without bloodshed—the change in public opinion—enemies giving way."[26]

Before the convention adjourned for the day, Gloucester spoke in support of Douglass, and Munro of Garnet. The discussion continued during the morning session of August 27 when a "large majority" voted in favor of Ray's motion. Beman, as presiding officer, appointed Garnet to chair the "special committee," which also included Douglass, Sumner, Davis, and Robert Banks of Detroit. Three of these— Douglass, Sumner, and Davis—later voted against the Address and two—Garnet and Banks—for it. Later that same day, the committee returned the Address, "with some very slight alterations," to the floor of the convention. The committee also reported a resolution calling for the printing of one thousand copies of the Address for circulation.[27] This suggests that Davis had not yet decided to vote against the Address, or that he believed the committee should not require Garnet to change it substantially, or that he—and perhaps the others opposed to it—determined that the entire convention should decide its fate.

The Address and the resolution to publish it became "the order of the day" during the morning session of August 18. So far Liberty abolitionists from New York City and Douglass had criticized the Address. Now Ohio Liberty abolitionists, led by Sumner, charged that an endorsement of the Address "would be fatal to the safety of the free people of color of the slave States, but especially so to those who lived on the borders of the free States." With the recent anti-black riots on his mind, Sumner asserted that black people in Cincinnati did not want "injudiciously to provoke difficulty."[28] William Watson of that city, David Jenkins of Columbus, and J. H. Malvin of Cleveland spoke in support of Sumner. Albert Outly of Lockport, New York, and the Garrisonian duo of Remond and Brown also spoke against the Address. Before the morning session ended, R. H. Johnson of Rochester, David Lewis of Toledo, and Garnet responded, with Garnet rejecting Sumner's contentions. As the afternoon session began, Douglass ended the debate with "forcible remarks" against the Address. The delegates then voted nineteen to eighteen against adopting and distributing it, with twenty-one of the delegates not voting. Those voting in favor included one from New York City and thirteen from upstate New York, three from Detroit, and one from Ohio. Among those opposed were the two from Massachusetts, nine from New York, four from Ohio, two from Detroit, one from Chicago, and one from Georgia.[29]

Following the vote, delegates began to leave, and the convention managers sought to finish other business. Meanwhile, some of those who favored the Address called for another vote on it. As the evening session—what was supposed to be the final session—began at 7:30, Ralph Francis of Rochester, who had voted with the majority, called for reconsideration. Ray, Sumner, and Banks opposed doing so. Ray said the Address had already consumed too much time. Sumner contended that those who favored it aimed to take unfair advantage of the departing delegates, and Banks, who had voted for the Address, agreed. Nevertheless, the convention voted to reconsider. J. P. Morris of Rochester joined Francis in announcing that he would change his vote from nay to yea. If they could have gotten a vote on the issue that evening, the Address might have passed!

But Beman, temporarily stepping down as president, spoke for an hour against it. Like others before him, he said it "had too much of the physical, and not enough of the moral weapon about it."[30] Garnet then spoke at length and Douglass, Remond, and Ray responded. At midnight, as some of the delegates called for an immediate vote on the Address, Beman first declared the convention over and then agreed to having it reconvene at 9:00 the following morning. When it did the delegates voted fourteen to nine to reject the Address, and it is likely that the delay cost Garnet dearly. Despite their announcement the previous evening, Francis and Morris did not vote; neither did Banks. While two delegates who had opposed the Address on the first vote now supported it, four who previously had not voted, including Beman and Ray, voted against it. Two, including Wright, who had voted for it, now voted against it. The number in favor from upstate New York dropped from thirteen to five.[31]

The delegates rejected Garnet's Address in part because, of the three Addresses, it came closest to endorsing slave revolt. But the main reason it failed was the greater ideological diversity among the delegates at Buffalo than among those at Peterboro and Boston. Yet Garnet's Address soon vied with Smith's as the most influential of the three. Among historians it is by far the best remembered and most analyzed. A landmark in African-American history, it is interpreted as an indication of emerging militancy among black abolitionists.[32]

Chapter Four

GOALS AND REACTIONS

By the early 1840s some abolitionists believed that their movement had to become more aggressive if it were to succeed. Looking back over the previous decade, they perceived that proslavery forces had put them on the defensive. The reaction to Nat Turner's revolt had led most of them publicly to forswear communicating with slaves and to mute their admiration for slave rebels. Northern antiabolitionist mobs had forced them to defend themselves. In the South the threat of proslavery violence had driven antislavery whites northward. In 1835 mobs forced James G. Birney from Kentucky, whipped northern abolitionist Amos Dresser in Nashville, and assisted in the arrest of another northern abolitionist, Ruben Crandall, in Washington, D.C. In 1836 mob attacks in Missouri led southern-born AASS agent David Nelson to retreat to Illinois. These events led most northern abolitionists to regard the slave states as too dangerous to enter. At the 1837 meeting of the MASS, Samuel J. May claimed that "there are 10,000 citizens of Massachusetts who would this day be lynched should they lisp their feelings or opinions south of Mason & Dixon's line."[1]

Abolitionist expressions of fear regarding antislavery activities in the South became the subject of antiabolitionist taunts. Since there were no slaves to free in the North, the antiabolitionists demanded to know why abolitionists, if they had a shred of manhood, did "not go among the slaveholders," "go to the slave states," "go to the South?" Yankee poet and essayist Ralph Waldo Emerson derided abolitionists for their "incredible tenderness for black folk a thousand miles off."[2] Abolitionists fended off this ridicule in several ways. Some maintained that they *were* being heard in the South through the propaganda they sent there and the excerpts of their writings published in southern newspapers. Others said that, since the North was proslavery, they had to change it before going on to the South. Still others admitted that they believed it was futile and dangerous for them to go there. Anticipating phrases in his Address to the Slaves, Garrison in 1835 asked, "Why . . . should we go into the slaveholding states, to assail their towering wickedness, at a time when we are sure we should be gagged, or imprisoned, or put to death, if we went thither?"[3]

So common during the late 1830s were abolitionist avowals that they must concentrate on the North, that for most of the twentieth century historians assumed that abolitionists had permanently given up action in the South.[4] But this was not the case. When they could, they preferred to point to a southern outpost of northern abolitionism and declare, *we are in the South!*[5] By the early 1840s a few abolitionists had begun to reestablish such outposts. Smith's Address encouraged them, and all three Addresses assumed that abolitionists could communicate with slaves. This chapter first analyzes how Smith, Garrison, and Garnet intended to do so. It then examines how abolitionists and nonabolitionists reacted to their rhetoric.

Abolitionists were clearly aware of the difficulties involved in contacting slaves. They understood that the great majority of slaves could not read. They knew that masters were vigilant and, at the very least, would insist on being present when northerners approached their bondpeople. Therefore abolitionists *sometimes* flatly denied that they could communicate with slaves. During the mid-to-late 1830s, antislavery stalwarts Arthur Tappan and Garrison not only rejected encouraging slaves to revolt, but they also denied that they had the means to do so. At the black national convention in Buffalo, one of the criticisms Frederick Douglass and other Garrisonians leveled against Garnet's Address to the Slaves was that it could not reach them. As late as 1858 Garrison declared that an "impassible barrier" cut northern abolitionists off from slaves.[6]

Smith, Garrison, and Garnet certainly had northern audiences in mind when they prepared their Addresses. They spoke in the North and they hoped to circulate printed versions of their remarks there. Smith stated that he intended to influence northern "public opinion" through his "intrepidity." He wanted to convince abolitionists that they had a "perfect moral right" to go south to help slaves escape. A few weeks after Garrison presented his Address, the *Liberator* printed an advertisement calling for scattering it "among the great multitude," without mentioning slaves. To a degree, Garnet and his black abolitionist colleagues considered *themselves* to be a slave audience.[7]

Yet the three men and other abolitionists assumed that their words *would* reach slaves. This was the case even among those, such as Garrison and Douglass, who sometimes denied that it could be done. Despite fierce proslavery resistance, abolitionists *had* sent large amounts of propaganda southward during the mid-1830s, and some of them persisted in doing so during the succeeding decades.[8] So Smith, Garrison, and Garnet *knew* that they could get their Addresses into that section. Getting them to literate slaves or to free African Americans who could communicate with slaves was by no means impossible. David Walker had relied on a network of black and white sailors to carry his *Appeal* to southern ports, and that network continued to exist.[9] In a letter as striking as it is rare, Charles T. Torrey's associate Abel Brown informed Smith during October 1843 that "the awful doctrine advocated in the address to the slave has gone into extensive practice." Brown reported that fugitive slaves who had reached Albany from North Carolina told him that northern sailors had "frequently told them that it would not be wrong to take a pilot boat and escape." Brown believed the sailors got this idea from "that Peterboro' Address."[10]

There were other means of contact. During the early 1840s, Torrey and others conversed with slaves in the Chesapeake. David Nelson met with slaves on the Ohio River between Illinois and Kentucky and found them to be less humble than previously. Some slaves who escaped to the North and some free African Americans who visited the North returned south with abolitionist motivations. Masters charged that free African Americans and northern abolitionists habitually interfered with their slaves.[11] Historian Merton L. Dillon contends that blacks forced from the borderlands by the domestic slave trade spread awareness of northern abolitionism among slaves in the deep South.[12]

Garnet's Garrisonian critics at Buffalo, who described his Address as a "flight of fancy," also regarded it as capable of sparking slave revolt. Earlier Garnet and Douglass had agreed that slaves could be influenced by northern abolitionists. As chapter 1 indicates, Garnet had in February 1842 contended that "the slaves *know* throughout the entire South, of the movement of the abolitionists, they know they have friends in the North in whom they may *confide* in case they are driven to desperation." Fifteen months later in New York City Douglass told those gathered at the 1843 annual meeting of the AASS, "It has been imagined that the slaves of the South are not aware of the movements made in their behalf, and in behalf of human freedom, every where, throughout the northern and western States. This is not true. They do know it. They knew it from the moment that the spark was first kindled in the land."[13]

When in 1848 Garnet finally published his Address to the Slaves, he expressed a hope that it would be "adopted by every slave in the Union." Smith had earlier expressed a similar hope for his Address. At the end of June 1843, Garrison's *Liberator* said of his Address, "Those who have friends or acquaintances at the South would do well to send them copies."[14] Although abolitionists often expressed doubts about reaching a slave audience, these three believed at the time that they could.

As Dillon maintains, the Addresses to the Slaves were part of an effort to form an alliance between slaves and abolitionists. They aimed to encourage the slave unrest that had already increased. The Addresses also aimed to reorient northern abolitionism toward the South. Smith urged slaves to escape northward *and* urged northerners to go into the South to help them on their way. Garrison used his Address to show how disunion would leave the white South defenseless against slave revolt. Garnet, while assuming that slaves would have to act on their own, called on black northerners to be more actively engaged with those in bonds. All three men sought to further an abolitionist self-image that embraced slaves. They also sought to lead their factions, to prevail over other factions, and to compete for the allegiance of black northerners. It was within this context that reactions to the Addresses occurred. The struggle was most closely fought in Buffalo's black national convention. But it began with what Smith said in Peterboro and continued long after the Buffalo meeting ended.

Of the three Addresses, Smith's had the broadest contemporary impact. It stirred furious debate among abolitionists and between abolitionists and nonabolitionists. In part this was because Smith was the first who dared to issue an address to slaves. In part it was because his Address was the most widely published. In part it was because his was the only one that advised slaves to take what they needed in both the slave and free states to achieve freedom.

Among slavery's defenders and the general public, Smith's Address gained an immediate and sustained notoriety far exceeding that ever gained by Garrison's and that gained by Garnet's prior to the Civil War. Religious weeklies like the *Observer* of New York City and large circulation dailies like that same city's *Journal of Commerce* condemned and ridiculed Smith's words. A few days after the Peterboro convention ended, a correspondent of the *New York Tribune* declared to that paper's editor, Horace Greeley, "Your readers will be astounded to learn that an *Address to the Slaves of the United States* was presented to the Convention by Gerrit Smith and adopted." Within two weeks of the convention, abolitionist Theodore D. Weld reported that Smith's Address had caused "a mighty stir" in slaveholding Washington, D.C., where John C. Calhoun denounced it on the floor of the U.S. Senate. Three weeks later, the influential *New York Evangelist* asserted that the "boldness and explicitness" of Smith's "language has already excited considerable remark."[15] As late as October 1845, N. L. Rice, a proslavery Presbyterian minister from Cincinnati, "condemned" Smith and the New York Liberty Party for advising slaves "not only to run from their masters, but to *steal*, along their route, in the free as well as the slave States, 'the horse, the boat, the food, the clothing, which they need!'" Rice spoke for many in the North as well as the South when he rebuked abolitionists "for sending emissaries into the slaveholding States, to render the slaves discontented, and induce them to run." He declared that "conduct and sentiments of this character are unscriptural and abominable."[16]

Abolitionists were not immune to Rice's argument or others like it. Smith raised a frightening image of slaves sweeping northward and stealing from everyone in their path. Many believed he had acted in a dangerously irresponsible manner. Advising escaping slaves to take what they needed seemed to violate Christian morality and to threaten the sanctity of law. Several of Smith's abolitionist critics charged that he had made the antislavery movement appear reckless. Initially there were mixed reactions from each of the major abolitionist organizations—the AASS, AFASS, and the Liberty Party. Then, as time passed, opposition became most pronounced among the Garrisonian leaders of the AASS and the Cincinnati leaders of the Ohio branch of the Liberty Party.

Liberty abolitionists in upstate New York and in New

England quickly rallied to support the Address.[17] Shortly after the Peterboro convention, local Liberty meetings in New York either endorsed Smith's Address or issued their own. In May 1843 a correspondent of Utica's *Liberty Press* went beyond Smith in declaring, "It is our duty to encourage and aid slaves to *rise* and take their liberty, and if the master attempts to shoot or kill the slave for taking his liberty, then that master must take the consequences of his folly; and if he loses his life, 'he dies as the fool dieth.'" In Boston the *Emancipator*, representing the views of New England's Liberty abolitionists, printed Smith's Address and declared it to be "decidedly the boldest production we remember to have seen from the anti-slavery press. It will make those ears, attuned to southern 'chivalry' and the right of property in man, tingle." The *Emancipator*'s editor, Joshua Leavitt, who was in Washington that winter, said of addressing slaves, "It is a shame that we have never done it before."[18]

Lewis Tappan, the white New York City merchant who led the AFASS, was at first more circumspect. Tappan's energy, organizational skill, and wealth made him a dominant figure in the antislavery movement. He was pious, cautious, sensitive to popular opinion, and as devoted as any abolitionist to peaceful means. During 1842 he still hoped to convert mainstream Protestant denominations to abolitionism and had not yet committed himself to the Liberty Party. In early February, he informed Smith that his "advice to slaves to take horses, &c, *en route*, from masters or *any other persons*" had "alarmed many abolitionists." Tappan indicated that, while he liked most of the Address, he believed Smith's advice that escaping slaves "take property in the *free* States" to be "wrong—very wrong." But Tappan soon adjusted his thinking to emerging circumstances. Not long after he wrote to Smith, he undertook with Nathaniel E. Johnson, a Presbyterian minister who edited the *New York Evangelist*, a remarkable analysis of the morality and legality of slaves taking property they needed to escape.[19] The two men consulted eighteenth-century English theologian William Paley's writings and Sir William Blackstone's commentaries on the common law. Then Johnson published a series of articles that appeared in the *Evangelist* from February to April 1842. While worrying about the expediency of Smith's Address, the series endorses and amplifies its radical implications.

For at least a decade, abolitionists had charged that slaveholders were sinners and thieves who stole the lives of other humans. Johnson begins the series by noting that Smith's critics charged that he now called on slaves also to become thieves. Like Tappan had initially, the critics maintained that Smith was especially wrong to urge escapees to take what they needed in the free states where many people were sympathetic to them. Johnson, however, reminds his readers that slavery violated the laws of God and nature. (That those laws had always been interpreted in masculine terms is inherent in Johnson's argument, which also helps define the masculine point of view embraced by all three Addresses to the Slaves.) Slaves, he emphasizes, were in a state of war with their masters. They were "by the law of Nature and of God" captives "in an enemy's land" (see p. 165). But an enslaved black man who had a family had greater responsibilities than a prisoner of war. He not only had a right to escape. He also had—as Garnet later emphasized—"a solemn obligation" to free "his wife and children." An enslaved man, Johnson maintains, was "bound by the law of Nature to protect his wife and children, if such protection be possible; and therefore, whatever he may submit to for himself, he has no right to consign his family to perpetual slavery" (see p. 164). The right "to destroy his domestic relations, and to traffic in him and his children as property" could "never be conceded by a slave, without his own violation of duty to God."[20]

Having established the inherent responsibility of enslaved men to free themselves and their families, Johnson proceeds to go beyond Smith on several points. First, like Smith, Johnson prefers that a slave escape peacefully, but he adds that "the law of nature will even justify him in using violence, *if escape can be accomplished in no other way*" (see p.

165). Second, Johnson defends at length the right of escaping slaves to expropriate property in the free as well as the slave states. Few northerners—abolitionist or nonabolitionist—who joined the debate over Smith's Address claimed that escapees who took property in the slave states had sinned or were guilty of theft. It was, Johnson maintains, "an original right" (see p. 166). Many abolitionists feared, however, that if fugitive slaves took what they needed in the free states, they would turn popular opinion against themselves. Johnson replies that under the Fugitive Slave Law of 1793, which required northerners to capture and return fugitive slaves—a requirement that had just been reaffirmed by the U.S. Supreme Court in *Prigg v. Pennsylvania*—escapees in the free states remained "in an enemy's country" (see p. 165). Or, as Garnet later put it, "the pharaohs were on both sides of the blood-red waters" (see p. 186). Only when fugitive slaves reached abolitionists who would protect them, Johnson argues, was it sinful for them to take things without paying. Otherwise an escapee could rightfully seize enemy property "all along his route" until he reached Canada (see p. 165).[21]

Third, Johnson reveals a great deal about abolitionist thought concerning the right of slaves to revolt. Because a state of war existed between masters and slaves, he contends that only two considerations allowed black men honorably *not* to revolt. They were the "prospect of deliverance through patient waiting" and the impossibility of successful insurrection. Both of these considerations, Johnson asserts, pertained to American slaves. Therefore Johnson, as Smith had earlier and Garrison would later, holds that slaves should not injure their "oppressors" so long as northern abolitionists might peacefully succeed in freeing them and so long as revolt would do them no good. Yet, if all else failed, Johnson maintains, the slaves' right of self-defense "justifies just as much force as is absolutely necessary" (see p. 166). In this analysis Johnson had a decided impact on Garnet, who in his Address quoted one of Johnson's later editorials. In July 1843, Johnson, despairing for the effectiveness of northern abolitionism, called for "some more effective door to be thrown open" in the struggle against slavery.[22] Garnet, still doubting that revolt could succeed, responded with his call for a general strike by slaves.

Johnson's series is even more ambivalent than Smith's Address concerning the slaves' role in achieving their freedom. Johnson insists that his aim is to demonstrate slavery's "total incurable depravity," *not* "to vindicate the expediency of the Peterboro' address, not being at all satisfied that it *was* expedient." After having carefully established the right of slaves to escape, take property, and rebel, he claims that his real intention is to convince northerners that they shared guilt for slavery unless they were "actively engaged for its abolition." In a passage that carries the same message as Goodman's paintings in Peterboro's Presbyterian church, and as some of the denunciations of Smith's Address, Johnson suggests that slaves did not, after all, have a role in their own liberation. Instead, it was up to northern abolitionists, through *their* "kindness and energy," to free "the . . . weeping slave, who can neither obtain freedom by force or flight." The rights of a "few thousands" of slaves who escaped northward, he asserts were "trifling compared to the right of millions to an immediate emancipation." Toward the end of his series, Johnson notes that six or seven newspapers had endorsed his analysis, that his articles had been "extensively republished," and that he had received "numerous private letters" from across the North. It was "rising indignation of the North," reflected in this response, that he hopes "will break the bonds of slaveholding obligations asunder" through peaceful political action.[23]

The Johnson-Tappan interpretation of Smith's Address is thorough and well grounded in the intellectual and theological authorities of its time. Despite its ambiguity, it provided strong support, as Smith himself put it, for "the morality of the Address" as well as for those abolitionists who favored an alliance with slaves and contemplated violent means. Precisely for these reasons it was far too radical to influence positively all abolitionists or such moderate northern opponents of slavery as William Ellery Channing, the famous Unitarian theologian and pacifist.[24] Channing, a Bostonian, held views on the roles of slaves and northerners in opposing slavery that were similar to those of some antislavery Whig politicians, some Liberty abolitionists, and, as it turned out, some leading Garrisonians. He stressed that slaves must patiently await deliverance. He maintained that northerners should limit their antislavery efforts to moral suasion and political efforts designed to separate their states and the national government from responsibility for human bondage.[25]

In an essay written shortly before his death in October 1842, Channing calls for "no crusade against slavery, no use of physical or legislative power for its destruction, no irruption into the South to tamper with the slaves, or to repeal or resist the laws." He denounces recent attempts by abolitionists to go south "to incite the slave to take flight." While he regarded those who had gathered at Peterboro to be "highly respected men," he charges that they were "wrong" in "preparing and publishing an address to the slaves, in which they are exhorted to fly from bondage." Channing correctly perceived growing frustration among abolitionists. There were signs, his essay notes, "that the enemies of slavery are losing their patience, calmness, and self-controlling wisdom; that they cannot wait for the blessing of Providence on holy efforts; that the grandeur of the end is in danger of blinding them to the character of the means."[26]

Smith's ostensibly peaceful Address raised violent images in Channing's mind, just as it had in Garrison's, Johnson's, and others. In his essay Channing calls on northerners to welcome fugitive slaves and wishes that slaves could leave the South without bloodshed. But he fears that abolitionist instigation of massive slave exodus would lead to "insurrection and massacre," which would convulse society amid "terrible crimes." Smith—and later Garnet—conceded that enslavement might limit one's ability to make moral judgments. But Channing, like other opponents of Smith's Address, stressed the ignorance of slaves rather than their natural rights. His essay insists that enlightened individuals must "beware of rousing that wild mass of degraded men to the assertion of their rights." Unlike Johnson, Channing did not believe a slave could "innocently adopt any and every expedient for vindicating his liberty."[27]

Instead Channing maintains that, despite their suffering, slaves had a high duty to treat their masters in a Christian manner. They could not expose households or communities "to brutal outrage and massacre." To avoid this, northern Christians, relying on solely moral influences, had to teach slaves "patience and love." If he were to visit an enslaved man, Channing contends, he would tell him that it was his Christian duty to "resist not evil; obey your master," to "not lie or steal," to "submit to . . . [his] hard fate," and look forward to God's reward for having been "a slave [rather] than a master."[28] This was a far less ambiguous issue for Channing than it was for Smith, who had said similar things about submission but also emphasized the right of slaves to revolt and escape.

Neither was the issue of abolitionist encouragement of slave resistance an ambiguous one for the Cincinnati leadership of the Ohio Liberty Party, nor for most Garrisonians. Both of these groups shared views similar to Channing's. They demonstrated that the aggressiveness that Smith advocated in his Address was no more acceptable in 1842 to most northern abolitionists than it was to nonabolitionists. Their responses to the Peterboro Address and to other radical political abolitionist undertakings represent a more profound division in the antislavery movement than had occurred when the AASS split in 1840. During the early 1840s, reformist political and Garrisonian abolitionists on one side and radical political abolitionists on the other rapidly diverged in their views concerning their relationship to slaves. This divergence foreshadowed a muted Garrisonian response to Garrison's Address to the Slaves and a hostile Garrisonian response to Garnet's. It also foreshadowed the disruption of the Liberty

Party in 1848 and a feud between the party's New York and
Ohio leaders that lasted into the 1850s. In a sense, the abolitionist reaction to Smith's Address established two lines of
development, one leading to Abraham Lincoln and the other
to John Brown. The first relied on peaceful agitation and
conventional party politics in the North to achieve antislavery goals. The second concentrated on direct action against
slavery in the South and against those who pursued escaping
slaves in the North.

Gamaliel Bailey, the editor of the *Philanthropist*, spoke
for the Ohio Liberty Party's dominant faction. As a white
abolitionist who had faced several mobs in the southern-
oriented city of Cincinnati, he shared the caution of the black
abolitionists from that city who in 1843 so strongly opposed
Garnet's Address to the Slaves. Depending on human law
for the survival of his press, Bailey was far less willing than
more northerly abolitionists to advocate disregarding an immoral law. He had in 1841 criticized the three young men
who had gone from Illinois into Missouri to help slaves escape. When he learned of Smith's Address and the resolutions passed at Williamsburg and Peterboro pledging not to
help quell slave revolts, he declared that he could not "keep
silent." His editorials on the subject denounce the resolutions for encouraging slave insurrection, but they deal most
heatedly with Smith's Address.[29]

Like Channing, Rice, and others, Bailey did not doubt
that Smith's message could reach slaves. Neither did he deny
that Smith had a right to address slaves. Instead his editorials
charge that Smith demonstrated poor judgement in exercis-
ing the right. "As for the Address," Bailey writes, "we are
utterly at a loss to understand what good can be accomplished
by it. A few slaves may be encouraged by it to run away, but
is slavery to be abolished by having its victims all run off to
Canada?" Antislavery societies, he maintains, aimed at "emancipation of the oppressed on the soil," not "colonization" in
Canada. Like many nonabolitionists, Bailey conceded that
slaves had a moral right to take what they needed to escape

from the South. But, unlike Tappan and Johnson, he denied that a right to self defense justified escapees in expropriating property in the free states. Ignoring northern support for the Fugitive Slave Law and Johnson's series of articles, Bailey's editorials maintain that escaping slaves could not morally take property in the North because the mass of northerners had not deprived them of liberty or earnings. Northerners, the editorials point out, often aided fugitive slaves.

Bailey's greatest concern, however, was the potentially negative impact of Smith's Address on southern and northern voters. Like his Cincinnati friend, the antislavery attorney Salmon P. Chase, Bailey hoped to create a Liberty Party that could appeal to a broad national electorate. He, Chase, and most other white abolitionists of the borderlands still believed that a majority of southern whites could be convinced to favor state legislation abolishing slavery. The Ohio Liberty abolitionists' version of antislavery aggressiveness was to spread their party southward. Bailey feared that Smith's Address would preclude this. It would, he charged, "needlessly irritate the [white] people of the Southern States, and tend to close up still more strongly the avenues to conviction in their minds." Bailey's Cincinnati associate William Henry Brisbane, formerly a South Carolina slaveholder who had freed his slaves at great personal expense, made a similar point in a letter to the *Philanthropist*. Brisbane labeled Smith's Address "evil" and noted that abolitionists had previously addressed themselves to masters not slaves. He charged that Smith had raised "impediments in the way" of "freeing two million slaves for the sake of a few thousand who might reach Canada."[30]

Bailey, Chase, Brisbane, and many other Liberty abolitionists, including northeasterners like Henry B. Stanton, took a more conventional view of their party's mission than did Smith and the radical political abolitionists. Smith and his colleagues regarded the party to be a holy biracial revolutionary vanguard that could not concede that slaveholders had rights. Bailey and his associates believed the party had to appeal, within the existing constitutional framework, to the average voter. In his editorials on Smith's Address, Bailey maintains that the "primary object of the Liberty party [in the North] is not the extinction of slavery in the [southern] States; for we at the North have no political power to legislate for its abolition." Instead the party's objects were "to release the citizens of the North from all political responsibility for the holding of men as property, to divorce the General Government from slavery, and to bring about a system of legislation favorable to Freedom and Free Labor." These, Bailey insists, were legitimate policies that could attract "a large majority of voters in the country" and push the South toward emancipation. "Why then," he asks, "should a Liberty Convention step out of its way to touch the political rights of the South, excite discontent in the minds of slaves, when it knows, or ought to know, that such action is calculated to repel nine-tenths of the people of the free states, and thus prevent the accomplishment of the great and legitimate objects of the Liberty Party?" If a Liberty national convention and other antislavery organizations adopted Smith's views, Bailey promised to separate from them and devote himself "simply to *individual* action against slavery."[31]

Garrisonians, meanwhile, reacted to Smith's Address with less unanimity than did the Ohio Liberty abolitionists. Within weeks of the Peterboro convention, Oliver Johnson and Garrison responded positively, if not wholeheartedly, to what Smith had said. In his firsthand account of the convention, Johnson mildly criticized some of the political abolitionists' assumptions. But he did not criticize the Address, which he declared, "cannot fail to electrify the country." A few weeks later at a local antislavery meeting in East Bloomfield, New York, Johnson anticipated Nathaniel E. Johnson by contending "that the advice given to the slaves respecting the means to be used in running away was consistent with sound Christian morality."[32] Garrison (as mentioned in chapter 2) also welcomed Smith's Address as "a novel procedure in the anti slavery movement" that would "doubtless add to the excitement of the times." Garrison defended the right of abolitionists to address slaves and praised Smith's instructions to those contemplating escape. Garrison only mildly objected to what he interpreted to be Smith's suggestion that most abolitionists wanted slaves to avoid violence on the basis of expediency rather than the "high ground of absolute morality."[33]

But the nonaggressive feminine values that most Garrisonians promoted—and some other assumptions that were not so laudable—soon produced a more negative assessment of Smith's Address. Lydia Maria Child, an accomplished author, an AASS executive committee member, and the editor of the *National Anti-Slavery Standard*—the faction's official newspaper—denounced the Address on February 24. While Smith's new departure impressed Oliver Johnson and Garrison, Child embraced a caution and distaste similar to that of Bailey, whom she quoted at length. In a manner that anticipated the Garrisonian reaction a year and a half later to Garnet's Address, Child smugly patronized Smith and the slaves he claimed to advise.

In late January Child and other AASS executive committee members, in their negative reaction to the Williamsburg resolutions, provided an advance warning of how they would respond to Smith's Address. Defining the antislavery movement as an exercise in white public relations, they maintained that the resolutions were "likely to excite causeless and dangerous irritation" and to "confirm" a widespread but "erroneous opinion . . . respecting the real character of and purpose of the anti-slavery movement." The committee's report notes that the resolutions violated the AASS constitution's pledge not to encourage "the oppressed" to free themselves by "resorting to physical force." In a conservative conclusion, the report declares that the AASS "aims at nothing illegal or unconstitutional" and "address[es] not the passions of the slaves, but the reason and conscience of the masters."[34]

Child further developed these themes when she turned to Smith. Like others on the subject, her editorial notes that his Address had "excited a good deal of curiosity." But, unlike Garrison, Oliver Johnson, and Nathaniel E. Johnson, and like Channing and Bailey, she believes it would do no good. In a manner similar to several other critics, Child claims that slave illiteracy and vigilant masters would keep the Address from reaching its designated audience. She fears, as did Bailey, that its real impact would be—like that of the Williamsburg resolutions—a negative one on white opinion in the North and South. To avoid harm to the antislavery movement, Child contends, "it behooves us to keep our old watch-fires steadily burning on the hill-tops, rather than throw up rockets with rush and crackle."[35]

Yet, having made these remarks, Child, once again like other critics, assumes that Smith's Address *would* reach the slaves. Turning to Smith's advice that escaping slaves expropriate property in the North as well as the South, she acknowledges the kindness of Smith's intentions while suggesting that he did not have an adequate understanding of moral philosophy. She charges that Smith failed to distinguish between what was appropriate advice for whites who might be held in unjust captivity and what was appropriate for enslaved African Americans. "The extreme moral degradation" suffered by the latter, she insists, rendered them "remarkably unfit to make moral distinctions." Smith need not assure them that they might "take the property of others without sin." The real danger was that they would not limit themselves in taking only what they needed to escape. Smith himself, she maintains, displayed a lack of moral rigor, "a strange flickering of lights and shadows in his own mind," in his apparent rejection of slave revolt on the basis of expediency rather than absolute morality. It was because dangerous logic, such as Smith's, might lead slaves to rise up violently when they thought they might succeed, she asserts, that the "best minds of our cause" would never be tempted to diverge from "our *original* anti-slavery principles."[36]

More than the remarks of any other critic, Child's demonstrate the contrast between Smith's new aggressive abolitionism and that of the 1830s. But, as it turned out, Child caused more difficulties for Garrison than she did for Smith. Of all his critics, Smith responded in print only to his Liberty colleagues Bailey and Brisbane in an effort to define the nature of political abolitionism. He could ignore Child and the others because his Address reflected an undeniable reality. Slave unrest and escape *were* increasing. Abolitionists associated with his radical political abolitionist faction *were* in contact with slaves. The reactions to his Address indicate that he startled abolitionists and nonabolitionists. They also reveal a great deal about what the various abolitionist factions stood for during the early 1840s. The reactions to Garrison's and Garnet's Addresses only confirmed the situation.

The most significant aspect of the immediate response to Garrison's is that there barely was a response. His Address to the Slaves is an important indication of the direction of abolitionism during the early 1840s. It links him to Smith, Garnet, and other non-Garrisonians during those years. It shows how Garrison tied disunion to slave revolt, how his acceptance of slave violence underlay a veneer of nonresistance, and how he was willing to embrace slaves as members of the antislavery movement. Initially a few commentators predicted that Garrison's Address would have a wide impact. It led one local Massachusetts antislavery society to call on slaves to escape to that state. Radical political abolitionist Charles T. Torrey noted with approval that the Address was "somewhat warlike, in its tone," which he attributed to the revolutionary ambiance of Faneuil Hall. Garrison's Address also reached at least one southern abolitionist—Samuel M. Janney of Virginia—who feared it would make masters more determined to prevent escapes. Yet overall the Address attracted so little attention that all Garrison's biographers but the most recent have ignored it.[37]

There are numerous reasons why it had such a small impact. Most obvious is that it was too similar to Smith's. Also, while it calls for disunion and employs more violent rhetoric than Smith's, it was in two respects less controversial: first, it does not justify fugitive slaves taking what they needed; second, it rejects Smith's proposal that northern abolitionists go south to help slaves escape. Therefore those who had reacted sharply to Smith's Address either did not respond to Garrison's or dismissed it as pointless and harmless. In a few lines under the title "Another Address to the Slaves," Bailey wrote, "We are inclined to think that two or three hundred thousand votes cast for Liberty would prove somewhat more effective than this. We attach little importance to means that can effect little good. The address, we believe, contains no exceptionable sentiments."[38]

To some extent, the very techniques that Garrison and other managers of the New England Anti-Slavery Convention used to attract participants and keep them united also undermined the impact of his Address. While those who responded to the Peterboro convention focused mostly on its resolutions and the content of Smith's Address, those who reported the Boston meeting focused on its great size, the extraordinary enthusiasm of those who attended, and "the thrilling music of the Hutchinsons." Emotion smothered content. A correspondent of the *New York Tribune* devoted a few sentences to Garrison's Address, noting that it was "drawn up in his peculiarly strong style," that it advised slaves "that their masters were tyrants and hypocrites, &c.," and that it called on slaves "to run away the first opportunity." But what impressed the correspondent was how the convention attracted "a great multitude of all classes," how "FANEUIL HALL . . . was crowded to the utmost," and how "the enthusiasm of the audience ran so high." Another observer emphasized the "multitudinous" attendance, Remond's and Douglass's "thrilling speeches," the Hutchinsons' "soul-stirring" songs, and the "racket of thumping canes, stamping feet, clapping hands and hurrahing mouths." The same observer declared, "The music of the Hutchinsons carries all before it. It was a most important charm to collect and attract people to the meetings of the Convention. Speechifying, even of the better sort, did less to interest, purify and subdue minds than this irresistible anti-slavery music."[39]

Two substantive issues also distracted interest from Garrison's Address to the Slaves. First there was the convention's appointment of a biracial delegation, including Latimer, Douglass, and Remond, to meet with President Tyler when he attended the commemorative ceremony at Bunker Hill. The committee hoped to present Tyler with Garrison's message calling on the president to free his slaves. The *Boston Post*, a Democratic newspaper, regarded the proposal, which was not carried out, to be "a gross breach of courtesy," and two newspapers from Tyler's home state of Virginia agreed. The *Richmond Enquirer* called it "a gross breach of hospitality." The *Old Dominion* of Portsmouth—a town from which many slaves surreptitiously left for the North—proposed that someone in the president's entourage "will on the spot cowhide the scoundrel who may attempt to introduce to him Latimer or any other negro for the purpose mentioned." Second, the delegates' criticism of the clergy had more resonance with Garrisonian opinion during the summer and fall of 1843 than did addressing the slaves.[40]

As Lydia Maria Child's earlier remarks on Smith's Address suggest, however, the main reason Garrison's Address failed to have much influence on other Garrisonians was that it advocated a strategy that diverged from the faction's fixation on agitation in the North. Persuaded by Smith's Address and frustrated with traditional tactics, Garrison had challenged the opinion of most of his associates. Because of his standing, and amid the enthusiasm of the New England Anti-Slavery Convention, he succeeded in having his Address adopted and published. But Douglass, Remond, and others at the convention who had rushed to endorse it soon realized that contacts with slaves were inconsistent with the Old Organization's modus operandi. Garrison's linking of disunion and slave revolt remained a subsidiary part of his faction's antislavery argument. But by May 1844, when the AASS officially adopted disunionism as its central antislavery slogan, Garrisonians emphasized that it would separate northerners from the guilt of slavery and serve as a *peaceful* means of pressuring the white South toward emancipation.[41]

Unlike radical political abolitionists, Garrisonians during the 1840s were not ready to help initiate slave escapes or to flirt with violent means. Garrison's Address itself calls on slaves to escape without matching Smith's contention that northern abolitionists go south to help them. While Garrisonians often praised northerners who engaged in such activities, they refrained from joining them. While Garrisonians aided fugitives who reached New England, they did so as individuals, not as representatives of organized abolitionism. Lydia Maria Child, Abigail Kelley Foster, and other Garrisonians gloried in agitating for general emancipation and resented diverting scarce resources into attempts to, as Foster later put it, "run off slaves."[42] Smith, in his Address, had employed violent images that Garrison carried a step further in his Address. But in 1843 Garrison's violent imagery made his colleagues uncomfortable. They believed such images would harm the antislavery cause and that repudiation of them would aid the Garrisonian faction. These motives become clear in their response to Garnet's Address.

The factors that determined how abolitionists responded to Garnet's call for slave action included the refusal of the National Convention of Colored Citizens to publish it, his initial failure to publish it himself, and the tendency of reporters in Buffalo to concentrate on his dramatic persona rather than on his words. Garrisonians at the convention had, of course, charged that his rhetoric was too violent. Delegates influenced by the priorities of the Ohio Liberty Party had said it was dangerous to the interests of free African Americans in the borderlands. In other words, they reacted in much the same manner that Bailey had when he contended that Smith's Address was inimical to the interests of white political abolitionists in that region. But only those who heard Garnet had a clear idea of what he had advocated. Everyone else who learned of Garnet's Address did so by word of mouth or through E. A. Marsh's very brief firsthand account.

These circumstances allowed for only a limited published response to Garnet's words, although not quite so limited as to Garrison's. Except that rumors of what Garnet had said contributed to a belief among Whig journalists in western New York that the Liberty Party advocated slave revolt, neither the proslavery nor antislavery newspapers of that state responded to it.[43] In Ohio, Bailey's *Philanthropist* mentioned neither Garnet nor the black convention. Yet there was a bifurcated Liberty-Garrisonian reaction to Garnet's Address, reflected on the one hand in the proceedings at the Liberty Party's national nominating convention, which met in Buffalo ten days after the black national convention, and on the other in the columns of the *Liberator.*

Garnet's success in having a national black convention endorse the Liberty Party made him the leading black political abolitionist. When he and two other black abolitionists— Charles B. Ray and Samuel Ringgold Ward—participated in the enormous Liberty National Convention, he drew most of the attention. With white radical political abolitionists Abel Brown, George W. Clark, William Goodell, James C. Jackson, Owen Lovejoy, Limaeus P. Noble, Alvan Stewart, and Charles T. Torrey in control of the convention, there was no public effort to contradict what Garnet had said a week earlier. Instead there was praise of his assertion of black masculinity. A correspondent of the *New York Evangelist* suggested that among those who witnessed Garnet's Address "*no doubt can remain of their* [black men] *being men!*" The Liberty convention resolved to "cordially welcome our colored fellow citizens to fraternity with us in the *Liberty* party." It also declared the fugitive slave clause of the United States Constitution to be "null and void," pledged not to help put down slave revolts, and advocated state laws prohibiting assistance in the capture of fugitive slaves.[44]

In contrast, the *Liberator,* during the fall of 1843, portrayed Douglass and Remond as the heroes of the black national convention because of their defense of nonviolence and opposition to the Liberty Party. The newspaper characterized Garnet as at best a clerical schemer and at worst a black dupe who foolishly followed the lead of white radical political abolitionists. At the time, Garrison, who understood the nuances of addressing slaves, was on an extended leave of absence from his newspaper as he oversaw medical care for his wife and mother-in-law, who had been injured in a carriage accident.[45] In his absence, Maria Weston Chapman, an aristocratic and able Bostonian who was similar to Lydia Maria Child in her imperious moral certainty and cultural insularity, edited the paper.

Chapman published a letter from Remond claiming responsibility for the turnout at the black national convention.[46] She also published Marsh's report on the convention, which included the fullest account then available of Garnet's Address to the Slaves. The account describes Garnet and his allies as would-be dictators. It portrays Douglass and Remond as defenders of freedom of debate. But it correctly reports that Garnet's Address called on slaves to strike, not revolt. According to Marsh, the Address "contained, among other things, advice to this effect: that the slave was to go to his master, tell of the injustice of slavery, the duty of immediate emancipation—to refuse to work another hour, unless paid; and if his master remained inexorable, '*then to strike for liberty.*'" In Marsh's view, it was only when pressed to defend his Address that Garnet talked of "war to the knife."[47]

In an editorial based on Marsh's letter, Chapman ignores this distinction. Certain that the Liberty Party was both proslavery and predisposed to violence, she charges that Garnet's Address expressed "the idea that the time for insurrection had come." Ignorant of the Address's subtleties and unsympathetic to assertions of black manhood, she regards the convention's rejection of it to be a victory of "love, forgiveness, and magnanimity" over "evil, hatred, force, revenge, and littleness." Contending that abolitionists must remain true to the AASS's original rejection of slave violence, she declares, "That man knows nothing of nature, human or Divine,—or of character,—good or evil, who imagines that a civil and servile war would ultimately promote freedom."

Chapman was more deliberately condescending toward Garnet than Child had been toward Smith. This was mainly because, like all Americans of her time, Chapman was heavily influenced by racial stereotypes. They led her to refuse to credit Garnet for his own words and to charge that white Liberty abolitionists had manipulated him. "We say emphatically to the man of color," her editorial declares, "trust not the counsels that lead you to the shedding of blood. . . . Little must the man of color have reflected, who does not see that the white man who now stimulates his feelings of revenge or his trust in violence, would be the first to desert or deny him should he be weak and rash enough to yield to such promptings." Chapman reminds Garnet of his duty as "a professed minister of the gospel of Christ" to follow "his Divine Master" in rejecting violence. She hopes "that Mr. Garnet had no further intentions, than merely to write what he thought a high-sounding address" and that "he would be shocked to find the counsels taking effect."[48]

White Garrisonian assumptions of moral superiority eventually helped drive Frederick Douglass out of their faction. Garnet, having himself criticized what he perceived to be the moral weakness of black men in slavery, was well aware of the implications of Chapman's posturing. Insulted by them, he waited two months before replying. To assure that his letter would be published, he sent it to the *Emancipator*, the leading Liberty newspaper in New England, rather than to the *Liberator*. In early December, with Garrison back in editorial control, the *Liberator* also published it.[49]

Garnet's letter reveals the angst that led to the outraged masculinity of his Address to the Slaves. It also indicts the factionalism that determined reactions to the Addresses and briefly refutes the contention that he had presented an unequivocal call for slave revolt. Emphasizing that he is a former slave, Garnet informs Chapman that he is astonished that she "should desire to sink me again to the condition of a *slave*, by forcing me to think as you do." He declares, "If it has come to this, that I must think and act as you do, because you are an abolitionist, or be exterminated by your thunder, then I do not hesitate to say that your abolitionism is abject slavery."

Garnet understood that it was Chapman's sectarian commitment to the AASS and her hatred of the Liberty Party that had motivated her attack. But he found her treatment of him as a black man and her willingness to rely on Marsh's secondhand report of his Address to be appalling. Chapman had claimed that he had "received bad counsel." Garnet responds, "You are not the only person who has told your humble servant that his humble productions have been produced by the '*counsel*' of some anglo-saxon. I have expected no more from ignorant slaveholders and their apologists, but I really looked for better things from Mrs. Maria W. Chapman." She had consigned his Address to "the most fiery trials." Yet, he notes, "madam, you have not seen the address—you have merely *heard* of it." In order to counter what he characterizes as Marsh's "false," "exaggerated," and "libelous" charges, Garnet promises to publish the Address in a "few days." Then Chapman could "judge how much treason there is in it." Meanwhile, he concludes, she could "be assured that there is one black American who dares to speak boldly on the subject of universal liberty."

As it turned out, five years elapsed before Garnet carried out his promise to publish his Address. During that time abolitionist contacts with slaves increased and the Liberty Party factions irrevocably split. The Ohioans led the great majority of political abolitionists into the Free Soil Party (a political alliance including former northern Democrats and Whigs), which opposed the spread of slavery rather than its existence in the South.[50] Meanwhile the radical political abolitionists of New York became increasingly dedicated to direct action, and many Garrisonians, including Douglass and Remond, began to reconsider their commitment to nonviolence.

The immediate reaction to the Addresses to the Slaves, like the Addresses themselves, reveals an antislavery movement attempting to deal with new circumstances. While the three Addresses had much in common, the reaction to them demonstrates how diverse was the movement that produced them. For a variety of reasons, Smith's Address had by far the greatest initial impact on abolitionists and nonabolitionists. It publicized an emerging abolitionist reorientation toward the South and the slaves. It revived the specter of antislavery violence that had been dormant since the early 1830s. It revealed the deep differences between the radical Liberty abolitionists centered in Peterboro and the reformist Liberty abolitionists centered in Cincinnati. In comparison, Garrison's and Garnet's Addresses had relatively less impact. Garrison's is significant as an indicator of changing conditions within the broader antislavery movement rather than as a turning point among Garrisonians. Seeking paradoxically to mix justification of slave violence and cooperation with slaves into his faction's abiding commitment to agitation in the North and pacifism, Garrison pointed to a path not taken. Garnet's Address became more controversial than Garrison's, but not as controversial as it might have been had it been published in 1843. Garnet's invocation of an assertive black masculinity disturbed white Garrisonians, such as Marsh and Chapman, who feared its violent potential. It also disturbed such black abolitionists as Douglass, Remond, and, to a lesser degree, Ray. Most important for the future, however, was that in 1850 the spirit of Smith's Address and Garnet's would combine.

Chapter Five

ABOLITIONISTS AND SLAVES

The Addresses to the Slaves and the reactions, or lack thereof, to them indicate a great deal about American abolitionism during the 1840s. Together they set advocates of aggressive antislavery apart from those who opposed direct action in the South. They separate those who embraced slaves as allies from those who appealed mainly to white audiences. Among the former were radical political abolitionists and church-oriented abolitionists. Among the latter were Garrisonians and the great majority of Liberty abolitionists. Garrisonians tended to ignore Garrison's Address, to criticize Smith's and Garnet's, and to advocate disunion as the only means of ending northern support for slavery. Meanwhile those Liberty abolitionists who concentrated their efforts on electoral politics feared that if abolitionists became involved with slaves they would alienate potential antislavery voters in the North and in the South. These factional differences would have been relatively unimportant, however, had the Addresses to the Slaves not reflected *action* undertaken by northern-based political and church-oriented abolitionists in cooperation with slaves in the upper South. While memory of Garrison's Address faded, Smith's and Garnet's, ambiguous as they are, encouraged an abolitionist presence in the South and an increased willingness to advocate *and* resort to violent means against slavery.

During the 1840s three forms of abolitionist engagement with slaves blossomed. They included missionary activity to encourage slaves to seek freedom, purchasing freedom, and helping slaves escape. Northern abolitionists first called for antislavery missionary activities in the South—involving preaching an abolitionist gospel and distributing Bibles to slaves—during the early 1830s. Even earlier, starting during the Revolutionary era, blacks and whites in the North and South had purchased the freedom of slaves and helped slaves escape.[1] But all three forms of aggressive abolitionism first became common during the 1840s. Because individuals who engaged in one form often engaged in one or two of the others, the undertakings became intertwined. Often purchase of freedom and antislavery religious missions led to efforts to help slaves escape.

Just as abolitionists reacted in a variety of ways to the Addresses to the Slaves, they also had varying responses to the interaction that Smith's Address in particular encouraged. Few northern abolitionists went south to work with slaves. Those who did during the 1840s were usually but not exclusively white radical political abolitionists or church-oriented abolitionists associated with the AFASS and American Missionary Association (AMA). Garrisonians, who themselves rarely went into the South, often criticized those who purchased the freedom of slaves or who advocated providing Bibles to slaves, but they did not usually criticize those who risked their lives in the South to help slaves escape. The Liberty abolitionists who led most of their party into the Free Soil coalition in 1848 frequently engaged in efforts to purchase freedom. But they took little interest in the missionary efforts, and most of them *did* oppose, at least in public, attempts in the South to help slaves escape.

Well before the Addresses to the Slaves, church-oriented abolitionists had debated whether they should communicate with slaves through missionary activities and provide them with Bibles. In 1831, John Rankin, a white Presbyterian minister who sheltered fugitive slaves at his home in the southern Ohio town of Ripley, lamented the lack of missions to slaves. In 1833 Simeon S. Jocelyn, the white minister of a black church in New Haven, Connecticut, who later helped send Bibles to slaves, responded that masters would never allow abolitionists to do such things. Yet one witness to this debate, Joshua Leavitt, never gave up on the idea. As editor of the *New York Evangelist* and later as editor—first in New York and later in Boston—of the *Emancipator*, he became its major proponent. In late 1839 he copied from the *Christian Reflector* an article that anticipated the first paragraph of Smith's Address. It declared, "We have agreed tacitly, with the slaveholder to pass by the poor slave and leave him to perish. It is said, this [preaching to slaves] will bring us into collision with the south. That is what we want. God has a controversy with them, shall his people have none? We wish to see Christian missionaries go there in the spirit of the Apostles, and preach the *gospel to the slaves.*"[2]

In March 1842, two months after Smith presented his Address and while Leavitt was away in Washington, the *Emancipator* contended that abolitionists would go south to provide "religious instruction" to slaves only if they could "preach the *whole* gospel," by which it meant an antislavery gospel. The newspaper's interim editor doubted that this would be allowed. But in 1846, with Leavitt back in Boston, the *Emancipator* promoted an emerging consensus among church-oriented abolitionists that slaves not only had a sacred right to the Bible but that having it would "soon make them free." A letter Leavitt copied from the *New York Observer* contended that God's word would teach the slave "to respect himself and understand his rights, to kindle in his bosom a keen appreciation of the blessings of liberty, and an intense thirst for its enjoyment." At a meeting held in Boston's Marlboro Chapel in May 1846, Leavitt declared that "a more incendiary doctrine than this . . . never appeared even in the columns of the *Emancipator*!" He maintained that Bibles could be distributed to slaves in cooperation with local churches in the District of Columbia, Kentucky, eastern Tennessee, and other parts of the upper South. He predicted that "the slaves will learn to read very fast when you give them the Bible."[3] During 1847 church-oriented abolitionists discussed how to put such an operation into effect.

At first they hoped to convince the American Bible Society (ABS) to employ abolitionists to distribute the Bibles. They believed that if they could portray the Bibles for slaves campaign as an alternative to slave escapes and revolts they could form an alliance with more conservative northern religious groups that supported the ABS.[4] But when that organization would not commit itself to such a controversial project, church-oriented abolitionist organizations prepared to carry it out themselves. The American Wesleyan Connection, an antislavery Methodist denomination, took the lead in early 1847. Then, in December of that year, the American Baptist Free Mission Society (ABFMS), centered in Gerrit Smith's Madison County, New York, declared that it would also act as an "aggressive agency upon slavery" by sending the Gospel to the slaves. The following spring, the AMA, assisted by the AFASS, began a better-funded cooperative effort, as Henry Bibb, a fugitive slave from Kentucky, emerged as the Bibles for slaves campaign's leading fund raiser and advocate.[5]

During the late 1840s and early 1850s, the Wesleyans, the ABFMS, and the AMA all initiated missionary efforts in the South. In 1847 the Allegheny Conference of the Wesleyan Connection sent Adam Crooks of Ohio to Guilford County, North Carolina. The next year the Conference sent Jarvis C. Bacon to southeastern Virginia. In 1849 it sent Jesse McBride to North Carolina to help Crooks. The three men preached to integrated audiences, including slaves. In August 1851 McBride reported, "We, of course, treated all the brethren, black and white, as men; at the communion, we make no other test than character. We invited seekers of all casts and complexions to the same altar for prayer." It was also in 1851 that the ABFMS sent northern abolitionist Edward Mathews to contact slaves in Virginia and Kentucky.

But the Wesleyans and the ABFMS did not have the resources to sustain their missionaries when they faced determined opposition from slaveholders. Shortly after McBride's report, pending criminal charges and threats of violence forced him, Crooks, and Bacon to retreat to the North. Meanwhile Mathews gave up his mission after a Kentucky mob nearly drowned him for preaching at a black church.[6]

The AMA was more resilient. It had agents in Maryland, Virginia, Tennessee, and Missouri, and for over a decade in central Kentucky it maintained a Bibles for slaves program. Local abolitionist John G. Fee, who headed a free church movement embracing slaves, free African Americans, and antislavery whites, directed the effort. It began during the spring of 1848 with one colporteur providing Bibles or New Testaments to "every slave that can read." By 1852 there were two engaged in this work, and by 1853 there were three active in six counties. As Fee pointed out, they "converse[d] and pray[ed] with bond and free." Despite mounting opposition from slaveholders, the effort continued until vigilantes expelled Fee and his associates from Kentucky in late 1859, following John Brown's raid.[7] Distributing Bibles to slaves and preaching to slaves were not the same as giving them one of the Addresses to the Slaves. There is no evidence that a missionary ever provided one of the Addresses to a slave. But, in communicating with slaves, the missionaries carried out the Addresses' major assumptions: that abolitionists could no longer deal only with masters and northerners, that it was possible to contact slaves, and that abolitionists had an obligation to inform slaves of their rights. By the early 1850s, missionaries in Kentucky helped slaves to escape.[8]

In part because they despised church-oriented abolitionists, Garrisonians ridiculed these missionary efforts. They charged that providing Bibles to slaves was a form of gradualism that, under the assumption that slaves had to be able to read the Bible before they could become free, would indefinitely delay general emancipation. Garrisonians also maintained that missionary efforts diverted attention and money that might better go to promoting northern sentiment in behalf of immediate emancipation. But, most of all, they denounced the Bibles for slaves campaign as "a sham, a delusion, and a snare" because it assumed that abolitionists could communicate with slaves and that slaves could play an active role in freeing themselves. These charges came from Stephen S. Foster, the official proceedings of the AASS annual meeting of 1847, and even Garrison himself. But Frederick Douglass and Wendell Phillips presented them most bluntly. In January 1848 Douglass criticized attempting to give Bibles to slaves in much the same terms that he and others had earlier criticized Smith's and Garnet's Addresses to the Slaves. "How do they mean to get the Bible among the slaves?" he asked. "It cannot go itself—it must be carried. And who among them all, has either the faith or the folly to undertake the distribution of Bibles among the slaves?" Douglass also wondered about who would teach the slaves to read. Phillips at the May 1849 AASS meeting declared, "The question . . . is, whether Northern sentiment, unclogged by Southern ownership, is permitted to link itself mentally and communicate with the oppressed race of the South." He asked, "Do you believe it possible?" He answered, "Why it is nonsense. . . . the rational method of course is to keep away."[9]

More than did other abolitionists, Garrisonians assumed that enslaved African Americans could not act in their own behalf until *after* they became free. In May 1847 the AASS declared that "the liberation of the slave is essential to his intellectual and religious elevation." In January 1848 Douglass expressed this sentiment more explicitly. "The slave," he pointedly, if ironically, contended, "is property. He cannot hold property. He cannot own a Bible. . . . The slave is a thing—and it is the all-commanding duty of the American people to make him a man."[10] Nothing could be further from the insistence in Garnet's Address—and to a lesser extent in Smith's and Garrison's—that enslaved black men had a responsibility to assert their manhood in behalf of the freedom of their people. By the early summer of 1849 a bitter debate had broken out among black abolitionists. On one side were Garnet, Bibb, and Samuel Ringgold Ward in favor of the Bibles for slaves effort. On the other were Douglass and Charles Lenox Remond against it. Relations between Douglass and Garnet, who had been at odds since 1843, became acrimonious. Garnet called Douglass a "sham and disgrace." Douglass charged that Garnet had the "spirit of a crafty priest." The Garrisonians were correct about the difficulties faced by abolitionists who attempted to bring the Bible to slaves. But their opposition even to trying reflected a conviction that slaves were passive recipients of abolitionist benevolence, rather than potential allies in the antislavery struggle.[11]

A similar, though less rigid, division of abolitionist opinion developed during the 1840s concerning the purchase of freedom. Like plans for government-sponsored compensated general emancipation, buying the freedom of individual slaves involved rewarding masters for their crimes. But, with the exception of Washington, D.C., during the Civil War, compensated emancipation proposals never went into effect in the United States.[12] In contrast, abolitionists frequently purchased freedom and in the process came into contact with slaves. As early as 1789, Quakers in New Jersey and Pennsylvania purchased freedom for some Virginian slaves. Later, during the first two decades of the nineteenth century, the Pennsylvania Abolition Society and its affiliates in the Chesapeake intervened in Maryland and the District of Columbia to either purchase freedom or protect slaves from sale south. In both instances, the abolitionists responded to appeals from African Americans who sought help in purchasing their own freedom or that of loved ones.[13] Yet the rise of immediate abolitionism during the late 1820s discouraged such interracial and intersectional relationships.

Throughout the 1830s immediatists unanimously denounced purchasing freedom and compensated general emancipation as immoral and ineffective means of ending slavery. Purchasing freedom was immoral, they maintained, because it recognized the right of the master to the slave. It was ineffective because it freed only a few slaves, leaving the great mass of them in perpetual bondage. Inadvertently, however, such reasoning provided abolitionists an additional rationale for dealing exclusively with masters, for trying to convince masters to free their slaves without compensation, and for curtailing contacts with individual slaves who sought financial assistance. Many abolitionists continued, as humanitarians, to help purchase freedom, but in conscious violation of apparently irrefutable moral logic.[14]

Two years before Gerrit Smith presented his Address to the Slaves, a family connection to slavery led him to challenge this logic. In 1822, three years after the death of his first wife, Smith had married Ann Carroll Fitzhugh. Her father, recently a Maryland slaveholder, had brought twenty slaves to New York, where state law freed them. But other Fitzhugh slaves remained in bondage in Maryland under the supervision of one of Ann's brothers. Meanwhile another brother took her former personal slave, Harriet, and Harriet's enslaved husband, Samuel Russell, to Kentucky, where he sold them to a Mississippian. When Ann's father died in 1840, she and Gerrit became slaveholders, and for them theories about the immorality of purchasing freedom ceased to make sense. They immediately joined with four of Ann's siblings who lived in New York to pay $4,000 to purchase the freedom of the ten family slaves who resided in Maryland. A year later Ann and Gerrit spent an additional $3,500 to buy the freedom of Harriet, Samuel, and their five children.[15]

This experience convinced Gerrit Smith that purchasing freedom was a legitimate abolitionist tactic. Shortly after he presented his Address to the Slaves, he told New York's abolitionist congressman, Seth M. Gates, "I have bought so many slaves, that I have none of the common abolitionist squeamishness about buying them." In January 1848 he claimed to have spent "many thousand dollars" in purchasing freedom and to have "within the last year . . . set ten of my fellow beings free from the irons of their slavery." Smith realized that purchasing freedom could be used as a means of presenting a moral argument to slaveholders in a manner that anyone who valued money could understand. More to the point, it brought abolitionists into contact with slaves. Smith sent his Quaker abolitionist friend James C. Fuller to Kentucky to negotiate the purchase of the Russells and to escort them back to Peterboro. Smith also encouraged southern abolitionists to purchase the freedom of slaves and send them north.[16] Most important, Smith's ability to publicize his departure from abolitionist orthodoxy encouraged others to do so as well. In May 1843, for example, Ohio Liberty abolitionist Salmon P. Chase sent radical political abolitionist Calvin Fairbank to Lexington, Kentucky, to purchase a woman sold at public auction.[17] It was in the vital Chesapeake region, however, that such efforts opened the most extensive contacts between abolitionists and slaves.

In 1844 Smith's close friend and associate William L. Chaplin arrived in Washington, D.C., a slaveholding city surrounded by slave states. Ostensibly Chaplin, the general agent of the New York Anti-Slavery Society, was there to report on proceedings in Congress for the *Albany Patriot*, the leading radical political abolitionist newspaper of the mid-1840s. Chaplin, who was white, quickly began to attend black church services, to establish ties to black families, and to provide considerable support to black efforts directed at purchasing freedom and initiating freedom suits. Since he and his black associates raised money in the North to finance these undertakings, they publicized far and wide that it was quite possible for abolitionists to become directly involved with slaves. In late 1845 Chaplin attempted to institutionalize the relationship by creating what he called a "Bureau of Humanity" designed to channel northern funds to freedom-seeking southern African Americans.[18]

By the late 1840s the interaction between abolitionists and slaves in and about Washington had grown intense. As masters—fearing congressional action against slavery in the District of Columbia—prepared to sell their human chattels south, slaves drew antislavery activists who were less militant than Chaplin into the struggle. Joshua R. Giddings, the abolitionist Whig congressman from Ohio's Western Reserve, spoke for others as well as himself when he reported to his wife, "I am constantly beset by the poor miserable wretches here who have their wives, their husbands or children sold to slave dealers." When Gamaliel Bailey moved from Cincinnati to Washington in late 1846 to publish the *National Era,* he joined in efforts to purchase freedom and in black freedom suits.[19] Abolitionists who engaged in these activities rejected the moral logic against purchasing freedom. But the logic was so strong that often the practice of ransoming slaves preceded an intellectual acceptance of doing so. As late as February 1848 Chaplin denied he favored "purchasing slaves even *into freedom,* as a general fact."[20]

Many of the more doctrinaire Garrisonians never made the transition. They remained very critical of anyone—including Garrison himself—who had. In early 1845 a Liberty abolitionist in Pennsylvania defended purchasing freedom by noting that Garrison and one of his associates had engaged in the practice. The *Pennsylvania Freeman,* a Garrisonian weekly published in Philadelphia, responded, "Many an act of impulsive humanity, when weighed in the balance of principles, is found by the performer to be wrong, both in morals and policy. Perhaps Mr. Garrison, and the individual alluded to, will be more careful when they find what a handle the adversary makes of their inconsistencies."[21] When in late 1846 British abolitionists purchased Frederick Douglass's freedom, while he was in England, in order to save him from possible recapture when he returned to the United States, Garrison supported them. But several Garrisonian stalwarts, as well as at least one prominent political abolitionist, condemned the purchase as immoral. The *Pennsylvania Freeman* recalled that Douglass himself had previously "protested against the ransom of slaves by purchase." In fact, as late as 1849 Douglass continued to oppose purchasing the freedom of those actually in bonds.[22]

In response to charges that purchasing freedom was sinful and counterproductive, radical political abolitionists emphasized contact with slaves, the power of sentiment, and a preference for action over abstract theory. In December 1846 Chaplin called on abolitionists "to *work* directly for the slave," to "thoroughly" identify "with desolate, forsaken humanity," and "to storm the castle of tyranny." By doing so, Chaplin suggested, abolitionists would improve their own character, help individual slaves, and spread "principles of equity, right and freedom." A few months later Smith reproved those who relied on "*calculation*" to contend that it was sinful to engage in heartfelt efforts to keep husbands and wives from being ripped apart by sale south. He charged that the more doctrinaire of the Garrisonians used only "cheap words" against slavery, while those who purchased freedom impressed slaveholders with their commitment and opened slaveholders' hearts "to the teachings of truth." In March 1848, as Chaplin's contacts with slaves led him into danger, he ridiculed "all that class of *cute* philosophers, who raise doubts about *buying people out of bondage!*" His white associate, Jacob Bigelow, a New Englander living in Washington, recalled in 1853 that "on the subject of paying for slaves, to secure their freedom, I acknowledge that I once *theorised* against it; but was, long ago very summarily cured of my theory, when I came to practise upon it."[23]

During the antebellum decades there existed a close relationship between purchasing freedom and helping slaves escape. Those in the borderlands who engaged in the former often became involved, to varying degrees, in the latter. Particularly when efforts to purchase freedom failed, slaves or their relatives called on abolitionists to help in the more dangerous business of escape. This happened all along the border between the free and slave states, but the record is best preserved for the Chesapeake.

Slave escapes in North America began in colonial times. During the Revolutionary Era, as the northern states initiated emancipation, some escapees began to head north. In many instances free blacks and in some instances whites—most notably Quakers—harbored them and helped them on their way. By the early nineteenth century, if not earlier, black and white sailors maintained a maritime escape route from southern ports to such northern cities as Philadelphia, New York, New Bedford, and Boston.[24] Since all of these were illegal clandestine activities, the number of escapees involved is unknown. Abolitionists assumed, nevertheless, that the number was small prior to the late 1830s and that at that time there occurred a great expansion.[25] There was certainly a large increase in reported arrests of people on charges that they had come from the free states to the South to help slaves escape.

Well-publicized cases of abolitionists going into the South to help slaves escape first became a part of antislavery culture in 1838. That year the governor of Ohio agreed to extradite an abolitionist named John B. Mahan to Kentucky on charges that Mahan had guided slaves northward. In 1839 Governor William H. Seward of New York, in a dispute that attracted national attention, refused to extradite three black sailors who had been charged by Virginia authorities with helping slaves escape. That same year authorities in Washington, D.C., arrested Leonard Grimes, a free black resident of that city, on charges that he too had successfully helped slaves escape from Virginia. In 1841, near Palmyra, Missouri, masters captured three white students—Alanson Work, James E. Burr, and George Thompson—from David Nelson's Mission Institute in Quincy, Illinois, as the young men attempted to convince slaves that they should escape. Later that year fugitive slave Madison Washington traveled, with abolitionist assistance, from Canada to Virginia in an attempt to rescue his wife from slavery. Recaptured and shipped aboard the *Creole*, with the New Orleans slave market as his intended destination, Washington led the successful revolt that attracted wide interest during late 1841 and early 1842.[26]

These were not the only cases between 1838 and 1841

in which black or white abolitionists went into slave states to help or attempt to help slaves escape. Radical political abolitionist Abel Brown, for example, quietly and successfully helped slaves escape in Kentucky and in the Chesapeake during the late 1830s. But it was the widely publicized cases of abolitionist involvement with slaves in physical antislavery action in the South that inspired the first of the Addresses to the Slaves. Of the three Addresses, only Smith's endorsed such activities, and it was radical political abolitionists who during the 1840s systematized slave rescues in the border South. In this version of the underground railroad, a few whites went to the Chesapeake to help local African Americans initiate escapes, and more than a few blacks and whites helped the escapees after they reached the free states.[27]

Arrests in the slave states of individuals accused of helping slaves escape peaked during the mid-1840s. Between 1844 and 1846 there were cases in South Carolina, Kentucky, Alabama, Florida, Missouri, Maryland, and Virginia. Not all of those arrested were white northerners; black and white southerners were also charged. But white northerners garnered the most publicity. Also, not all of the arrested northerners were radical political abolitionists. One of the best known was Jonathan Walker, who had ties to the Garrisonians and to the Massachusetts branch of the Liberty Party.[28] But radical political abolitionists, working closely with local African Americans in the Chesapeake between 1842 and 1850, maintained the largest, best organized, and longest lasting escape network of the 1840s.

It came into existence several months after Smith's colleague Charles T. Torrey arrived in Washington, D.C., in December 1841. Torrey was a church-oriented political abolitionist from Massachusetts, who prior to heading south and allying with Smith had clashed with Garrison on the issues of the role of churches in abolitionism, political action, and women's rights. While living in Washington as a congressional reporter for several antislavery newspapers, Torrey interacted with slaves in the District of Columbia, Maryland,

and Virginia. During the spring of 1842, he and local free black abolitionist Thomas Smallwood began taking escapees northward along a predetermined route. That fall Torrey went to Albany, New York, to edit the *Tocsin of Liberty*, which in 1843 became the *Albany Patriot*. While he was there, Torrey helped lead the Liberty Party and, in cooperation with Abel Brown, established the Albany Vigilance Association dedicated to protecting fugitive slaves who reached that city. Then, in the fall of 1843, he returned to the Chesapeake to resume his underground railroading. Over a year earlier, Garnet's town of Troy, located a few miles from Albany, had become a way station in this particular network. Despite his Address's depreciation of escape as a means of emancipation, and despite his wooden leg, Garnet was by 1848, if not earlier, going south to Philadelphia to take charge of fugitives who had arrived in that city.[29]

Because Torrey and Smallwood aimed to drive slavery out of the Chesapeake, they were not as discreet in their operations as they might have been. They taunted the masters whose slaves they had helped liberate and threatened to kill black informers and white constables. In October 1843, with police closing in, Smallwood moved with his family to Toronto. When he and Torrey returned to Washington the following month to lead another group of slaves to freedom, police foiled their plan and nearly captured them. Thereafter Smallwood remained in Toronto, and Torrey, still working closely with free African Americans and slaves, expanded his activities into Maryland and Virginia. He claimed to have helped four hundred slaves escape by the time Baltimore authorities arrested him in June 1844. Sentenced to serve six years at the Maryland Penitentiary, he died there of tuberculosis on May 9, 1846. Torrey had demonstrated more dramatically than anyone else that the premise of the Addresses to the Slaves was correct: abolitionists could communicate with slaves. He inspired slaves, who escaped in even greater numbers following his arrest.[30] He frightened slaveholders with the prospect of an abolitionist-slave alliance. His martyrdom encouraged other radical political abolitionists to take up where he left off.

Chief among Torrey's northern successors was Chaplin, who had replaced him as editor of the *Patriot*. With Smith's financial backing, Chaplin, like Torrey before him, immersed himself in the local black community. At first he concentrated on his Bureau of Humanity. Then in early 1848, in coopera- tion with African Americans, he organized the attempt by seventy-seven slaves to escape down the Potomac River aboard the schooner *Pearl*. When that April the attempt failed and angry masters sold the *Pearl* fugitives south, Chaplin led the effort to raise money for their redemption. Suspected but never charged in the incident, he continued to cooperate with slaves until August 1850 when Washington police ar- rested him following a vicious gunfight as he drove a car- riage, with two escaping slaves inside, on a northward route out of the city. Much as the Addresses to the Slaves raised images of violence, actual abolitionist communication with slaves led to real violence.[31]

The abolitionist factions differed in opinion concern- ing those who helped slaves to escape, but they were never so strictly divided on this issue as they were in regard to mis- sionary activities and purchasing freedom. No abolitionist ever opposed assisting fugitive slaves who had reached the free states. Radical political abolitionists who, by definition, denied that masters had a legal right to their slave property also unanimously supported their colleagues who went into the South to rescue people from bondage. They heeded Chaplin when he declared that Torrey had done more to- ward abolishing slavery by his actions in the South than had either northern speeches or votes. They continued through- out the 1840s to link helping slaves to escape with Smith's Address to the Slaves and with biracialism.[32]

Other abolitionist groups were not so united in regard to slave rescuing. Black Garrisonians, none of whom went south themselves, approved those who did. Especially fol- lowing the *Pearl* escape attempt, Frederick Douglass found that in assisted escapes black men could assert their manhood and become more than things.[33] But white Garrisonians, the more moderate white Liberty abolitionists, and many white church-oriented abolitionists were less supportive. White Garrisonians who expressed admiration for those who went south to help slaves escape did so in response to the arrests of Walker, Fairbank, Webster, and Torrey. Later they lamented Torrey's death and the recapture of the *Pearl* fugitives. Garrison, the MASS, the AASS, and J. Miller McKim of the *Pennsylvania Freeman* all praised the courage and humanity of slave rescuers. They often maintained that it was their own commitment to agitation in the North that produced escapes. In January 1848, for example, the MASS attributed "the increasing armies of fugitives" to slaves having "heard the good tidings of the preached Gospel of their deliverance."[34]

Other white Garrisonians, however, regarded slave rescues just as they did missions to the slaves and purchasing freedom. In 1840 Nathaniel P. Rogers contended that none of these tactics came "within the scope of our Society policy." In regard to assisted escapes, he declared, "We are for abolishing slavery itself, not by aiding it to run away, but so that slaves need not run away to get their liberty." Lydia Maria Child insisted in 1842 that "it has always been urged that it was not a legitimate use of our society funds to pay the expenses of runaways, or help them to buy their wives and children." Abolitionists, she maintained, had to concentrate their "funds and . . . energies . . . on the destruction of the *system* . . . and therefore . . . must not waste . . . efforts upon [fugitives] however painfully they might appeal to our sympathies."[35] Sydney Howard Gay reflected a common abolitionist sentiment when, following Torrey's and Walker's arrests, he wrote in the AASS's official newspaper, "It behooves us that our zeal shall not outrun our discretion, and in our eagerness to relieve a few cases of individual suffering . . . we shall not overlook the consequences of our actions on the whole mass." In 1849 Wendell Phillips cited Torrey's and Fairbank's fates as evidence that abolitionists should not dare to go south.[36]

Rogers and Gay worried that cooperation with slaves in illegal ventures would counteract the positive impact of abolitionist propaganda on whites. AFASS leader Lewis Tappan expressed this view in a private letter following Torrey's arrest. "My own opinion is no abolitionist has a right to go into a slave State with the avowed design of trampling upon its laws," he wrote in July 1844. "The cause is injured by them doing so." But by September other church-oriented abolitionists on the AFASS executive committee convinced Tappan that the organization should fund Torrey's and Walker's legal expenses and aid their families. Thereafter Tappan and the AFASS favored helping slaves escape. A month after the *Pearl* sailed, Tappan presented resolutions to the organization's annual meeting expressing sympathy "with nations and individuals who cast off oppressors and cast off tyrannical power whether wielded by the head of a nation or of a plantation." Neither he nor his organization, however, criticized abolitionists who did not agree with them on this point.[37]

White Liberty abolitionists and others who emphasized electoral politics and became Free Soilers in August 1848 never reached a consensus similar to that of the AFASS on this issue, even though they had a great deal in common with the church-oriented abolitionists. Leavitt, who led the Liberty Party in New England into the Free Soil coalition and who had worked with slaves in Washington during the early 1840s, advocated violence in helping slaves escape. In April 1845 he declared, "We go for a wise, humane and just application of physical force, so far as it is necessary to the business of rescuing from oppression." Congressman Joshua R. Giddings, who led many fervently antislavery Whigs in Ohio's Western Reserve into the new party, maintained that there existed a moral, if not legal, right to help slaves escape.[38] But Bailey spoke for most Liberty, and later Free Soil, abolitionists when, like some Garrisonians, he denounced assisted slave escapes as counterproductive. As an antislavery journalist in Cincinnati and Washington, he had worked directly with slaves in purchasing freedom and funding freedom suits. Yet he was primarily an advocate of drawing northern *and southern* whites into an antislavery party. Having weathered mob attacks while working on slavery's northern border, he was also determined to placate local public opinion. Both of these goals alienated him from those who emphasized an abolitionist-slave alliance.

In 1841 Bailey had "condemn[ed] in decided terms" Work, Burr, and Thompson's attempt to entice slaves to escape from Missouri. In remarks that angered Smith and Torrey, he declared that "it is impossible that aggression like this on the citizens of other states should effect the abolition of slavery, while it could not fail to involve the anti-slavery cause in unnecessary odium." Following the *Pearl* incident, Bailey denied that he would "support illegal or unconstitutional measures to end slavery" and would not engage in "a clandestine policy."[39] In response, radical political abolitionists condemned him for his "respect for slave laws," his lack of "heart," and his failure to recognize "the negro . . . [as] fully a man, and fully possessed of the rights of man." After Chaplin's arrest, Bailey publicly rejected helping slaves escape and suggested that both Chaplin and Torrey were misguided. In turn, Smith denounced Bailey's "cowardly and heartless disclaimers." Both men believed Smith's Address to the Slaves to have been the turning point in their relationship.[40] Bailey worked to convert the oppressors and Smith sought community with the oppressed.

These disagreements between and within abolitionist factions over missions to the slaves, purchasing freedom, and helping slaves escape reflect the forces that produced the Addresses to the Slaves and the reactions to them. Those who opposed the Addresses and the initiatives in behalf of an abolitionist-slave alliance—whether they belonged to the Liberty/Free Soil, church-oriented, or Garrisonian factions— believed the antislavery movement would succeed by peacefully changing white opinion.

Garrisonians, following their disunion doctrine, addressed almost exclusively a northern audience, although they hoped that their agitation would have an indirect impact on southern whites. Many of them reacted negatively to Smith's and Garnet's Addresses, ignored Garrison's, and disdained strategies that brought abolitionists into contact with slaves, who, they contended, must be freed through the transformation of white opinion.[41] While most Garrisonians came to admire those who went south to help slaves escape, they did not themselves engage in such aggressive and risky undertakings. Their strategy, which by the mid-1840s had diverged from the reality of an abolitionist-slave alliance in the South's borderlands, became difficult for Garrisonians in general and black Garrisonians in particular to maintain. This disjuncture helps to explain the gradual transformation from Garrisonian to radical political abolitionist that Frederick Douglass completed in 1851.

The Liberty/Free Soil, church-oriented, and radical political abolitionist factions were all more aggressive toward the South than were Garrisonians. Bailey's *National Era* was part of a strategy to spread political abolitionism among whites in the upper South. Unlike Garrisonians, Bailey interacted with slaves throughout his career. But, much to the displeasure of radical political abolitionists, he always subordinated that interaction to his effort to make antislavery politics appealing to white men. Meanwhile church-oriented and radical political abolitionists developed ties with African Americans in the same region. Because the memberships of these non-Garrisonian abolitionist factions overlapped, contradictory impulses were common. Smith, Torrey, Chaplin, and other radical political abolitionists engaged in electoral politics, but emphasized a revolutionary interracial strategy reflected in Smith's and, to a lesser degree, Garnet's Addresses. Joshua Leavitt and Lewis Tappan were each simultaneously church-oriented and Liberty abolitionists. Because he believed white abolitionists had to engage slaves, Leavitt at times sounded like a radical political abolitionist, but he helped lead Liberty abolitionists into the Free Soil Party in 1848. Because Tappan, like Bailey, believed that the peaceful persuasion of whites could bring about real freedom for African Americans, he sometimes sounded like Bailey or some of the Garrisonians in opposing clandestine abolitionist activities in the South. But Tappan's commitment to an abolitionist-slave alliance proved to be stronger than his commitment to mass political parties. He voted for radical political abolitionist Gerrit Smith in the presidential election of 1848.[42]

By then radical political abolitionists and Garrisonians together constituted a small but influential minority within the broader antislavery movement. In their critiques of American society and in their efforts to convince first Free Soilers and later Republicans that they must embrace immediate abolition and black rights, the two groups were quite similar.[43] But the radical political abolitionists remained the more aggressive of the two groups. This was clear in August 1850 when the Fugitive Slave Convention, held at Cazenovia, New York, produced the striking Letter to the Slaves.

Chapter Six

CONVERGENCE

As the sectional struggle intensified during the late 1840s and thereafter, what became of the Addresses to the Slaves? Nothing became of William Lloyd Garrison's. Because it was incompatible in 1843 with the views of most of the members of his faction, it had negligible long-term impact. In contrast, Gerrit Smith's and Henry Highland Garnet's Addresses helped shape the direction of radical political, most black, and some Garrisonian abolitionist thought and action. They became key documents in an evolving northern abolitionist relationship with slaves and with violent means.

The visions of antislavery action in Smith's and Garnet's Addresses differ. Smith's counsels against slave violence because it was inexpedient rather than immoral. It promotes escape as an effective antislavery measure, advises slaves to expropriate what property they need to reach the North or Canada, and urges northern abolitionists to go south to help them. Garnet's rejects escape as an antislavery measure and assumes that enslaved men must act on their own. Its major theme is that they must assert their manhood by striking for freedom, and it warns that they must expect a violent response from masters. But, as the 1840s passed, assisted slave escape, assertions of black masculinity, and advocacy of antislavery violence became intertwined, and so did Smith's and Garnet's Addresses as symbols of abolitionist militancy. In August 1850, on the eve of Congress's passage of a new fugi-

117

tive slave law, the legacies of the two Addresses merged at the village of Cazenovia, New York, where Smith presented a Letter to the Slaves.

Nothing better illustrates the twists and turns occasioned by the contradictory impulses in American abolitionism than the history, during the late 1840s, of Garnet, his Address to the Slaves, and his rival, Frederick Douglass. Like other abolitionists, Garnet could not resolve tensions between his conviction that black freedom would very likely be won by force and his Christian commitment to nonviolence. Shortly before he prepared his Address, Garnet accepted a commission from the peaceable and conservative American Home Missionary Society. In 1847 and 1848 he served on the executive committee of the aggressive but firmly nonviolent AMA, which led to his involvement in the Bibles for slaves effort. In 1850 he went to England to lecture in behalf of the peaceable, and not at all aggressive, free produce movement. That same year, he spoke at the World Peace Conference in Frankfurt, Germany.[1] Garnet's subsequent sojourn as a missionary in Jamaica strengthened his association with peaceful means. His time in Europe and Jamaica also removed him from the American antislavery struggle until he returned to the United States in 1855 with altered priorities. From then until the Civil War he was more interested in black migration to Africa than confronting slavery in the South.

   During the years prior to his departure for Europe, Garnet had nevertheless continued to promote his Address to the Slaves. But the opposition of other black abolitionists and his own ambivalence limited his effectiveness. In October 1847, he presented the Address at an evening session of the National Convention of Colored People and Their Friends, held at his Liberty Street Church in Troy. Although Garnet dominated the proceedings and his Address once again "produced much sensation," this time he did not try to have it adopted. The forces in favor of relying solely on peaceful northern agitation were too strong. Of the sixty-six delegates, forty-four were from New York. But the Massachusetts delegation, including William Wells Brown, Douglass, and William C. Nell, was larger and even more influential than it had been at Buffalo four years earlier. This became clear as the delegates overwhelmingly voted to adopt a Garrisonian-style report, written by Douglass, that labeled calls for slave violence inexpedient and "the result of an unpardonable impatience or an atheistic want of faith in the power of truth as a means of regenerating and reforming the world." Garnet himself voted with the majority after having deleted from the report such explicitly Garrisonian aspects as the term *moral suasion* and a denunciation of all organized religion.[2]

A few months later, however, Garnet finally succeeded in publishing his Address. He did so in a manner that directly linked it with David Walker's *Appeal* and indirectly with Smith's Address. The pamphlet *Walker's Appeal, with a Brief Sketch of his Life by Henry Highland Garnet. And also Garnet's Address to the Slaves of the United States of America* appeared in a limited edition in early 1848. It indicates that Garnet's Address had by that time been "slightly modified," while retaining "all of its original doctrine." It also expresses Garnet's hope that his Address "may be borne on the four winds of heaven, until the principles it contains shall be understood and adopted by every slave in the Union."[3]

Just as significantly, by praising Walker's constant involvement with fugitive slaves—which was in fact similar to his own—Garnet suggests in the pamphlet that his view of the northern abolitionist relationship to slaves was actually very close to that of his friend Smith. Also, Garnet suggests that inculcating fear among masters was as important as inculcating manhood among slaves. In a manner reminiscent of Smith's 1842 portrayal of a weakened slavery begging to be left alone, Garnet writes of Walker's *Appeal*, "When the fame of this book reached the South, the poor, cowardly, pusillanimous tyrants grew pale behind their cotton bags, and armed themselves to the teeth. They set watches to look after their happy and contented slaves."[4] With his own black critics in mind, Garnet charges that only cowards contended that Walker had gone too far. He had come to believe, to a much greater degree than he had in 1843, that northern abolitionism had a role, a potentially violent role, in the South.

Garnet was not the only one to have reached this conclusion. The highly publicized *Pearl* incident of April 1848 encouraged many other black and white abolitionists, regardless of factional identification, to accept Smith's contention that organized slave escapes were effective means of weakening slavery. In particular, accounts of the *Pearl* fugitives, of other organized slave escapes, and of the masters' outraged reaction to them influenced how black abolitionists interpreted Garnet's Address once it became available in print. In September 1848, the National Colored Convention, meeting in Cleveland, linked the aura of violent action associated with Garnet to Smith's call for assisted escapes. The convention declared, "We pledge ourselves individually to use all justifiable means in aiding our enslaved brethren in escaping from the Southern Prison House of Bondage."[5] In January 1849 black abolitionists in Ohio specifically linked Garnet's Address to escape rather than to a general strike. A black state convention, meeting in Columbus, resolved, "that we still adhere to the doctrine of urging the slave to leave immediately with his hoe on his shoulder, for the land of liberty, and would accordingly recommend that five hundred copies of Walker's Appeal, and Henry H. Garnet's Address to the Slaves be obtained in the name of the Convention and gratuitously circulated."[6]

The *Pearl* escape attempt also encouraged convergence among abolitionist factions by convincing more Garrisonians, especially black Garrisonians, that assisted slave escapes must become an abolitionist priority. A month after the *Pearl* set sail from Washington, the AASS annual meeting for 1848 adopted the key radical political abolitionist principle that slaveholders had no rights, that no law protected their claim to own human beings. Garrisonians clung until the Civil War to their contention that the Constitution was proslavery. But by 1848 most of them had begun to recognize an abolitionist obligation to help slaves escape.[7] No Garrisonian better reflected this changed perspective than Douglass, who had moved to Rochester, New York, in 1847 to begin publishing his *North Star*. A month after the AASS meeting, he traveled to Buffalo to attend his first radical political abolitionist function—the national nominating convention of those Liberty abolitionists who refused to participate in the formation of the Free Soil Party. In his account of the convention, Douglass presents himself as a loyal Garrisonian defending his faction's interpretation of the Constitution and its contention that only disunion could bring about general emancipation. But he admits that the convention had "done much to remove prejudice from our mind respecting some of the prominent men engaged in it" and praises Smith's "Address of the Liberty Party to the Colored People of the Northern States," which called on black men to help the antislavery cause by becoming more moral and enterprising than white men. Douglass had no difficulty, as a Garrisonian, in endorsing Smith's call on black men to withdraw from proslavery churches and proslavery political parties. He was, however, part of a major shift away from earlier Garrisonian doctrine when he endorsed the radical political abolitionist contention that "all men" had a duty to go south to help slaves escape.[8]

This was not an easy transition for Douglass and other black Garrisonians who, as late as the Troy convention, had insisted that slaves must depend for their deliverance on nonviolent abolitionist agitation in the North. As late as July 1849, Douglass charged in the *North Star* that Garnet was a hypocrite in his plan to go to England to appeal to its people's "moral sense" because "Mr. Garnet has again and again declared that he has no faith in moral means for the overthrow of American Slavery. That his hope for success was in the sword." Yet Garnet knew that by then Douglass himself was much more favorable to violent means than he had been earlier. In a letter to Douglass written at Smith's home, Garnet emphasized the paradoxical reality that, while he himself believed in peaceful persuasion, he also believed that "the slave has a moral right to use his physical power to obtain his liberty." Garnet asserted that his motto was "give me liberty, or give me death" and asked, "Dare you, Frederick Douglass, say otherwise?"[9] Douglass, and other formerly pacifistic black abolitionists, could not.

The issue of black manhood, as much as uncertainty concerning the effectiveness of moral suasion in the North, had led Douglass and other black Garrisonians to lurch toward a reevaluation of their rhetoric. In a speech he delivered in Ireland in October 1845, Douglass had praised Madison Washington for engaging in "physical warfare" and demonstrating that not just white men could fight for freedom. Back in the United States in June 1848—less than a year after he had promoted strictly peaceful northern agitation at the Troy convention—Douglass had informed white northerners that there were "many Madison Washingtons and Nathaniel Turners in the South, who would assert their rights to liberty, if you would take your feet from their necks, and your sympathy and aid from their oppressors."[10] Two months before he charged Garnet with hypocrisy, Douglass had declared that without immediate abolition, "that spirit in man which abhors chains . . . will lead those sable arms that have long been engaged in cultivating . . . the South, to spread death and destruction there." Insisting that he was "a peace man," he nevertheless recognized that "a *state of war*" existed in the South and wanted southern whites "to know that at least one coloured man in the Union, peace man though he is, would greet with joy the glad news . . . that an insurrection had broken out in the Southern States."[11]

The other black Garrisonians who had opposed Garnet's Address at Buffalo in 1843 paralleled Douglass's course toward a more favorable view of slave violence. At a meeting in Abingdon, Massachusetts, in June 1847, Charles Lenox Remond declared that based on the principles of the American Revolution the slaves were bound by their love of justice to "RISE AT ONCE, *EN MASSE*, AND THROW OFF

THEIR FETTERS; and [that] he, for one, *would counsel them to do so.*" That same year, William Wells Brown compared Nat Turner to Moses.[12]

Another factor that encouraged convergence among radical political, Garrisonian, and church-oriented abolitionists was the decision of Gamaliel Bailey, Salmon P. Chase, and most Liberty abolitionists to join the Free Soil Party in 1848. Although the rise of free-soilism did not immediately end the participation of such former Liberty abolitionists as Bailey and Chase in the AFASS, it did set church-oriented abolitionists led by Lewis Tappan on their way into the radical political abolitionist ranks. The departure of what had been the largest group of immediatists did not end rivalry between the remaining Liberty abolitionists and Garrisonians, but it did encourage confluence and a grudging Garrisonian admission that the remaining non-Garrisonian immediatists *were* abolitionists.[13] That these non-Garrisonian abolitionists had begun more clearly to acknowledge antislavery women as co-laborers facilitated the process. So did the Compromise of 1850 which, with its new, stronger fugitive slave law, brought all immediatists into cooperation with fugitive slaves in the North.[14]

The Fugitive Slave Convention at Cazenovia, held August 21 and 22, 1850, and its "Letter to the American Slaves from those who have fled from American Slavery" constitute a milestone in convergence. The convention, initiated by white radical political abolitionists, aimed to embrace black radical political abolitionists, the black leaders of the New York State Vigilance Association, black and white Garrisonians, and antislavery women of both races. It aimed to meld all the constituencies that had endorsed the Addresses to the Slaves, and some that had not. It proposed to do so on the basis of Smith's call on northern abolitionists to help slaves escape and on the basis of Garnet's demand that black men assert their masculinity in the struggle against slavery. Although the Cazenovia Convention preceded the passage of the Fugitive Slave Law of 1850 by several weeks, it anticipated a struggle *in the North* against the law, which would overshadow but not end direct action against slavery *in the South*.[15] The convention promoted biracialism, cooperation among abolitionist factions, and a less ambiguous embrace of violent means. It presaged the physical character of abolitionism during the following decade.

Smith, Douglass, and most other immediatists never gave up their effort to push the Free Soil Party and, later, the Republican Party toward endorsing general emancipation and black rights. But, during the summer of 1850, as Smith planned the Cazenovia Convention, he aimed at a more radical constituency and at a more direct challenge to slavery. In conjunction with the New York State Vigilance Association, headed by Charles B. Ray, Smith in early August issued a call through the *Liberty Party Paper,* published in Syracuse as his faction's official journal, inviting "free men, free women and fugitives" to meet at Cazenovia for "mutual counsel and encouragement."[16] Influenced by the Women's Rights Convention, held in 1848 at nearby Seneca Falls, his increased engagement with African Americans, and his continued contacts with Garrisonians, Smith organized a gathering that would be more diversified than any of those that had produced the Addresses to the Slaves.[17]

He invited black Garrisonians Douglass, William Craft, and Ellen Craft, of whom Douglass and, perhaps, Ellen Craft attended. He invited white Garrisonian Samuel Joseph May, who lived in nearby Syracuse and accepted. In his letter to May, Smith hoped that Massachusetts Garrisonians Wendell Phillips, Edmund Quincy, Charles C. Burleigh, and Garrison himself might attend, but none of them did. Smith also invited fugitive slaves who were affiliated with his radical political faction and the AFASS. Among them were James Baker and Jermain Wesley Loguen, who both attended, and Samuel Ringgold Ward, Henry Bibb, Henry Box Brown, and James McCune Smith, all of whom did not. Baker was a locally prominent abolitionist, whom Charles T. Torrey had helped escape from Washington, D.C., in 1842. Three years later William L. Chaplin had acted as the agent of radical political abolitionists who purchased the freedom of Baker's wife and children. Among the white abolitionists who adhered to his faction, Smith invited Beriah Green and William Goodell, neither of whom attended, as well as Joseph C. Hathaway, James C. Jackson, Samuel Thomas Jr., Chaplin's fiancée Theodosia Gilbert, and antislavery minstrel George W. Clark, all of whom did.[18] Either Smith or Chaplin arranged for the attendance of famous former *Pearl* fugitives Mary and Emily Edmonson.

Smith hoped to unite black and white abolitionists in direct action against slavery on the basis of aspects of his and Garnet's Addresses to the Slaves. At the time, he and other radical political abolitionists envisioned the border South in general and the District of Columbia in particular as the theater for this struggle. Not only had Torrey and Chaplin previously worked with slaves in the District, but considerable indirect evidence indicates that Smith planned the Cazenovia Convention in conjunction with a scheme, originated by Chaplin, to showcase the ability of abolitionists to carry out clandestine biracial attacks on slavery in the national capital. They hoped to weaken slavery at this strategic and symbolic point and to disrupt efforts in Congress to pass compromise legislation. They also hoped to strengthen their own political power by forcing Gamaliel Bailey's *National Era*, the most important abolitionist newspaper in favor of the Free Soil Party, to alienate either abolitionists or nonextensionists.[19]

During that summer, four slaves belonging to southern congressmen had escaped. Free African-American residents of Washington harbored them for several weeks. Then, on the evening of August 8, Washington police arrested Chaplin as he attempted to drive a carriage containing two of the slaves northward from the city. The police reported that Chaplin and the slaves all had pistols and put up a ferocious resistance before being captured. Although he denied being armed, Chaplin gloried in having helped slaves in an attempt to gain freedom. Later several newspaper reports maintained that he had intended to bring the fugitives to the Cazenovia convention in order, in the words of the *New York Tribune*, "to give it *eclat*."[20] Their appearance would have been even more dramatic and provocative than Goodwin's pictures of slaves at Peterboro in 1842, Latimer at the New England Anti-Slavery Meeting in May 1843, and Garnet's own persona at Buffalo in August of that year. Instead, because of the arrest of Chaplin and the two fugitives, the Edmonson sisters and Chaplin himself, though he was present only in spirit, filled this vital role. The convention became as much a Chaplin meeting as a fugitive slave meeting. It symbolized the union of abolitionists and slaves that Smith's Address to the Slaves had called for years earlier.

The ambiance of the Cazenovia Convention was similar to that of the meetings that in 1842 and 1843 had heard the Addresses to the Slaves. Like the Peterboro and Boston gatherings, it attracted a large, enthusiastic crowd, which observers estimated to have been between two and three thousand. As in the case of other large abolitionist gatherings, people were attracted by the promise of the dramatic oratory and freewheeling debate. When the convention convened at the village's Free Congregational Church, which had a seating capacity of four hundred, many were unable to enter, just as had been the case at Peterboro's Presbyterian church over eight years earlier. But, in contrast to the cold weather that gripped upstate New York in January 1842, the warmth of August allowed the convention managers to accommodate the crowd by moving the second day's session to an apple orchard offered by its owner, Grace Wilson, a leader among local abolitionist women.[21] The Cazenovia meeting also diverged from that at Peterboro in regard to religion, entertainment, and, most significantly, diversity.

There were far fewer ministers at Cazenovia in 1850 than there had been at Peterboro in 1842 (or at Buffalo in 1843), indicating that by 1850 the level of anticlericalism among radical political abolitionists had drawn closer to that of the Garrisonians. In his report to the convention on Chaplin's imprisonment, Joseph C. Hathaway declared that "American religion" was "a stench" and that "American ministers" were "false to man and rebels against God." When asked about exceptions to these pronouncements, he replied, "I was speaking of their general characteristics. An anti-slavery religion is not American religion—it is anti-American." Only black clergy and white clergy who represented independent or "free" churches had prominent roles at Cazenovia. Loguen, an African Methodist Episcopal Zion minister, had organized a black "Abolition Church" in Syracuse and was very active in New York as an underground railroad agent. One of the white ministers, Edward Mathews, had engaged in aggressive abolitionism in the border South and another white minister, Francis Hawley, soon would. Mathews, who represented the Free Baptist Missionary Society, spoke at the convention about his experiences in Virginia. Gerrit Smith's friend Hawley, whose church hosted the initial meeting of the convention and who served as one of its vice presidents, became active during the mid-1850s in John G. Fee's church-oriented antislavery campaign in Kentucky.[22]

In regard to entertainment, while those attending the Peterboro Convention had frequently united in prayer, there is no indication that they had united in song. This contrasted with the New England antislavery and black national conventions of 1843. But at Cazenovia songs by Clark and the Edmonsons raised emotion and encouraged solidarity among those gathered. Douglass reported that Mary and Emily Edmonson "favored the Convention with occasional songs." Among them, according to local tradition, was a stirring rendition of "I Hear the Voice of Lovejoy on Alton's Bloody Plain," which recounted the 1837 murder of white abolitionist Elijah P. Lovejoy by a proslavery mob in southern Illinois. One of the several songs Clark presented was a musical rendition of John G. Whittier's poem "Stanzas for the Times." In light of Chaplin's arrest, many at the convention must have reacted emotionally when Clark sang, "Shall ruffian threats of cord and steel / The dungeon's gloom—th' assassin's blow, / Turn back the spirit roused to save / The Truth— our Country—and the Slave?"[23]

The most striking difference between the Peterboro and Cazenovia conventions, however, involved degrees of diversity. The Peterboro gathering had been the least diverse racially, sexually, and ideologically of all the meetings that heard Addresses to the Slaves during the early 1840s. It left no record of black attendance. Like the black national convention at Buffalo, it had no female delegates. Like the New England Anti-Slavery Convention, one faction dominated. But the level of diversity achieved at Cazenovia was unsurpassed during the nineteenth century. A correspondent of the *New Englander* wrote of the second day's session in the apple orchard: "A large number of persons of every sect in religion, of every party in politics, and every shade of complexion, met in this magnificent temple of nature."[24]

While it is likely that not a single African American attended the Peterboro Convention, the *Utica Daily Gazette* noted that there was "a smart sprinkling of blacks" among the thousands of whites at Cazenovia. Between thirty and fifty fugitive slaves sat together. In addition, black men held positions of authority: Douglass chaired the convention and Charles B. Ray and Loguen were on the nominating committee. James Baker served on the business committee. During the first day, Douglass, Baker, and Ray each addressed those assembled and Douglass read a letter from Samuel Ringgold Ward. The *Madison County Whig* reported that, during the second day, some of the fugitives "presented narratives of their escapes." One of the Edmonson sisters spoke "words of simple and touching eloquence" regarding Chaplin's "arrest and imprisonment."[25]

Their youth and their gender, as well as their status as former fugitives, made the Edmonsons impressive embodiments of resistance to slavery's oppressiveness. Their presence—and that of many other women, both black and

Leaders of the Cazenovia Fugitive Slave Convention, August 22, 1850. This daguerreotype shows former slaves Emily and Mary Edmonson, wearing patterned shawls and standing to the right and left respectively of Gerrit Smith, who is gesturing with his left arm. Directly in front of Smith and seated at the table are Theodosia Gilbert and Frederick Douglass. (From the Collection of the Madison County Historical Society, Oneida, New York.)

white—at Cazenovia indicates that by 1850 radical political abolitionists had approached Garrisonians in their commitment to feminism. A now famous daguerreotype taken at the apple orchard shows the sisters, Theodosia Gilbert, perhaps Ellen Craft, and several other women on the convention's platform, along with Smith, Douglass, and a number of men. There are also many women facing the platform. Two women served on the meeting's business committee, and one served along with Smith's son-in-law as a recording secretary. Douglass's assistant Julia Griffiths reported the proceedings for the *North Star.* Another woman delivered a speech castigating antiabolitionsts.[26]

The factional mixture at Cazenovia was as significant as the convention's embrace of African Americans and women. It was a radical political abolitionist meeting, but not exclusively so. Its managers were black and white men who, regardless of their faction, were committed to asserting black manhood and to aggressive, if not necessarily violent, antislavery tactics. Gerrit Smith, who organized the meeting, was the most responsible for this. He was also the most important figure in attendance. Yet the absent Chaplin had nearly as great an influence through the presence of his friends James C. Jackson, who had worked with him on the *Albany Patriot*, Joseph C. Hathaway, who reported on his condition in jail, Gilbert, who had nursed his wounds, and William H. Smith, who led the effort to raise funds for his bail. Although others—including Free Soilers, Whigs, and supporters of the American Colonization Society—who gathered at Cazenovia were more conservative, in all the Letter to the Slaves emerged from a more radical, as well as more diverse, constituency than had any of the Addresses to the Slaves.

By the time the Cazenovia Convention convened at 10:00 A.M. on August 21, Smith, May, and the other managers had agreed that its goal was to identify the entire antislavery movement—black and white, political, church-oriented, and Garrisonian—with fugitive slaves and those northerners who

aided them. Although the major means were to be Smith's
Letter to the Slaves and recognition of Chaplin's martyrdom,
the proceedings themselves symbolized this convergence.
White radical political abolitionist Jackson called the meeting to order. White Garrisonian May served as temporary
chairman. Black Garrisonian Douglass became permanent
chairman. In short order the convention's morning session
created a committee to raise funds for Chaplin's defense, a
committee of women to provide him with an inscribed silver
pitcher, and a committee, chaired by Loguen, to report an
"address or addresses from the fugitive slaves."[27]

At the start of the afternoon session, Loguen reported
two documents: the Letter to the Slaves and an address to
the Liberty Party. Smith presented both of them, and an extended debate, involving him, Ray, Douglass, Clark, Loguen,
and May, began. The debate extended into the convention's
second day and overlapped with an intense discussion of the
seventeen resolutions that Smith reported from the business
committee. The nature of those resolutions provides additional context for understanding the significance of the Letter. Douglass attempted unsuccessfully to defeat a resolution
that appeared to endorse voting and another that praised the
free produce movement.[28] In the end, those assembled passed
all seventeen, by no means unanimously. Several of them
called on Congress to act against slavery in the District of
Columbia. One sought to appeal to both Garrisonians and
radical political abolitionists by calling for either "disband-
ing th[e] Government or wielding it for the overthrow of
Slavery in every part of the Nation." Others reflected Garnet's
Address, Johnson's *New York Evangelist* articles, and Smith's
Address in demanding that "men" in bondage had a duty "to
get out of it" and that "others" had a duty to help them. They
praised Torrey, Chaplin, and other slave rescuers. They
threatened "CIVIL REVOLUTION" if Chaplin, his accom-
plices, and all the slaves of the District of Columbia were not
freed. When called on to explain this pronouncement, Smith
remained ambivalent concerning violent means, but less so

than he had been earlier. He said the resolution "implied no bloodshed, but a revolution in civil things. It did not ask for blood and did not forbid bloodshed."[29]

The convention's Letter to the American Slaves developed themes similar to those in the resolutions. Smith, in preparing the draft he presented, had relied on his Address to the Slaves and on Johnson's *Evangelist* articles, both of which had been published over eight years earlier. As in Smith's Address, the emphasis in the Letter is on escape and northern assistance to escapees. Smith in 1842 had offered to supply slaves with pocket compasses and that same offer is in the Letter. In both his Address and Letter, Smith advises slaves to take what they needed to escape, although the Letter avoids the controversial suggestion that fugitives appropriate property in the free states. Both Smith's Address and Letter end with the admonition, "Lift up your heads, for your redemption draweth nigh." The impact of Johnson's articles, on which Smith had relied to defend his Address and which had helped shape Garnet's, emerges in the Letter's discussion of the right of slaves to escape and to take what they needed. The Letter deals with this in two ways. First it invokes the radical political abolitionist doctrine, which many Garrisonians had come to accept, that slaveholders had no rights. Second, following Johnson, it maintains that even if slaveholders had rights, slaves, as "prisoners of war, in an enemy's country" were "exempt from all obligations to respect them." Slaves had "the fullest liberty to plunder, burn, and kill" in effecting their escapes (see p. 192).

Among the Letter's many departures from Smith's Address, the most important is that it purports to be from the fugitive slaves gathered at Cazenovia. It claims to relate, in their own voice, their experiences, to express their views, and to provide their advice to slaves. Although this is a literary device, rather than literal truth, the fugitives *did* have a role in writing the letter, which symbolizes the convergence of black and white immediatists on a militant agenda involving cooperation with slaves.

In assuming to write from a black point of view, Smith produced a document more similar to Garnet's Address to the Slaves than would have been the case had Smith merely written in behalf of the fugitives. Portions of the Letter discuss the positive role of white immediatists, especially in helping fugitives escape. But, while the Letter contains no call for a general strike as a means of gaining emancipation, it emphasizes, as Garnet had, what African-American men must do. It insists that slaves act for themselves in escaping. It advises them that, on reaching the North, they must maintain their "self-respect" by not joining churches that had "negro pews" and not supporting political parties that discriminated against them. It also admonishes them not to send their children to segregated schools and not to support the American Colonization Society. In a passage reminiscent of Garnet's assertion of black masculinity, the Letter declares, "It is not to be disguised, that a colored man is as much disposed, as a white man, to resist, even unto death, those who oppress him" (see p. 191). With less ambiguity than any of the Addresses to the Slaves, the Letter pledges to enslaved men that in the event of an "insurrection of the Southern slaves . . . the great mass of colored men of the North . . . will be found by your side, with death-dealing weapons in their hands" (see p. 191).[30]

This is far from Garrisonian nonresistance and reliance on abolitionist agitation in the North, and by 1850 most Garrisonians were less doctrinaire pacifists than they had been earlier. Even during the early 1840s, Smith's and Garrison's Addresses had acknowledged that, while some abolitionists were nonresistants, most regarded slave violence to be a matter of expediency. The Letter makes the same point more strongly in the name of fugitive slaves. It contends that only a "handful" of the fugitives had "become non-resistants" and, therefore, would not furnish slaves "with deadly weapons" even if they could (see p. 191). In addition—and in a manner similar to Garrison's Address—the Letter reminds those who heard or read it that even nonresistants recognized that "if the American revolutionists had excuse for shedding but one drop of blood, then have the American slaves excuse for making blood flow 'even to the horse-bridles'" (see p. 192).

The Letter seeks to bind together the fugitives, the Garrisonians, and the radical political remnant of the Liberty Party by portraying all of them as equally opposed to northern political and religious subservience to the South. It contends that the only abolitionists that African Americans could trust "are, almost all of them, members of the American Anti-Slavery Society, or of the Liberty Party." It maintains that the Free Soil Party was too inconsistent and that the country's major political parties and major religious denominations were linked to the South and, therefore, "adverse to the colored population" (see p. 190). It gives the AASS and the Liberty Party equal credit for revealing "the callousness of American religion and American democracy" and prays "that soon, not a shred of the current religion, nor a shred of the current politics of this land, may remain" (see p. 191). Only then would Christianity triumph and whites recognize blacks as having equal rights with themselves.

For the more immediate future, the Letter, like the Cazenovia Convention itself, sought to link radical political abolitionists, Garrisonians, fugitive slaves, and those still in bondage in a physical challenge to slavery and the laws that protected it. The Letter reaffirms abolitionist commitment to helping slaves escape, *and* their readiness to protect those who had reached the North. Like Smith's and Garrison's Addresses, the Letter gives northern abolitionists credit for rising numbers of slave escapes. It rhetorically informs its designated slave audience that more African Americans were leaving the "Southern prison house," because "the Liberty Party, the Vigilance Committee of New York, individuals, and companies of individuals in various parts of the country, are doing all they can, and it is much, to afford you a safe and cheap, passage from slavery to liberty" (see p. 196). While the Letter emphasizes Chaplin's efforts, it praises the abolitionists of New York and New England—the radical political abolitionists and the Garrisonians—for providing fugitives with the only safe havens in the North.

Most significant, the Letter notes "the industrious efforts, which are now in making to get new facilities at the hands of Congress for re-enslaving those, who have escaped from slavery." In response it proposes interracial cooperation in the North against the enforcement of what soon became the Fugitive Slave Law of 1850. The Letter correctly predicts that there would be resistance in New York and New England, maintaining that "the colored people . . . will 'stand for their life,' and what is more, the white people . . . will not stand against them." It warns masters and federal authorities that "a regenerated public sentiment has, forever, removed these States beyond the limits of the slaveholders' hunting ground. Defeat—disgrace—and it may be death—will be their only reward for pursuing their prey into this *abolitionized* portion of our country" (see p. 221).[31]

The *Madison County Whig* reported that Smith wrote the Letter to the Slaves "at Peterboro, and brought [it] to the Convention, exactly as it was adopted." But this was not quite the case. Like Smith's and Garnet's Addresses, the Letter immediately became the subject of extended debate, and it underwent some revision before it passed. Edward Mathews maintained that "the majority of the Convention were peace men, designing to use the press and pen as their weapons."[32] Yet, since none of those who dominated the debate—Smith, Ray, Douglass, Clark, and May—were at that time adverse to violent rhetoric, the threats of violence in the Letter do not appear to have been a major issue. Douglass and May, in contrast to Douglass and the other Garrisonians who criticized Garnet's Address in 1843, were not in August 1850 concerned with the issue of violent versus peaceful means. Instead—revealing a great exception to Garrisonian rhetoric—they objected to Smith's representation of abolitionist influence on northern public opinion. In his presentation, Smith repeated an assertion, which both he and Garrison had made in their Addresses to the Slaves, that "the population in the Free States are, with few exceptions, the fugitive slaves' friends." Douglass now contended that this "overestimated" the "abolition feeling in the North." Insisting that only those, such as Chaplin, who helped slaves escape were their friends, Douglass succeeded not only in having the offending passage deleted from the Letter but in signaling his embrace of a more aggressive form of abolitionism. Douglass and May also objected that Smith had put words "into the mouths of the fugitives" and that therefore the Letter had to be approved by the fugitives present. After some debate, the fugitives got this opportunity and endorsed the modified version of the Letter before the entire convention adopted it.[33]

The abolitionist debate over the Letter ended, for all intents and purposes, with the adjournment of the Cazenovia Convention. In part this was because the large segment of abolitionist opinion represented by Gamaliel Bailey now identified with the Free Soil Party. But, more significantly, in another indication of convergence, it was because Garrisonian opposition to physical cooperation with slaves had greatly diminished. Appeals to the spirit of the American Revolution, Garnet's association of violence with manhood, Johnson's depiction of slaves as prisoners of war, and dramatic reports of actual slave rebellions and escapes had finally convinced most of them that slaves and fugitive slaves might rightfully resort to violence in order to free themselves. By the late 1840s the remaining immediatists, prodded by the contention that there could be no law protecting slavery and by rising slave unrest, had also come to believe that black and white northerners were justified in employing illegal and violent means in behalf of escaping slaves. The majority of immediatists who gathered at Cazenovia, as well as the great majority of those who had not, were ready for action. As historian Lawrence J. Friedman pointed out in 1982, immediatists remained ambivalent regarding violence throughout the 1850s. Nevertheless they were far less ambivalent than they had been during the early 1840s. The immediatist press published the Letter to the Slaves, but had very little to say about it. This included one Garrisonian journal that mildly dissented from it.[34]

In contrast, nonabolitionist northern and southern newspapers had a great deal more to say about the Letter than they had about any of the Addresses. In part this was the result of technology, as railroads and the telegraph—the latter of which came into public use in 1844—facilitated the dissemination of news. In part it was a result of increased sectional tensions. Many northern journalists and politicians sought to allay anger and fear among white southerners by dismissing those who attended the Cazenovia meeting as deranged fanatics out of step with northern public opinion. The *Buffalo Morning Express* denounced "the absurdities and atrocities perpetuated by the Abolitionists at Cazenovia, under the auspices of Gerrit Smith." Like several other northern newspapers, it concluded that Smith had "become insane." The *New York Observer* wryly commented, "Even fanaticism has its limits." While acknowledging that "this is a free country" in which anyone might express an opinion, the relatively sympathetic *New York Tribune* labeled "the whole [Cazenovia] affair mistaken and unwise."[35] In the South, however, journalists and politicians who advocated disunion in order to protect slavery claimed that the abolitionists at Cazenovia were typical northerners whose aggressive behavior required defensive measures. Immediately following the convention, during Congress's debate over the Fugitive Slave bill, Senator David L. Yulee of Florida noted the convention's "incendiary address" and called "the attention of the people of the South to it as a sample of the opinions and feelings of the North in relationship to the rights of the South." Despite warnings that the Letter must be kept from slaves, at least two disunionist southern newspapers published it in full in order to convince white southerners of the danger they faced.[36]

The northerners and southerners who commented on the Cazenovia Convention and its Letter to the Slaves were each partially right and partially wrong. The abolitionists, of course, were not insane in opposing slavery and favoring human equality. But the majority of those who gathered at Cazenovia *were* zealous in their determination to defy state and national law. They would, if necessary, resort to violent means against slavery. Whether or not they were in or out of step with northern public opinion on this point is a matter of degree. Very few in the North approved slave revolt or going south to help slaves escape. But many were sympathetic to fugitive slaves and a majority did not like the federal interference in local affairs that the fugitive slave laws entailed. Rather than being entirely out of step with northern public opinion, those gathered at Cazenovia were in advance of it. As for the southern claim that aggressive action by abolitionists in concert with slaves required defensive measures, it was, in light of the events discussed in this book, undeniable. Yulee and other proslavery advocates could observe potentially powerful northern politicians, including William H. Seward, Salmon P. Chase, Joshua R. Giddings, and Charles Durkee, publicly demonstrating in Washington their sympathy for Chaplin.[37]

The Addresses to the Slaves of 1842 and 1843 marked the beginning of a momentous change in American abolitionism. They were ambiguous, contingent, and contradictory statements of the determination of some northerners to become active allies of the slaves in a physical struggle for freedom. They marked a point at which some black and white abolitionists began to realize that they had to embrace slaves as allies, become more aggressive in helping slaves escape, and accept the legitimacy of violent means on the part of slaves. In 1850 the Letter to the Slaves demonstrated that the remaining immediatists had become less ambivalent concerning their relationship to slaves, the centrality of slave escape to the antislavery struggle, and the morality of violent action undertaken not only by slaves but by themselves. At Cazenovia they converged on a plan of action. They were ready actively to aid slaves to escape, and, if necessary, to revolt; the same reasoning that produced the Letter produced John Brown's raid in 1859.[38]

But those gathered at Cazenovia were also committed to rallying against the new Fugitive Slave Law *as soon as it went into effect*. This new, harsher law pushed most of the physical antislavery struggle northward as interracial mobs repeatedly clashed with those who attempted to enforce it.[39] In February 1851 black and white abolitionists forcibly rescued a fugitive slave known as *Shadrack* from a Boston courtroom. Nine months later a mob led by Smith, Loguen, and May stormed a Syracuse, New York, police station to free *Jerry*. Similar violent confrontations continued throughout the 1850s. Rather than build on Torrey's and Chaplin's contacts with slaves in order to plan and carry out in the border South more mass escape attempts like that aboard the *Pearl*, the more militant antislavery northerners for years devoted much of their time and resources to rescuing fugitive slaves captured in the North. If this had not been necessary, something similar to Brown's raid would have occurred much earlier.

CONCLUSION

Following the national election of 1856, there were rumors that slaves in the upper South might revolt. In response, Henry C. Wright, a prominent white Garrisonian, *suggested* that abolitionists call on them to do so. "We owe it as our duty to ourselves and to humanity, to excite every slave to *rebellion* against his master," Wright declared. A year later Charles L. Remond, one of the black Garrisonians who had opposed Garnet's Address to the Slaves, responded to the Dred Scott decision by *proposing* to prepare another, more explicitly incendiary, address to the slaves. "If we recommend to the slaves of South Carolina to rise up in rebellion," he contended, "it would work greater things than we imagine."[1] But unlike the early 1840s and in 1850 when perceptions of slave unrest led respectively to the Addresses to the Slaves and the Letter to the Slaves, no formal document resulted from either Wright's or Remond's call.

This was not because abolitionists had once again given up on communicating with slaves, or appearing to communicate with them, or because they no longer sought to ally with slaves against masters. Instead it was because during the 1850s actual abolitionist cooperation with slaves had already become, more than ever before, a prominent feature of the antislavery movement. Wright's and Remond's words were superfluous because what the Addresses called for had, to a degree, become reality. Gerrit Smith made this point in November 1852 on the first anniversary of the *Jerry* fugitive slave rescue in Syracuse. Critics, he recalled, had declared him to be crazy for issuing his "letter to the slaves," but now radical political and Garrisonian abolitionists, in preventing the enforcement of the Fugitive Slave Law, had implemented his doctrine that no law could protect slavery.[2]

Clandestine escape networks had entered their heyday. Harriet Tubman in Maryland and other black and white underground railroad agents elsewhere in the borderlands did not personally gain wide renown during the 1850s. Even most abolitionists did not know their names because they acted in secret and, unlike Torrey and Chaplin, were not caught. But Americans knew that many abolitionists engaged to varying degrees in helping slaves escape from the border South to the North or Canada. And, unlike Torrey, Chaplin, and Tubman, the great majority of them did so in the North. They had the luxury of taking direct action in behalf of the oppressed without leaving home. Neither did they have to take great risks, since northern juries during the 1850s rarely convicted those charged with violating the Fugitive Slave Law. Nevertheless helping escapees revitalized abolitionism.[3] Fugitive slaves had, since the early 1840s, been prominent as antislavery speakers. Their heroism had helped shape the Addresses to the Slaves. It was, however, during the 1850s that they became the emotional core of the movement.

In a context in which black and white abolitionists and some Free Soilers—and later some Republicans—cooperated with fugitive slaves, there were bound to be echoes of the Addresses and Letter to the Slaves. Among them was John Brown's "Words of Advice," which he presented on January 15, 1851, to a group of African-American residents of Springfield, Massachusetts. This brief speech differed from the Addresses to the Slaves in several respects. Brown directed it to a single audience of fugitive slaves rather than to multiple audiences of auditors, readers, and faraway slaves. In addition, he was calling on African Americans in the North to organize resistance to the Fugitive Slave Law rather than on slaves in the South to escape, resist, or revolt. But Brown's assumptions that black men must prove their masculinity, that they needed the help of friendly whites, and that they must act forcefully reflected aspects of the Addresses.[4] There is a legend that Brown published Garnet's Address in 1848. Whether he did or not, his phraseology reflected Garnet's when he demanded that black men must be in "earnest." He was very much in the radical political abolitionist tradition when he demanded that they recall the aggressive efforts of Jonathan Walker and Charles T. Torrey.[5]

Brown began developing his own plan for aggressive abolitionism during the years following the Addresses to the Slaves. His raid on the federal arsenal at Harpers Ferry, Virginia, in October 1859 constituted the culmination not only of those plans but of the spirit of the Addresses. According to Brown biographer Richard O. Boyer, Brown met Garnet and Jermain W. Loguen in 1846 and discussed his plan with them at that time. It may be that contact with the charismatic Brown changed Garnet's mind about the efficacy of mass escape as an abolition measure.[6] Brown met Gerrit Smith in April 1848 when the two men agreed that Brown would live, work with, and lead African Americans on land Smith provided in New York's Adirondack Mountains. It seems very likely that Brown at this time informed Smith of his plans for action in the South. The two men began a long association, and Smith later became a principal financier of Brown's raid. But it was the less militant Frederick Douglass who years later provided the only account of Brown's plan as Brown conceived it during the late 1840s. Douglass recalled that Brown told him in November 1847 that slavery could not be peacefully abolished in the South and that he hoped to lead a small detachment of armed men into the mountains of Virginia. There they would "induce" the "most restless and daring" slaves to join them, and send "large numbers" of other slaves "to the north by the underground railroad."[7]

Brown was already less ambivalent concerning violent

means than Smith, Garrison, and Garnet—and certainly less so than Douglass. Unlike all four of these men as well, but like Torrey and Chaplin, Brown was also willing and able to do more than claim to address slaves from a distance. He went into the South. But Brown's statements, during the late 1840s and well into the 1850s, tended, like Smith's and Garrison's Addresses, to emphasize escape rather than rebellion as the key to abolition.

This was true as well of another abolitionist who echoed the Addresses to the Slaves. Three years after Brown spoke to fugitive slaves in Springfield, James Redpath, a young Scottish-born antislavery journalist, traveled from the Northeast into the deep South to carry out the proposition that abolitionists could communicate directly with slaves even in the heart of slaveholding power. Redpath later fought beside Brown against proslavery forces in Kansas Territory and after the Harpers Ferry raid became one of Brown's more dedicated defenders. During his three southern journeys, undertaken in 1854 and 1855, Redpath traveled through Virginia, North Carolina, South Carolina, Georgia, Alabama, and Louisiana. He spoke with enslaved men and women, though mostly with men. In letters published in the *Liberator*, Redpath noted the ignorance and complacency of some slaves. But he found that most of them expressed discontent and willingness to risk northward escape attempts. Like Garnet, over a decade earlier, Redpath emphasized that enslaved men had a responsibility to act in behalf of their outraged wives and daughters. In his conversations, he repeatedly drew them out on this subject.

Redpath described those who were willing to escape as "resolute and bold men." Like Smith in his Address and Letter, Redpath urged abolitionists to supply them with pocket compasses. Unlike Smith, Redpath also wanted to supply them with "revolving pistols" and money. Slavery, he believed could best be destroyed by sending into the border South northern agents who would engage in such activities and expand the underground railroad. Redpath later contended that he went south to "prepare the way" for rebellion and that it was the duty of abolitionists to "teach, urge, and encourage insurrection." But, like Brown during the late forties and early fifties, Redpath, during 1854 and 1855, counseled escape.[8]

Neither Brown nor Redpath claimed, as Smith and Garrison had in their Addresses to the Slaves, that escape was a peaceful alternative to revolt (see pp. 156–57, 176–77). Instead, they celebrated the courage of men, slave and free, black and white, who dared to take up arms in the freedom struggle. But it was not until the two men experienced civil war between antislavery and proslavery forces in Kansas Territory that they began to think in terms of a war against slavery in the South rather than of assisted escape. By the late 1850s many other abolitionists, including Smith and Garnet but not Garrison, had reached a similar conclusion.[9] The raid Brown and his tiny, interracial band carried out at Harpers Ferry in the hope of sparking a slave rebellion, Brown's arrest, his execution in December 1859, and the reactions to these events in the North and South helped precipitate the Civil War that began sixteen months later.

This war, the most costly and most important in American history, brought a violent end to slavery. It thereby vindicated those abolitionists who, beginning with David Walker, had doubted that peaceful means would be enough to achieve their goal. Recently some historians have characterized the Civil War as the largest American slave revolt, or have contended that a slave uprising accompanied the war.[10] Although there was actually more escape than revolt, many men who were slaves under southern law fought as Union soldiers for black freedom. In this sense the war echoed warnings in Smith's, Garrison's, and Garnet's Addresses to the Slaves, as well as in Smith's Letter to the Slaves, that, without peaceful emancipation, black men would rise up against their masters.

Two wartime documents also echo the Addresses in their ambivalence and their insistence that black men must prove their manhood in order to gain freedom for themselves and their families. The first is Abraham Lincoln's Emancipation Proclamation, issued on January 1, 1863. In declaring slavery abolished in states, or portions of states, in rebellion against the United States, Lincoln included two paragraphs addressed to people (but actually men), who in fact were still held as slaves in the South. The paragraphs are reminiscent of the Addresses to the Slaves in their indecisiveness concerning black violence in behalf of freedom. On the one hand, Lincoln writes, "I hereby enjoin upon the people so declared to be free to abstain from all violence, unless in necessary self-defense." On the other, he announces that enslaved men "of suitable conditions, will be received into the armed service of the United States" so that they might fight against their masters. Earlier in the war, Lincoln had refused to allow black men to enlist in Union armies, in part because he believed that to do so would further alienate white southerners. With the Emancipation Proclamation he reached a conclusion that Smith, Garrison, and Garnet had reached twenty years earlier on the question of which racial group to rely on in the South.[11]

The second wartime document is a March 1863 editorial written by Douglass in response to Lincoln's proclamation. It echoes the substance of Charles T. Torrey's 1842 call for a black invasion of the South and the tone of Garnet's Address to the Slaves. Douglass was a thoroughgoing integrationist. Throughout his journalistic career he usually addressed his editorials to an audience of undifferentiated reformers. But in this case Douglass addressed black men, including enslaved black men, exclusively. Urging them to enlist in Union armies in general and Massachusetts's new black regiment in particular, he declared, "Only a moderate share of sagacity was needed to see that the arm of the slave was the best defense against the arm of the slaveholder. Hence with every reverse to the national arms, with every exulting shout of victory raised by the slaveholding rebels, I have implored the imperiled nation to unchain against her foes, her powerful black hand."[12]

Just as two decades earlier Smith, Garrison, and Garnet had claimed to be prodding black men to action, so did Douglass in 1863. He declared that "liberty won by white men would lose half its luster" and that they "Who would be free themselves must strike the blow." Like Garnet's Address, Douglass's editorial counsels, "Better even die free, than to live slaves." Circumstances had changed greatly since the early 1840s. The United States government no longer supported slavery; slaves were escaping by the thousands; abolitionists had become popular in the North.[13] Yet Douglass stressed that real freedom would come to African Americans only if black men fought for it. Like Garnet had two decades earlier, Douglass called on them to remember Denmark Vesey and Nat Turner. In addition, he invoked the names of Shields Green and John Copeland, two black men "who followed noble John Brown" to Harpers Ferry.

More important than echoes, however, is what the Addresses to the Slaves—and the Letter to the Slaves as well—indicate about the direction of American abolitionism from the early 1840s to the Civil War years. Well into the twentieth century, historians placed the Liberty Party within an exclusively northern political context and found it wanting in principle as well as in electioneering. At best it seemed to be a precursor to the nonabolitionist Free Soil and Republican Parties. Even the Neo-abolitionist historians of the 1960s placed post-1840 abolitionism in the context of northern party politics. Aileen Kraditor, for example, contended that Garrisonians had a more sophisticated understanding than did the Liberty abolitionists of how to influence the political system. From the 1970s through the early 1980s, however, it was not just political abolitionists whom historians found wanting in effectiveness. The predominant assumption during those years was that American abolitionism in general was ineffective because white male abolitionists, mired in racism and sexism, had retreated into isolation.[14] Not until 1990 did a new way of understanding the role of the abolitionists in the sectional struggle emerge with the publication of Merton L. Dillon's *Slavery Attacked*. Dillon indicated that the abolitionists' relationship with slaves might be more significant than their relationship with northern politics. Since 1990 there have also been numerous studies emphasizing interracial abolitionism in America.[15]

The three Addresses to the Slaves mark the point when northern abolitionists realized that they had to embrace slaves as allies, communicate with them, and help them physically in seeking freedom. The order in which the Addresses appeared and the contemporary response to them reveal the primacy of Gerrit Smith and the radical political wing of the Liberty Party in this process. They envisioned and implemented an abolitionism that transcended both agitation and party politics by seeking directly to impact slavery in the South. William Lloyd Garrison's Address is important as an indication of the force of the convictions that abolitionists must communicate with slaves and that slaves might justifiably resort to violence in order to liberate themselves. Of the three Addresses, Garnet's most directly reveals the centrality of the issue of black manhood, not only in contemplating antislavery violence but as a factor in biracial abolitionism.

The devotion of black and white Garrisonians to feminism, nonresistance, disunionism, and reliance on agitation in the North made it difficult for them to embrace aggressive abolitionism. In fact, no abolitionist, black or white, radical political or Garrisonian, was during the 1840s entirely comfortable in advocating violent means. All abolitionists remained reluctant advocates of force even during the 1850s. But the primacy of radical political abolitionists, during the 1840s, in cooperating with slaves in dangerous and illegal ventures is a corrective to the nearly universal assumption that Garrisonians were the real radicals. So is the initiative of Smith in organizing the Cazenovia Fugitive Slave Convention, which brought together black and white abolitionists in support of the Letter to the Slaves. This convention and Smith's Letter set the agenda for aggressive, physical abolitionism during the 1850s and 1860s. Influenced by

Smith's and Garnet's Addresses to the Slaves, those who met at Cazenovia were ready to resist the Fugitive Slave Law of 1850, to support expanded underground railroading, and to invade the South. They anticipated John Brown's raid and the Civil War.

THE ADDRESSES
AND RELATED DOCUMENTS

From the Friend of Man.
Address of the Anti-Slavery Convention
OF THE STATE OF NEW-YORK
Held in Peterboro', January 19th, 1842,
TO THE
SLAVES IN THE U. STATES OF AMERICA
[Gerrit Smith]

AFFLICTED BRETHREN:
The doctrine obtains almost universally, that the friends of
the slave have no right to communicate with him—no right
to counsel and comfort him. We have, ourselves, partially at
least, acquiesced in this time-hallowed delusion: and now,
that God has opened our eyes to our great and guilty error,
we feel impelled to make public confession of it; to vindicate
publicly our duty to be your advisers, comforters and helpers;
and to enter upon the discharge of that duty without delay.

Why do abolitionists concede, that their labors for the
slave must be expended directly upon his master: and that
they are to seek to improve the condition of the one, only
through favorable changes wrought in the mind of the other?
Is it not because they are not yet entirely disabused of the
fallacy, that slavery is a legitimate institution? that it has
rights? that it creates rights in the slaveholder, and destroys
rights in the slave? Were they, as they should do, to regard
slavery in the light of a sheer usurpation, and none the less
such for the hoariness of the abomination; they would have
as little respect for the protest of the man-stealer against the
direct agency of others upon his stolen property, as they would

153

for the protest of the horse-stealer against a similar liberty with his stolen property. With a vision so clear, they would no more acknowledge a possible acquisition or loss of rights by theft in the one case, than in the other. The same rights, which the slave had, before he "fell among thieves," he has now; and amongst them is his right to all the words of consolation, encouragement and advice, which his fellow-men can convey to him.

To make the abolitionist most odious, he is charged with the supposedly heinous, and almost matchless offence of communicating with the slave: and the abolitionist, instead of insisting on the right to do so, and instead of publicly lamenting the great difficulties in the way of practicing the right, impliedly disclaims it, by informing his accusers, that the abolition doctrine is to address the master, and not the slave. No slaveholding sophistry and blustering could obtain such a disclaimer from Paul. That heaven-directed Apostle not only himself communicated with the slave on the subject of his slavery, but directed others to do so. He declared it to be as well the duty of Timothy and Titus, as of himself: and far was he from conditioning the duty on the consent of the master. Paul carried out more fully and fearlessly than the modern abolitionist the doctrine that the slave is a man, and not a chattel. He wrote to slaves: and, in doing so, implied not only that they are beings to be reasoned with, but that it is their duty, and therefore right to read the Scriptures, of which his writings to them constitute a part. Indeed, he expressly commands them to read his epistles. That he did not acknowledge the rightfulness of subjecting one man absolutely to the will of another man, is manifest from his saying to slaves: "Be not ye servants of men." This injunction forbids their rendering any service incompatible with the claims of God; and forbids that they should suffer even their masters to invade the sacred precincts of conscience.

Although much has been gained by the bold positions that abolitionists have taken, much also has been lost by their timidly hesitating to take other positions, which, if bolder, are not less truthful or advantageous. When the abolitionists first demanded that the Amistad captives should be set free, few were found to respond to the justice of a demand, in which our whole nation now acquiesces. The northern press, with few exceptions, pronounces the recent insurrection on board of the Creole to be justifiable and heroic. But had this insurrection occurred before that on board of the Amistad, scarcely any other than an abolition newspaper would have failed to denounce and stigmatize it. No less extensive conquests of public opinion will be achieved by the future instances of our intrepidity. Let abolitionists fully and solemnly utter the doctrine, that they are bound to enter into and maintain all practicable communications with the slave; and the candid and intelligent will not only respond to it, but, ere they are aware, they will have been carried along by its trains of consequences and influences to the conviction, that the abolitionist has a perfect moral right to go into the South, and use his intelligence to promote the escape of ignorant, and imbruted slaves from their prison-house. The motto of the abolitionists, as well as of our Commonwealth, should be "HIGHER"; and they should feel, that unless they are continually rising higher and higher in their bold and righteous claims, all the past attainments of their cause are left unsure.

Having vindicated the right of abolitionists to address you, we will very briefly enumerate some of the things, which they are doing for you, and some of the things which you should do, and some of the things which you should not do, for yourselves.

First. We ask the God of the oppressed to have mercy on you, and deliver you.

Second. We ask our National and State Legislatures to exert all their respective constitutional power for the overthrow of slavery.

Third. We deny, that any but an anti-slavery man has a view of the Christian scheme so large and just as to fit him to be a preacher of the gospel.

Fourth. We deny that any but an anti-slavery man is a republican, or fit to make laws for republicans.

Fifth. The arguments to justify our course are to be read in the innumerable pamphlets and scores of newspapers, which we publish; and are to be heard from the lips of lecturers, amongst whom are men eminent for learning, logic and eloquence.

And now with respect to your own duties. Woeful as is slavery, and desirable as is liberty, we entreat you to endure the former—rather than take a violent and bloody hold of the latter. Such, manifestly, was the teaching of Paul to the slaves of his time. Whatever was his, the reason for our similar teaching is that recourse to violence and blood-shed for the termination of slavery, is very likely, in the judgment of a large portion of us, to result in the confirmation and protraction of the evil. There are, it is true, some persons in our ranks who are opposed to the taking of human life in any circumstances; and whose doctrine it is, that, however certain might be your success, it would be sinful for you to undertake to fight your way to liberty. But the great majority of abolitionists justify their forefathers' bloody resistance to oppression; and can, therefore, dissuade you from such resistance to a ten thousandfold greater oppression, not on the high ground of absolute morality, but on the comparatively low one of expediency. And now, after repeating to you that some abolitionists believe the taking of human life, under whatever provocations, to be sin; and that others are convinced, that your insurrection would result in nought but evil to yourselves, to your oppressors, and the innocent ones bound up with them; we add, that it is on the condition, that you shall not stain it with blood, that you will be entitled to expect that we shall continue to advocate your cause unitedly and hopefully. It is about ten years since the anti-slavery movement in this country began. During all this time, there has been no servile insurrection at the South. Whilst we rejoice in the strong probability, that this remarkable forbearance of the swelling numbers of slaves is owing to their reliance on the philanthropic efforts in their behalf; we tremble, lest, discouraged by the tardy results of these efforts, they should extinguish their waning hopes in bloody despair.

Do not infer, from what we have said against violent attempts to recover your freedom, that we object to your availing yourselves of any feasible, peaceable mode to accomplish it. We but concur with the great apostle, when we say: "if thou mayest be free, use it rather." Although to run away from slavery is, slaveholders being judges, the most black-hearted ingratitude, and although the adviser to such a requital of the unequaled loving-kindness of a slaveholding master is pronounced by the same tribunal to be indelibly disgraced and ineffably mean: we, nevertheless, call on every slave, who has the reasonable prospect of being able to run away from slavery, to make the experiment.

We rejoice with all our hearts, in the rapid multiplication of escapes from the house of bondage.—There are now a thousand a year; a rate more than five times as great, as that before the anti-slavery effort. The fugitive need feel little apprehension, after he has entered a free State. Seven years ago, a great majority of the people of the border free States were in favor of replunging into slavery their poor, scarred, emaciated, trembling brother, who had fled from its horrors. But now, under the influence of anti-slavery lessons, nineteen-twentieths of them have come to be ashamed of and to revolt at such monstrous inhumanity. We add, that the fugitive slave may safely continue in some of the free States—especially in those where a jury passes on the question whether "service or labor may be due" from a man, merely because he has had the misfortune to fall into the hands of kidnappers, and be reduced to slavery. We leave him, however, to his own free choice, between taking up his abode with us and in the British dominions. If he prefer the latter, we will gladly furnish him with facilities for realizing his preference. The abolitionist knows no more grateful employment than that of carrying the dog and rifle-hunted slave to Canada.

It may be well to say here, that it has often occurred to us, that those inhabitants of the South, who pity the slave, would render him an inestimable service by supplying him with a pocket compass.—could every slave who encounters the appalling perils of flight from bondage, have access to this little and cheap, but unerring guide, he might dispense with the shining of the North star. An occasional match light to show him the needle of this compass would suffice for his direction in the darkest night.

This is also the place for saying a few words to you on the subject of theft. We are aware, that an almost irresistible tendency of slavery is to make thieves of its victims. But we entreat you not to steal. "Not purloining" is an apostolic injunction on slaves as well as other servants. Let all your toil go unrequited, rather than seek an equivalent, at the expense of trampling on conscience, and polluting the soul by violating a Divine command. "Say not thou, I will recompense evil, but wait on the Lord, and he shall save thee." In your poorest estate, you will still be infinitely better off than they who "rob the poor, because he is poor"; "for the Lord will spoil the soul of those that spoiled them." Do not, however, suppose, that we forbid your innocent yieldings to necessity. We are aware of the dreadful straits to which some of you are, at times, reduced: and God forbid, that we should tell you to starve or freeze, when relief is possible. In those straits you have the permission of Him, who says, that "the life is more than meat, and the body is more than raiment," to count as your own that, of which you stand in perishing need. And when too, you are escaping from the matchless horrible Bastille take, all along your route, in the free, as well as the slave States, so far as is absolutely essential to your escape, the horse, the boat, the food, the clothing, which you require; and feel no more compunction for the justifiable appropriation than does the drowning man for possessing himself of the plank, that floats in his way.

But we proceed to offer you our advice on another point. We do not wonder, that slave ships witness thousands of cases of suicide. We do not wonder, that so many of the slaves of the South lay violent hands on themselves and on their little ones, who inherit the frightful doom of slavery. But the heaviest load of life, which the malignity and ingenuity of oppressors can devise, is to be borne patiently. Least of all, is it to be thrown off by the black crimes of self-destruction and murder. Only trust in God, beloved brethren, and you will soon be where you will "hear not the voice of the oppressor," and where "the wicked cease from troubling, and the weary be at rest."

Cherish no vindictive or unkind feelings toward your oppressors. Early and late, and with all possible cheerfulness, yield them your unrecompensed toil. Submit to stripes and to every exaction, which you can submit to, without sin. Your consent to violate God's law, let no bribes, no menaces, nor sufferings, be able to obtain.

If you would have Him, who hears "the sighing of the prisoner," grant you a speedy deliverance, then pray earnestly and perseveringly to Him for yourselves and your oppressors.

Have no confidence in pro-slavery preachers.—Those sham ministers of the gospel, whether at the North or South, who dare not rebuke oppression, would barter away your souls for one smile of the proud tyrants, on whom they fawn. Reject their teaching with holy indignation; and God's Spirit will supply their place with His own perfect lessons of truth.

Perilous as it is, you should, nevertheless, snatch all your little opportunities to learn to read. The art of reading is an abundant recompense for the many stripes it may have cost you to acquire it. The slave, who has learned to read a map, has already conquered half the difficulty in getting to Canada; and the slave, who has learned to read the Bible, can learn the way to heaven. Have no conscience against violating the inexpressibly wicked law which forbids you to read it;—nor indeed against violating any other slaveholding law. Slaveholders are but pirates; and the laws, which piracy enacts, whether upon land or sea, are not entitled to trammel the consciences of its victims.

We shall get as many copies of this Address, as we can into the hands of your white friends in the slave States. To these, as also to the few (alas how few!) of the colored people of the South, who, some by permission and some by stealth, have obtained the art of reading, we look to acquaint you with its contents. Communications of similar design—that of enlightening and comforting you—will probably be made from time to time hereafter. We close the present one with a brief reference to a few of the facts, which argue the speedy overthrow of slavery in the United States.

There are now but two nations in all of continental America, that uphold slavery. These are our own and Brazil. In the West Indies, slavery has received its death blow, and will expire, ere the close of another five years. The literature of Europe—and especially the America-swaying literature of England—is well imbued with hostility to slavery. Texas will be speedily re-annexed to anti-slavery Mexico, unless the favor of European nations prevent it; and the favor she will enjoy, on no less condition than that of following the fashion of the times, and running up the abolition flag.

The South would quickly give up slavery, were she deprived of her English market for cotton and her northern market for sugar. But India will soon enable England to dispense with blood-stained cotton; and northern conscience is fast coming to revolt at the consumption of blood-stained sugar.

The principles of abolition have already struck their root deep in the genial soil of the free states of our Union; and even at the South, abolitionists are multiplying rapidly. The idea, that a pro-slavery man is fit to preach to Christians, and that a pro-slavery man is fit to legislate for republicans, is becoming exceedingly abhorrent and ludicrous all over the North; and this idea is too absurd to enjoy a greatly prolonged favor, even at the South.

Wounded, writhing slavery still cries, "let me alone—let me alone." But the people will not let it alone: and such providences, as the insurrections on board of the Amistad and Creole, show that God will not let it alone. His decree has gone forth, that slavery shall continue to be tortured, even unto death. "Lift up your heads," then brethren, "for your redemption draweth nigh."

Liberator, February 11, 1842.

Rights of a Fugitive Slave
[Nathaniel E. Johnson]

The State Anti-Slavery Convention have published an address to the slaves of the South, in which the following passage occurs:

> This is also the place for saying a few words to you on the subject of theft. We are aware that an almost irresistible tendency of slavery is to make thieves of its victims. But we entreat you not to *steal.* "Not purloining" is an apostolic injunction on slaves as well as other servants. Let all your toil go unrequited, rather than seek an equivalent, at the expense of trampling on conscience, and polluting the soul by violating a divine command. "Say not thou, I will recompense evil; but wait on the Lord and he shall save thee." In your poorest estate, you will still be infinitely better off than they who "rob the poor because he is poor"; "for the Lord will spoil the soul of those that spoiled them." Do not, however, suppose that we forbid your innocent yieldings to necessity. We are aware of the dreadful straits to which some of you are at times reduced; and God forbid, that we should tell you to starve or freeze, when relief is possible. In these straits you have the permission of Him, who says, that "the life is more than meat, and the body is more than raiment," *to count as your own* that of which you stand in perishing need. And when, too,

you are escaping from the matchless, horrible
Bastille, *take* all along your route, in the free as
well as the slave State, so far as is absolutely essential to your escape, the horse, the boat, the food,
the clothing which you require; and feel no more
compunction for the justifiable appropriation, than
does the drowning man for possessing himself of
the plank that floats his way.

The boldness and explicitness of this language has already excited considerable remark, and the Convention have
been charged with advising the slave to commit the very sin
which they professedly condemn. Even those who exhibit
very little care or feeling respecting the enormous system of
outrageous theft and robbery of which the Southern States
are guilty, become very zealous for moral principle, when
the right of a flying slave to the means absolutely necessary
to his escape is asserted.

As the subject requires to be discussed with candor and caution, we propose to suggest a few things for the consideration of
our readers, which may help them to definite conclusion.

The law of slavery, it must be remembered, is entirely
local, and of no moral obligation upon the slave. His obedience to it is simply a matter of prudence, or of self-denial, or
of the necessity of choosing the least of two evils. It is in all
its principles directly against the law of nature and of God.
So, it is declared to be by Blackstone, and all the most profound writers on law.

From such a law, the slave, therefore, has a right to escape if he can. Indeed, not only has he a right; but he is under a solemn obligation to do the same, if thereby his wife
and children may be delivered from its curse. He is bound by
the law of Nature to protect his wife and children, if such
protection be possible; and therefore, whatever he may submit to for himself, he has no right to consign his family to
perpetual slavery if he can prevent it by escape. In the exercise of his right he becomes an antagonist of the local and

unrighteous law of slavery. So long as he is within the grasp of that law, he is in an enemy's land, and has a right to use the necessary means for a peaceful escape. The law of nature will even justify him in using violence, *if escape can be accomplished in no other way*.

A slave starts from Virginia, with whose law making him the property of his masters, he is by the law of nature and of God necessarily at war. So long as he is within the bounds of Virginia, he is in an enemy's land. He has a right, if his master, armed with the authority of an unrighteous law, is pursuing him, to seize upon a horse belonging to one of his enemies and use it for his purpose. If he comes to a river, and finds a boat belonging to one of his enemies, he has a right to seize it and row himself over, thereby facilitating his own escape and impeding the pursuit of his merciless foe. He has the same right in his flight through Pennsylvania and New York, if those free States have pledged themselves to Virginia, that they will catch him and restore him to slavery if they can. Such a contract does exist. He is not, therefore, free from the reach of slave law, until he is entirely beyond the bounds of the United States. Hence he is in an enemy's country "all along his route," until he has reached a soil free from the contaminating law of slavery, and blessed with the municipal recognition of the great primary authority of natural law under which he has acted.

Such are the principles, we presume, on which the Convention founded the direction given to the slave. They do not advise them to insurrection nor to plunder, nor to the taking of their enemy's goods beyond *what is absolutely essential to effect their purpose of peaceful escape*.

It may be said, that these principles, if carried out, would justify insurrection. In reply to this, we recur again to the statements we made in the case of the Creole. We then said that there were only two considerations which obliged—we might have said justified—men in submitting to slavery. One was, the prospect of deliverance by patient waiting; and the other was, the impossibility of it by insurrection. Such is the condition of the slaves at the South. These principles correspond entirely with the principles of the law of nature and of revelation. We are not to seek redress for any wrongs, however great, by violence, so long as it can possibly be obtained by peaceful means. Neither are we to inflict injuries on our oppressors which can do us no good, and only gratify our revenge. Even the man whose life is assaulted, must retreat as far as he can, and take every possible means to preserve it before he takes the life of the assailant. Yet when all these fail, and the final method will succeed, the right of self-defense, which Blackstone declares can never be taken away by the laws of society, remains and justifies just so much use of force as is absolutely necessary.

If then, such be the nature of the principle, and such be the peculiar position of the slave, the right to escape, and to avail himself of the property of his *enemies* for the purpose of escaping, seems to be an original right, lying back of all the foundations of *meum* and *tuum,* or of the division of goods, which rests alone on municipal law. Such taking of goods as the Convention recommend, is, therefore, entirely free of the guilt of theft, both by the law of nature, and the unchangeable law of God. The question, therefore, is it a sin to steal? which the New-York Observer raises in view of this case, does not belong to the subject. The Convention have not authorized theft, if the above argument is valid.

Is IT A SIN TO STEAL? Let that question be repeated. Is it a sin to take so much food as we need to satisfy the gnawings of extreme hunger? Blackstone decides that it is. Is it then a sin to take a whole man, body and mind, and force him from his native country, and sell him as the PROPERTY of another? Is it a sin to pay that thief and robber his price, and, then carry out the deed?

Is it a sin to appropriate the whole of that slave's labor according as we please? Is it a sin to lay our claim upon his children and his children's children? Is it a sin to carry out that robber's claim, by selling the slave or his wife, or his children, to the highest bidder, for the sake of gain? Is it a sin to frame iniquity by law, and to establish a system of legislation authorizing these enormities? Is it a sin to sanction and tolerate such conduct and such laws in the church of God? Is it a sin for religious men and religious papers to apologize for these abominations? We repeat the question, IS IT A SIN *TO STEAL*? Let that question resound far and wide, until it penetrate the parlor of every slaveholder, the heart of every slave driver in every cotton field, the bosom of every Southern legislator, the halls of national government, and the altars of every church. Is it a sin to steal, and sanction stealing—to rob, and sanction robbery? Let those "few religious papers" which are still willing to wipe the feet of the slaveholder, prepare an answer.

New-York Evangelist, February 24, 1842.

Address to the Slaves of the United States
William Lloyd Garrison

Brethren and Fellow-Countrymen:
Assembled in Convention, from all parts of New-England, in Faneuil Hall, the old CRADLE OF LIBERTY, in the city of Boston, we, the friends of universal emancipation—the enemies of slavery, whether at home or abroad—your advocates and defenders—would improve this opportunity to address to you words of sympathy, of consolation, of encouragement and hope.

We wish you to know who you are—by whom and for what purpose you were created—who are your oppressors, and what they profess to receive as self-evident truths, in regard to the rights of man—who are your friends, and in what manner they stand ready to aid you—what has been effected in your cause within the last ten years in the United States— and what is the prospect of your emancipation from chains and servitude.

In the first place, then, you are men—created in the same divine image as all other men—as good, as noble, as free, by birth and destiny, as your masters—as much entitled to "life, liberty, and the pursuit of happiness," as those who cruelly enslave you—made but a little lower than the angels of heaven, and destined to an immortal state of existence— equal members of the great human family. These truths you must believe and understand, if you desire to have your chains broken, and your oppression come to a speedy end.

Know this, also, that God never made a slave-master, nor a slave. He abhors cruelty and injustice in every form, and his judgments have been poured out on those nations that have refused to let the oppressed go free. He pities all who are sighing in bondage, and will work out their redemption, at whatever cost to those who are crushing them in the dust. He "has made of one blood all nations of men, to dwell on all the face of the earth"—not to war with each other—not to defraud, degrade, torment, persecute, or oppress each other—but to enjoy equal rights and perfect liberty, to love and do good to each other, to dwell together in unity. His is no respecter of persons, but has given to all the stamp of his divinity, and his tender mercies are over all the works of his hands. "Thus saith the Lord, Execute judgment and righteousness and deliver the spoiled out of the hand of the oppressor; and do no wrong, do no violence to the stranger, the fatherless, nor the widow, neither shed innocent blood." Such is your Creator, Father, and God!

Your masters say that you are an inferior race; that you were born to be slaves; that it is by the will and direction of God, that you are held in captivity. Your religious teachers declare that the Bible, (which they call the word of God) sanctions slavery, and requires you to submit to it as of rightful authority. Believe them not! They all speak falsely, and the truth is not in them. They libel the character of God, and pervert the teachings of the Bible in the most awful manner. They combine to take from you all your hard earnings; they cover your bodies with stripes; they will not allow you to obtain light and knowledge; they call you their property, and sell you and your children at auction, as they do their cattle and swine. If they will steal, will they not die? Listen not to what they tell you. They are the enemies of God and man. Their religion is of Beelzebub, the prince of devils; not of Jesus, the Son of God. As long as they keep you in slavery, they deny Jehovah, reject Christ, and grieve the Holy Spirit.

God made you to be free—free as the birds that cleave the air, or sing on the branches—free as the sunshine that gladdens the earth—free as the winds that sweep over sea and land;—free at your birth, free during your whole life;

free to-day, this hour, this moment! He has given you facul-
ties to be improved, and souls to live forever. He has made
you to glorify him in your bodies and spirits, to be happy
here and hereafter, and not to be a degraded and miserable
race.—Your masters have no more right to enslave you, than
you have to enslave them—to sell your children, and lacer-
ate your bodies, and take your lives, than you have to inflict
these outrages on them and theirs. The complexion of your
masters is no better than yours—a black skin is as good as a
white one. It is for you to say when, or where, or for whom
you will work—where you will go, or in what part of the
country or the world you will reside. If your masters prevent
you from doing as you wish, they rob you of an inalienable
right, and your blood will be required at their hands. If you
submit unresistingly to their commands, do it for Christ's
sake (who died the just for the unjust,) and not because they
claim a rightful authority over you—for they have no such
authority.

Your masters tell us that you do not wish to be free; that
you are contented and happy as slaves; that you are much
attached to their persons, and ready to lay down your lives to
save them from harm; that you have an abundance of good
clothes, good food, and all that you need to make your situation comfortable; that your tasks are light and easily per-
formed; and that you are much better off than such of your
number as have been liberated from bondage. We do not
believe any of what they say. We know, from the natural desire for liberty that burns in the bosom of every human being—from the horribly unjust code of laws by which you are
governed—from the attempts of slaves, in all countries, to
obtain their freedom by insurrection and massacre—from
the vigilance with which all your movements are watched, as
though you waited for an opportunity to strike an effectual
blow for your rights—from the testimony of thousands of
slaves who have escaped to the North and to Canada—from
the numerous advertisements in southern newspapers, of
runaways from the plantations—that your masters are trying

to deceive us. We are sure that there is nothing in the world you desire so much as liberty.

We know that you are driven to the field like beasts, under the lash of cruel overseers or drivers, and there compelled to toil from the earliest dawn till late at night; that you do not have sufficient clothing or food; that you have no laws to protect you from the most terrible punishment your masters may choose to inflict on your persons; that many of your bodies are covered with scars, and branded with red hot irons; that you are constantly liable to receive wounds and bruises, stripes, mutilations, insults and outrages innumerable; that your groans are borne to us on every southern breeze, your tears are falling thick and fast, your blood is flowing continually; that you are regarded as four-footed beasts and creeping things, and bought and sold with farming utensils and household furniture. We know all these things, and a great deal more in regard to your condition.

Who, O unhappy countrymen, are your oppressors? They are the descendants of those who, in 1776, threw off the British yoke, and for seven years waged war against a despotic power, until at length they secured their independence. In a certain Declaration which they published to the world, at that period, and which is now read and subscribed to on the fourth of July annually, they said—"We hold these truths to be self-evident—that all men are created equal; that they are endowed by their Creator with certain inalienable rights; that among these are life, liberty, and the pursuit of happiness:—That, to secure these rights, governments are instituted among men, deriving their just powers *from the consent of the governed*; that whenever any form of government becomes destructive of these ends, it is the right of the people to alter or abolish it, and to institute a new government, laying its foundation on such principles, and organizing its powers in such form, as to them shall seem most likely to effect their safety and happiness. . . . When a long train of abuses and usurpations, pursuing invariably the same object, evinces a design to reduce them under absolute despotism, it is *their right*, it is THEIR DUTY, to *THROW OFF SUCH GOVERNMENT*, and to provide new guards for their future security."

In acknowledging the truths set forth in this Declaration, to be self-evident, your masters, in reducing you to slavery, are condemned as hypocrites and liars, out of their own mouths. By precept and example, they declare that it is both your right and your duty to wage war against them, and to wade through their blood, if necessary, to secure your own freedom. They glory in the revolutionary war, and greatly honor the names of those heroes who took up arms to destroy their oppressors. One of these heroes—Patrick Henry, of Virginia—exclaimed, "Give me liberty, or give me death!" Another—Joseph Warren, of Massachusetts—said, "My sons, scorn to be slaves!" Their cry was,

> Hereditary bondmen! know ye not,
> Who would be free, themselves must strike the blow.

When, a few years since, the Poles rose in insurrection against the Russian power—and the Greeks rushed to the strife of blood against their Turkish oppressors—and the South Americans broke in pieces the Spanish yoke, and made themselves free and independent—your masters, in common with all the people of the North, cheered them on to the conflict, and sent them banners and arms, to enable them to triumph in the cause of liberty—exclaiming,

> O, where's the slave so lowly,
> Condemned to chains unholy,
> Who, could he burst his bonds at first,
> Would pine beneath them slowly?

Yet, should you attempt to gain your freedom in the same manner, you would be branded as murderers and monsters, and slaughtered without mercy! But the celebrated Thomas Jefferson, of Virginia, has truly said, that in such a contest, the Almighty has no attribute that can take the side with your oppressors; and, though a slaveholder himself, he was forced many years ago to exclaim, in view of your enslavement—"I tremble for my country when I reflect that God is just; that his justice cannot sleep forever; that, considering numbers, nature, and natural means only, a revolution of the wheel of fortune, an exchange of situation, is among possible events; that it may become probable by supernatural interference!" And he concluded by expressing the hope that the way was "preparing, under the auspices of heaven, for a total emancipation, and that this was disposed, in the order of events, to be with the consent of the masters, rather than by their extirpation."

Thomas Jefferson wrote in this manner more than sixty years since. At that period, your number was a little more than half a million; now it is more than two millions and a half. Sad and dreary has been your existence up to the present hour; and, doubtless, you have almost given up all hope of ever celebrating the day of jubilee—your emancipation—on this side of the grave.

Take courage! be filled with hope and comfort! Your redemption draws nigh, for the Lord is mightily at work in your behalf. Is it not frequently the darkest before day-break? The word has gone forth that you shall be delivered from your chains, and it has not been spoken in vain.

Although you have many enemies, yet you have also many friends—warm, faithful, sympathizing, devoted friends—who will never abandon your cause; who are pledged to do all in their power to break your chains; who are laboring to effect your emancipation without delay, in a peaceable manner, without the shedding of blood; who regard you as brethren and countrymen, and fear not the frowns or threats of your masters. They call themselves abolitionists. They have already suffered much, in various parts of the country, for rebuking them who keep you in slavery—for demanding your immediate liberation—for revealing to the people the horrors of your situation—for boldly opposing a corrupt public sentiment, by which you are kept in the great southern prison-house of bondage. Some of them have been beaten with stripes; others have been stripped, and covered with tar and feathers; have had their property taken from them and burnt in the streets; others have had large rewards offered by your masters for their seizure; others have been cast into jails and penitentiaries; others have been mobbed and lynched with great violence; others have lost their reputation, and been ruined in their business; others have lost their lives.—All these, and many other outrages of an equally grievous kind, they have suffered for your sakes, and because they are your friends. They cannot go to the South, to see and converse with you, face to face; for, so ferocious and bloody-minded are your taskmasters, they would be put to an ignominious death as soon as discovered. Besides, it is not yet necessary that they should incur this peril; for it is solely by the aid of the people of the North, that you are held in bondage, and therefore, they find enough to do at home, to make the people here your friends, and to break up all connection with the slave system. They have proved themselves to be truly courageous, insensible to danger, superior to adversity, strong in principle, invincible in argument, animated by the spirit of impartial benevolence, unwearied in devising ways and means for your deliverance, the best friends of the whole country, the noblest champions of the human race. Ten years ago, they were so few and feeble as only to excite universal contempt; now they number in their ranks, hundreds of thousands of the people.—Then, they had scarcely a single anti-slavery society in operation; now they have thousands. Then they had only one or two presses to plead your cause; now they have multitudes. They are scattering all over the land their newspapers, books, pamphlets, tracts, and other publications, to hold up to infamy the conduct of your oppressors, and to awaken sympathy in your behalf. They are continually holding antislavery meetings in all parts of the free States, to tell the people the story of your wrongs. Wonderful has been the change effected in public feeling, under

God, through their instrumentality. Do not fear that they will grow weary of your service. They are confident of success, in the end. They know that the Lord Almighty is with them—that you are with them. They know, too, that your masters are cowardly and weak, through conscious wrong-doing, and already begin to falter in their course. Lift up your heads, O ye despairing slaves! Yet a little while, and your chains shall snap asunder, and you shall be tortured and plundered no more! Then, fathers and mothers, your children shall be yours, to bring them up in the nurture and admonition of the Lord. Then, husbands and wives, now torn from each other's arms, you shall be reunited in the flesh, and man shall no longer dare to put asunder those whom God has joined together.—Then, brothers and sisters, you shall be sold to the remorseless slave speculator no more, but dwell together in unity. "God hasten that joyful day!" is now the daily prayer of millions.

The weapons with which the abolitionists seek to effect your deliverance are not bowie knives, pistols, swords, guns, or any other deadly implements. They consist of appeals, warnings, rebukes, arguments and facts, addressed to the understandings, consciences and hearts of the people. Many of your friends believe that not even those who are oppressed, whether their skins are white or black, can shed the blood of their oppressors in accordance with the will of God; while many others believe that it is right for the oppressed to rise and take their liberty by violence, if they can secure it in no other manner; but they, in common with all our friends, believe that every attempt at insurrection would be attended with disaster and defeat, on your part, because you are not strong enough to contend with the military power of the nation; consequently, their advice to you is, to be patient, long-suffering and submissive, yet a while longer, trusting that, by the blessing of the Most High on their labors, you will yet be emancipated without shedding a drop of your master's blood, or losing a drop of your own.

The abolitionists of the North are the only true and

unyielding friends on whom you can rely. They will never deceive nor betray you. They have made your cause their own, and they mean to be true to themselves and to you, whatever may be the consequence. They are continually increasing in number, in influence, in enterprise and determination; and, judging from the success which has already attended their measures, they anticipate that, in a comparatively short period, the entire North will receive you with open arms, and give you shelter and protection, as fast as you escape from the South.—We, who now address you, are united with them in spirit and design. We glory in the name of abolitionist, for it signifies friendship for all who are pining in servitude. We advise you to seize every opportunity to escape from your masters, and, fixing your eyes on the North star, travel on until you reach a land of liberty. You are not the property of your masters. God never made one human being to be owned by another. Your right to be free, at any moment, is undeniable; and it is your duty, whenever you can, peaceably to escape from the plantations on which you are confined, and assert your manhood.

Already, within a few years, twenty thousand of your number have successfully run away, many of whom are now residing at the North, but a very large proportion of whom are living in Canada, enjoying safety and freedom under the British flag. To that country the slave-hunters dare not go; nor will they much longer dare to come to the North, in pursuit of fugitive slaves. But, while we thus invite and encourage you to transform yourselves from things into men by flight, we would counsel you to use the utmost caution in attempting to escape; for many dangers yet lurk in the path of every fugitive, and should any of you be caught, you know that your fate would be a terrible one. Still, we assure you that there are now thousands in the free states to succor you, where, a few years since, scarcely an individual could be found to hide the outcast. If you come to us, and are hungry, we will feed you; if thirsty, we will give you drink; if naked, we will clothe you; if sick, we will administer to your necessities;

if in prison, we will visit you; if you need a hiding-place from the face of the pursuer, we will provide one that even blood-hounds cannot scent out. This is the pledge we sacredly give to you.

We are not in favor of sending you to Africa, for we regard you as fellow-countrymen, and, with few exceptions, you have a right to claim this as your native land, for you were born on its soil. We do not, therefore, make your removal out of the country a condition of freedom, but demand for you all that we claim for ourselves—liberty, equal rights, equal privileges.

Your masters threaten, that if we do not stop pleading your cause, and assailing their slave system, they will dissolve the Union. Such a dissolution has for us no terrors; for we regard it as far preferable to a perpetuity of slavery. Such a dissolution you would have no occasion to lament; for it would enable you to obtain your freedom and independence in a single day. Your masters are only two hundred and fifty thousand in number; you are nearly three millions; and what could they do, if they should be abandoned to their fate by the North? If it were not now for the compact existing between the free and the slave States, by which the whole military power of the nation is pledged to suppress all insurrections, you would have long ere this been free. Your blood is the cement which binds the American Union together; your bodies are crushed beneath the massy weight of this Union; and its repeal or dissolution would ensure the downfall of slavery. We tell your masters that we shall not be intimidated by their threats, but shall continue to expose their guilt, to rebuke their oppression, to agitate the public mind, to demand your release, until there shall be none to help them, and they be separated from all political and religious connection with the people of the North—or (what we most earnestly desire as a matter of choice) until liberty be proclaimed thro'-out all the land unto all the inhabitants thereof, with the hearty consent of the whole people.

Done in Faneuil Hall, May 31, 1843.

Liberator, June 2, 1843.

AN ADDRESS
TO THE SLAVES OF THE UNITED STATES OF AMERICA. (REJECTED BY THE NATIONAL CONVENTION, 1848.) BY HENRY HIGHLAND GARNET.

PREFACE.

The following Address was first read at the National Convention held at Buffalo, N.Y., in 1843. Since that time it has been slightly modified, retaining, however, all of its original doctrine. The document elicited more discussion than any other paper that was ever brought before that, or any other deliberative body of colored persons, and their friends. Gentlemen who opposed the Address, based their objections on these grounds. 1. That the document was war-like, and encouraged insurrection; and 2. That if the Convention should adopt it, that those delegates who lived near the borders of the slave states, would not dare to return to their homes. The Address was rejected by a small majority; and now in compliance with the earnest request of many who heard it, and in conformity to the wishes of numerous friends who are anxious to see it, the author now gives it to the public, praying God that this little book may be borne on the four winds of heaven, until the principles it contains shall be understood and adopted by every slave in the Union.
Troy, N.Y., April 15, 1848.   H.H.G.

ADDRESS TO THE SLAVES OF THE U.S.

Brethren and Fellow Citizens:
Your brethren of the north, east, and west have been accustomed to meet together in National Conventions, to sympathize with each other, and to weep over your unhappy condition. In these meetings we have addressed all classes of the free, but have never until this time, sent a word of consolation and advice to you. We have been contented in sitting still and mourning over your sorrows, earnestly hoping that before this day, your sacred liberties would have been restored. But, we have hoped in vain. Years have rolled on, and tens of thousands have been borne on streams of blood, and tears, to the shores of eternity. While you have been oppressed, we have also been partakers with you; nor can we be free while you are enslaved. We therefore write to you as being bound with you.

Many of you are bound to us, not only by the ties of a common humanity, but we are connected by the more tender relations of parents, wives, husbands, children, brothers, and sisters, and friends. As such we most affectionately address you.

Slavery has fixed a deep gulf between you and us, and while it shuts out from you the relief and consolation which your friends would willingly render, it afflicts and persecutes you with a fierceness which we might not expect to see in the fiends of hell. But still the Almighty Father of Mercies has left to us a glimmering ray of hope, which shines out like a lone star in a cloudy sky. Mankind are becoming wiser, and better—the oppressor's power is fading, and you, every day, are becoming better informed, and more numerous. Your grievances, brethren, are many. We shall not attempt, in this short address, to present to the world, all the dark catalogue of this nation's sins, which have been committed upon an innocent people. Nor is it indeed, necessary, for you feel them from day to day, and all the civilized world look upon them with amazement.

Two hundred and twenty-seven years ago, the first of our injured race were brought to the shores of America. They came not with glad spirits to select their homes, in the New World. They came not with their own consent, to find an unmolested enjoyment of the blessings of this fruitful soil. The first dealings which they had with men calling themselves Christians, exhibited to them the worst features of corrupt and sordid hearts; and convinced them that no cruelty is too great, no villainy, and no robbery too abhorrent for even enlightened men to perform, when influenced by avarice, and lust. Neither did they come flying upon the wings of Liberty, to a land of freedom. But, they came with broken hearts, from their beloved native land, and were doomed to unrequited toil, and deep degradation. Nor did the evil of their bondage end at their emancipation by death. Succeeding generations inherited their chains, and millions have come from eternity into time, and have returned again to the world of spirits, cursed, and ruined by American Slavery.

The propagators of the system, or their immediate ancestors [descendants] very soon discovered its growing evil, and its tremendous wickedness, and secret promises were made to destroy it. The gross inconsistency of a people holding slaves, who had themselves "ferried o'er the wave," for freedom's sake, was too apparent to be entirely overlooked. The voice of Freedom cried, "emancipate your Slaves." Humanity supplicated with tears, for the deliverance of the children of Africa. Wisdom urged her solemn plea. The bleeding captive plead his innocence, and pointed to Christianity who stood weeping at the cross. Jehovah frowned upon the nefarious institution, and thunderbolts, red with vengeance, struggled to leap forth to blast the guilty wretches who maintained it. But all was vain. Slavery had stretched its dark wings of death over the land, the church stood silently by—the priests prophesied falsely, and the people loved to have it so. Its throne is established, and now it reigns triumphantly.

Nearly three millions of your fellow citizens, are prohibited by law, and public opinion, (which in this country is stronger than law), from reading the Book of Life. Your intellect has been destroyed as much as possible, and every ray of light they have attempted to shut out from your minds. The oppressors themselves have become involved in the ruin. They have become weak, sensual, and rapacious. They have cursed you—they have cursed themselves—they have cursed the earth which they have trod. In the language of a Southern statesman, we can truly say, "even the wolf, driven back long since by the approach of man, now returns after the lapse of a hundred years, and howls amid the desolations of slavery."

The colonists threw the blame upon England. They said that the mother country entailed the evil upon them, and that they would rid themselves of it if they could. The world thought they were sincere, and the philanthropic pitied them. But time soon tested their sincerity. In a few years, the colonists grew strong and severed themselves from the British Government. Their Independence was declared, and they took their station among the sovereign powers of the earth. The declaration was a glorious document. Sages admired it, and the patriotic of every nation reverenced the godlike sentiments which it contained. When the power of Government returned to their hands, did they emancipate the slaves? No; they rather added new links to our chains. Were they ignorant of the principles of Liberty? Certainly they were not. The sentiments of their revolutionary orators fell in burning eloquence upon their hearts, and with one voice they cried, LIBERTY OR DEATH. O, what a sentence was that! It ran from soul to soul like electric fire, and nerved the arm of thousands to fight in the holy cause of Freedom. Among the diversity of opinions that are entertained in regard to physical resistance, there are but a few found to gainsay that stern declaration. We are among those who do not.

SLAVERY! How much misery is comprehended in that single word. What mind is there that does not shrink from its direful effects? Unless the image of God is obliterated from the soul, all men cherish the love of Liberty. The nice discerning political economist does not regard the sacred right, more than the untutored African who roams in the wilds of Congo. Nor has the one more right to the full enjoyment of his freedom than the other. In every man's mind the good seeds of liberty are planted, and he who brings his fellow down so low, as to make him contented with a condition of slavery, commits the highest crime against God and man. Brethren, your oppressors aim to do this. They endeavor to make you as much like brutes as possible. When they have blinded the eyes of your mind—when they have embittered the sweet waters of life—when they have shut out the light which shines from the word of God—then, and not till then has American slavery done its perfect work.

TO SUCH DEGRADATION IT IS SINFUL IN THE EXTREME FOR YOU TO MAKE VOLUNTARY SUBMISSION. The divine commandments, you are in duty bound to reverence, and obey. If you do not obey them you will surely meet with the displeasure of the Almighty. He requires you to love him supremely, and your neighbor as yourself—to keep the Sabbath day holy—to search the Scriptures—and bring up your children with respect for his laws, and to worship no other God but him. But slavery sets all these at naught, and hurls defiance in the face of Jehovah. The forlorn condition in which you are placed does not destroy your moral obligation to God. You are not certain of Heaven, because you suffer yourselves to remain in a state of slavery, where you cannot obey commandments of the Sovereign of the universe. If the ignorance of slavery is a passport to heaven, then it is a blessing, and no curse, and you should rather desire its perpetuity than its abolition. God will not receive slavery, nor ignorance, nor any other state of mind, [as a substitute] for love, and obedience to him. Your condition does not absolve you from your moral obligation. The diabolical injustice by which your liberties are cloven down, NEITHER GOD, NOR ANGELS, OR JUST MEN, COMMAND YOU TO SUFFER FOR A SINGLE MOMENT. THEREFORE IT IS YOUR SOLEMN AND IMPERA-

TIVE DUTY TO USE EVERY MEANS, BOTH MORAL, INTELLECTUAL, AND PHYSICAL, THAT PROMISE SUCCESS. If a band of heathen men should attempt to enslave a race of Christians, and to place their children under the influence of some false religion, surely, heaven would frown upon the men who would not resist such aggression, even to death. If, on the other hand, a band of Christians should attempt to enslave a race of heathen men and to entail slavery upon them, and to keep them in heathenism in the midst of Christianity, the God of heaven would smile upon every effort which the injured might make to disenthral themselves.

Brethren, it is wrong for your lordly oppressors to keep you in slavery, as it was for the man thief to steal our ancestors from the coast of Africa. You should therefore now use the same manner of resistance, as would have been just in our ancestors, when the bloody foot prints of the first remorseless soul thief was placed upon the shores of our fatherland. The humblest peasant is as free in the sight of God, as the proudest monarch that ever swayed a scepter. Liberty is a spirit sent out from God, and like its great Author, is no respecter of persons.

Brethren, the time has come when you must act for yourselves. It is an old and true saying, that "if hereditary bondmen would be free, they must themselves strike the blow." You can plead your own cause, and do the work of emancipation better than any others. The nations of the old world are moving in the great cause of universal freedom, and some of them at least, will ere long, do you justice. The combined powers of Europe have placed their broad seal of disapprobation upon the African slave trade. But in the slave holding parts of the United States, the trade is as brisk as ever. They buy and sell you as though you were brute beasts. The North has done much—her opinion of slavery in the abstract is known. But in regard to the South, we adopt the opinion of the New York Evangelist—"We have advanced so far, that the cause apparently waits for a more effectual door to be thrown open than has been yet." We are about to point

you to that more effectual door. Look around you, and behold the bosoms of your loving wives, heaving with untold
agonies! Hear the cries of your poor children! Remember
the stripes your fathers bore. Think of the torture and disgrace of your noble mothers. Think of your wretched sisters, loving virtue and purity, as they are driven into
concubinage, and are exposed to the unbridled lusts of incarnate devils. Think of the undying glory that hangs around
the ancient name of African:—and forget not that you are
native-born American citizens, and as such, you are justly
entitled to all the rights that are granted to the freest. Think
how many tears you have poured out upon the soil which
you have cultivated with unrequited toil, and enriched with
your blood; and then go to our lordly enslavers, and tell them
plainly, that YOU ARE DETERMINED TO BE FREE.
Appeal to their sense of justice, and tell them that they have
no more right to oppress you, than you have to enslave them.
Entreat them to remove the grievous burdens which they
have imposed upon you, and to remunerate you for your labor. Promise them renewed diligence in the cultivation of
the soil, if they will render to you an equivalent for your
services. Point them to the increase of happiness and prosperity in the British West Indies, since the act of emancipation. Tell them in language which they cannot misunderstand,
of the exceeding sinfulness of slavery, and of a future judgement, and of the righteous retributions of an indignant God.
Inform them that all you desire, is FREEDOM, and that
nothing else will suffice. Do this, and for ever after cease to
toil for the heartless tyrants, who give you no other reward
but stripes and abuse. If they then commence the work of
death, they, and not you, will be responsible for the consequences. You had far better all die—*die immediately*, than live
slaves, and entail your wretchedness upon your posterity. If
you would be free in this generation, here is your only hope.
However much you and all of us may desire it, there is not
much hope of Redemption without the shedding of blood. If
you must bleed, let it all come at once—rather, *die freemen*,

than live to be slaves. It is impossible, like the children of Is-
rael, to make a grand Exodus from the land of bondage. THE
PHARAOHS ARE ON BOTH SIDES OF THE BLOOD-
RED WATERS! You cannot remove en masse, to the dominions of the British Queen—nor can you pass through
Florida, and overrun Texas, and at last find peace in Mexico.
The propagators of American slavery are spending their blood
and treasure, that they may plant the black flag in the heart
of Mexico, and riot in the halls of the Montezumas. In the
language of the Rev. Robert Hall, when addressing the vol-
unteers of Bristol, who were rushing forth to repel the invasion of Napoleon, who threatened to lay waste the fair homes
of England, "Religion is too much interested in your behalf,
not to shed over you her most gracious influences."

You will not be compelled to spend much time in order
to be inured to hardships. From the first moment that you
breathed the air of heaven, you have been accustomed to
nothing else but hardships. The heroes of the American Revolution were never put upon harder fare, than a peck of corn,
and a few herrings per week. You have not become enervated
by the luxuries of life. Your sternest energies have been beaten
out upon the anvil of severe trial. Slavery has done this, to
make you subservient to its own purposes; but it has done
more than this, it has prepared you for any emergency. If
you receive good treatment, it is what you could hardly expect; if you meet with pain, sorrow, and even death, these are
the common lot of the slaves.

Fellow-men! Patient sufferers! behold your dearest
rights crushed to the earth! See your sons murdered, and
your wives, mothers, and sisters, doomed to prostitution! In
the name of the merciful God! and by all that life is worth,
let it no longer be a debatable question, whether it is better
to choose LIBERTY or DEATH!

In 1822, Denmark Veazie, of South Carolina, formed a
plan for the liberation of his fellow men. In the whole history of human efforts to overthrow slavery, a more compli-
cated and tremendous plan was never formed. He was

betrayed by the treachery of his own people, and died a martyr to freedom. Many a brave hero fell, but History, faithful to her high trust, will transcribe his name on the same monument with Moses, Hampden, Tell, Bruce, and Wallace, Touissaint L'Overture, Lafayette and Washington. That tremendous movement shook the whole empire of slavery. The guilty soul thieves were overwhelmed with fear. It is a matter of fact, that at that time, and in consequence of the threatened revolution, the slave states talked strongly of emancipation. But they blew but one blast of the trumpet of freedom, and then laid it aside. As these men became quiet, the slaveholders ceased to talk about emancipation: and lo, behold your condition to-day! Angels sigh over it, and humanity has long since exhausted her tears in weeping on your account!

The patriotic Nathaniel Turner followed Denmark Veazie. He was goaded to desperation by wrong and injustice. By Despotism, his name has been recorded in the list of infamy, but future generations will number him among the noble and brave.

Next arose the immortal Joseph Cinque, the hero of the Amistad. He was a native African, and by the help of God he emancipated a whole ship-load of his fellow men on the high seas. And he now sings of liberty on the sunny hills of Africa, and beneath his native palm trees, where he hears the lion roar, and feels himself as free as the king of the forest. Next arose Madison Washington, that bright star of freedom, and took his station in the constellation of freedom. He was a slave on board the brig Creole, of Richmond, bound to New Orleans, that great slave mart, with a hundred and four others. Nineteen struck for liberty or death. But one life was taken, and the whole were emancipated, and the vessel was carried into Nassau, New Providence. Noble men! Those who have fallen in freedom's conflict, their memories will be cherished by the true hearted, and the God-fearing, in all future generations; those who are living, their names are surrounded by a halo of glory.

We do not advise you to attempt a revolution with the

sword, because it would be INEXPEDIENT. Your numbers are too small, and moreover the rising spirit of the age and the spirit of the gospel, are opposed to war and bloodshed. But from this moment cease to labor for tyrants who will not remunerate you. Let every slave throughout the land do this, and the days of slavery are numbered. You cannot be more oppressed than you have been—you cannot suffer greater cruelties than you have already. RATHER DIE FREEMEN, THAN LIVE TO BE SLAVES. Remember that you are THREE MILLIONS.

It is in your power so to torment the God-cursed slaveholders, that they will be glad to let you go free. If the scale was turned and black men were the masters, and white men the slaves, every destructive agent and element would be employed to lay the oppressor low. Danger and death would hang over their heads day and night. Yes, the tyrants would meet with plagues more terrible than those of Pharaoh. But you are a patient people. You act as though you were made for the special use of these devils. You act as though your daughters were born to pamper the lusts of your masters and overseers. And worse than all, you tamely submit, while your lords tear your wives from your embraces, and defile them before your eyes. In the name of God we ask, are you men? Where is the blood of your fathers? Has it all run out of your veins? Awake, awake; millions of voices are calling you! Your dead fathers speak to you from their graves. Heaven as with a voice of thunder, calls on you to arise from the dust.

Let your motto be RESISTANCE! RESISTANCE! RESISTANCE!—No oppressed people have ever secured their liberty without resistance. What kind of resistance you had better make, you must decide by the circumstances that surround you, and according to the suggestion of expediency. Brethren, adieu. Trust in the living God. Labor for the peace of the human race, and remember that you are three millions.

Henry Highland Garnet, *Walker's Appeal, with a Brief Sketch of His Life by Henry Highland Garnet. And also Garnet's Address to the Slaves of the United States of America* (New York: [Garnet], 1848)

A Letter to the American Slaves from those who have fled from American Slavery
[Gerrit Smith]

AFFLICTED AND BELOVED BROTHERS:—The meeting which sends you this letter, is a meeting of runaway slaves. We thought it well, that they, who had once suffered as you still suffer, that they, who had once drank of that bitterest of all bitter cups, should come together for the purpose of making a communication to you.

The Chief object of this meeting is, to tell you what circumstances we find ourselves in—that, so, you may be able to judge for yourselves, whether the prize we have obtained is worth the peril of the attempt to obtain it.

The heartless pirates, who compelled us to call them "master," sought to persuade us, as such pirates seek to persuade you, that the condition of those, who escape from their clutches, is thereby made worse, instead of better. We confess, that we had our fears that this might be so. Indeed, so great was our ignorance, that we could not be sure, that the abolitionists were not the fiends, which our masters represented them to be. When they told us, that the abolitionists, could they lay hands upon us, would buy and sell us, we could not certainly know, that they spoke falsely; and when they told us that abolitionists are in the habit of skinning the black man for leather, and of regalling [*sic*] their cannibalism on their flesh, even such enormities seemed to us to be possible. But owning to the happy change in our circumstances, we are not as ignorant and credulous now, as we once were; and if we did not know it before, we know it now, that slaveholders are as great liars, as they are great tyrants.

The abolitionists act the part of friends and brothers to us; and our only complaint against them is, that there are so few of them. The abolitionists, on whom it is safe to rely, are, almost all of them, members of the American Anti-Slavery Society, or of the Liberty Party. There are other abolitionists: but most of them are grossly inconsistent; and, hence, not entirely trustworthy abolitionists. So inconsistent are they, as to vote for anti-abolitionists for civil rulers, and to acknowledge the obligation of laws, which they themselves interpret to be pro-slavery.

We get wages for our labor. We have schools for our children. We have opportunities to hear and learn to read the Bible—that blessed book, which is all for freedom, notwithstanding the lying slaveholders say it is all for slavery. Some of us take part in the election of civil rulers. Indeed, but for the priests and politicians, the influence of most of whom is against us, our condition would be every way eligible. The priests and churches of the North, are, with comparatively few exceptions, in league with the priests and churches of the South; and this of itself, is sufficient to account for the fact, that a caste-religion and a negro-pew are found at the North, as well as at the South. The politicians and political parties of the North are connected with the politicians and political parties of the South; and hence, the political arrangements and interests of the North, as well as the ecclesiastical arrangements and interests, are adverse to the colored population. But, we rejoice to know that all this political and ecclesiastical power is on the wane. The callousness of American religion and American democracy has become glaring and every year, multitudes, once deluded by them, come to repudiate them. The credit of the repudiations is due in a great measure, to the American Anti-Slavery Society, to the Liberty Party, and to anti-sectarian meetings, and conventions. The purest sect on earth is the rival of, instead of one with, christianity. It deserves not to be trusted with a deep and honest and earnest reform. The temptations, which beset the pathway of such a reform, are too mighty for it to resist. Instead of going forward for God, it will slant off for itself. Heaven grant, that, soon, not a shred of sectarianism, nor a shred of the current religion, nor a shred of the current politics of this land, may remain. Then will follow, aye, that will itself be, the triumph of christianity; and then, white men will love black men, and gladly acknowledge that all men have equal rights. Come, blessed day—come quickly.

Including our children, we number in Canada, at least, twenty thousand. The total of our population in the free States far exceeds this. Nevertheless, as we are poor, we can do little more to promote your deliverance than pray for it to the God of the oppressed. We will do what we can to supply you with pocket compasses. In dark nights, when his good guiding star is hidden from the flying slave, a pocket compass greatly facilitates his exodus.—Besides, that we are too poor to furnish you with deadly weapons, candor requires the admission, that some of us would not furnish them, if we could; for some of us have become non-resistants, and have discarded the use of these weapons: and would say to you: "love your enemies; do good to them, which hate you; bless them that curse you; and pray for them, which despitefully use you." Such of us would be glad to be able to say, that all the colored men of the North are non-resistants. But, in point of fact, it is only a handful of them, who are. When the insurrection of the Southern slaves shall take place, as take place it will, unless speedily prevented by voluntary emancipation, the great mass of the colored men of the North, however much to the grief of any of us, will be found by your side, with deepstored and long-accumulated revenge in their hearts, and with death-dealing weapons in their hands. It is not to be disguised, that a colored man is as much disposed, as a white man, to resist, even unto death, those who oppress him. The colored American, for the sake of relieving his colored brethren, would no more hesitate to shoot an American slaveholder, than would a white American, for the sake of delivering his white brother, hesitate to shoot an Algerine slaveholder. The State motto of Virginia: "Death to Tyrants"; is as well the black man's, as the white man's motto. We tell you these things not to encourage, or justify, your resort to physical force; but simply, that you may know, be it to your joy or sorrow to know it, what your Northern colored brethren are, in these important respects. This truth you are entitled to know, however the knowledge of it may affect you, and however you may act, in view of it.

We have said, that some of us are non-resistants. But, while such would dissuade you from all violence toward the slaveholder, let it not be supposed, that they regard it as guiltier than those strifes, which even good men are wont to justify. If the American revolutionists had excuse for shedding but one drop of blood, then have the American slaves excuse for making blood to flow "even to the horse-bridles."

Numerous as are the escapes from slavery, they would be far more so, were you not embarrassed by your misinterpretations of the rights of property. You hesitate to take even the dullest of your master's horses—whereas it is your duty to take the fleetest. Your consciences suggest doubts, whether in quitting your bondage, you are at liberty to put in your packs what you need of food and clothing. But were you better informed, you would not scruple to break your master's locks, and take all their money. You are taught to respect the rights of property. But no such rights belong to the slaveholder. His right to property is but the robber-right. In every slaveholding community, the rights of property all center in them, whose coerced and unrequited toil has created the wealth, in which their oppressors riot. Moreover, if your oppressors have rights of property, you, at least, are exempt from all obligation to respect them. For you are prisoners of war, in an enemy's country—of a war, too, that is unrivaled for its injustice, cruelty, meanness—and therefore, by all the rules of war, you have the fullest liberty to plunder, burn, and kill, as you may have occasion to do to promote your escape.

We regret to be obliged to say to you, that it is not

every one of the Free states, which offers you an asylum. Even within the last year, fugitive slaves have been arrested in some of the Free States, and replunged into slavery. But, make your way to New York or New England, and you will be safe. It is true, that even in New York and New England, there are individuals, who would rejoice to see the poor fly-ing slave cast back into the horrors of slavery. But, even these are restrained by public sentiment. It is questionable whether even Daniel Webster, or Moses Stuart, would give chase to a fugitive slave; and if they would not, who would?—for the one is chief-politician and the other chief-priest.

We do not forget the industrious efforts, which are now in making to get new facilities at the hands of Congress for re-enslaving those, who have escaped from slavery. But we can assure you, that as to the State of New York and the New England States, such efforts must prove fruitless. Against all such devilism—against all kidnappers—the colored people of these States will "stand for their life," and what is more, the white people of these States will not stand against them. A regenerated public sentiment has, forever, removed these States beyond the limits of the slaveholders' hunting ground. Defeat—disgrace—and it may be death—will be their only reward for pursuing their prey into this *abolitionized* portion of our country.

A special reason why you should not stop in that part of the Nation which come within the bounds of John McLean's judicial district, is, that he is a great man in one of the reli-gious sects, and an aspirant for the Presidency. Fugitive slaves and their friends fare hard in the hands of this Judge. He not only puts a pro-slavery construction on the Federal Consti-tution, and holds, that law can make property of man—a marketable commodity of the image of God, but, in various other ways, he shows, that his sympathies are with the op-pressor. Shun Judge McLean, then, even as you would the Reverend Moses Stuart. The law of the one is as deadly an enemy to you, as the religion of the other.

There are three points in your conduct, when you shall

have become inhabitants of the North, on which we cannot refrain from admonishing you.

1st. If you will join a sectarian church, let it not be one which approves of the negro-pew, and which refuses to treat slaveholding as a high crime against God and man. It were better, that you sacrifice your lives than that by going into the negro-pew, you invade your self-respect—debase your souls—play the traitor to your race—and crucify afresh Him who died for the one brotherhood of man.

2d. Join no political party, which refuses to commit itself fully, openly, and heartfully, in its newspapers, meetings, and nominations, to the doctrine, that slavery is the grossest of all absurdities, as well as the guiltiest of all abominations, and that there can no more be a law for the enslavement of man, made in the image of God, than for the enslavement of God himself. Vote for no man for civil office; who makes your complexion a bar to political, ecclesiastical, or social equality. Better die than insult yourself and insult every person of African blood, and insult your Maker, by contributing to elevate to civil office he who refuses to eat with you, to sit by our side in the House of Worship, or to let his children sit in the school by the side of your children.

3d. Send not your children to the school which the malignant and murderous prejudice of white people has gotten up exclusively for colored people. Valuable as learning is, it is too costly; if it is acquired at the expense of such self-degradation.

The self-sacrificing, and heroic, and martyr-spirit, which would impel the colored men of the North to turn their backs on pro-slavery churches and pro-slavery politics, and pro-slavery schools, would exert a far mightier influence against slavery, than could all their learning, however great, if purchased by concessions of their manhood, and surrenders of their rights, and coupled, as it then would be, by characteristic meanness and servility.

And now, brethren, we close this letter with assuring you, that we do not, cannot forget you. You are ever in our minds, our hearts, our prayers. Perhaps, you are fearing, that the free colored people of the United States will suffer themselves to be carried away from you by the American Colonization Society. Fear it not. In vain is it, that this greatest and most malignant enemy of the African race is now busy in devising new plans, and in seeking the aid of government, to perpetuate your enslavement. It wants us away from your side, that you may be kept in ignorance. But we will remain by your side to enlighten you. It wants us away from your side, that you may be contented. But we will remain by your side, to keep you, and make you more, discontented. It wants us away from your side to the end, that your unsuccored and conscious helplessness may make you the easier and surer prey of our oppressors. But we will remain by your side to sympathize with you, and cheer you, and give you the help of our rapidly swelling members. The land of our enslaved brethren is our land, and death alone shall part us.

We cannot forget you, brethren, for we know your sufferings; and we know your sufferings, because we know from experience, what it is to be an American slave. So galling was our bondage, that, to escape from it, we suffered the loss of all things, and braved every peril, and endured every hardship. Some of us left parents, some wives, some children. Some of us were wounded with guns and dogs, as we fled. Some of us, to make good our escape, suffered ourselves to be nailed up in boxes, and to pass for merchandise. Some of us secreted ourselves in the suffocating holds of ships. Nothing was so dreadful to us, as slavery; and hence, it is almost literally true that we dreaded nothing, which could befall us, in our attempt to get clear of it. Our condition could be made no worse, for we were already in the lowest depth of earthly woe. Even should we be overtaken, and resubjected to slavery, this would be but to return to our old sufferings and sorrows: and should death itself prove to be the price of our endeavor after freedom, what would that be but a welcome release to men, who had, all their lifetime, been killed every day, and "killed all the day long."

We have referred to our perils and hardships in escaping from slavery. We are happy to be able to say, that every year is multiplying the facilities for leaving the Southern prison house. The Liberty Party, the Vigilance Committee of New York, individuals, and companies of individuals in various parts of the country, are doing all they can, and it is much, to afford you a safe and cheap, passage from slavery to liberty. They do this however, not only at great expense of property, but at great peril of liberty and life. Thousands of you have heard, ere this, that, within the last fortnight, the precious name of William L. Chaplin has been added to the list of those, who, in helping you gain your liberty, have lost their own. Here is a man, whose wisdom, cultivation, moral worth, bring him into the highest and best class of men:— and, yet, he becomes a willing martyr for the poor, despised, forgotten slave's sake. Your remembrance of one such fact is enough to shed light and hope upon your darkest and most-desponding moments.

Brethren, our last word to you is to bid you be of good cheer, and not to despair of your deliverance. Do not abandon yourselves, to the crime of suicide. Live! live to escape from slavery, live to serve God! live till He shall Himself call you into eternity! Be prayerful—be brave—be hopeful. "Lift up your heads, for your redemption draweth nigh."

North Star, September 5, 1850.

NOTES

For complete publication information see Bibliography.

Abbreviations

AASS	American Anti-Slavery Society
AFASS	American and Foreign Anti-Slavery Society
AMA	American Missionary Association
AP	*Albany Patriot*
MASS	Massachusetts Anti-Slavery Society
NASS	*National Anti-Slavery Standard*
NE	*National Era*
NS	*North Star*
NYDT	*New York Daily Tribune*
NYE	*New York Evangelist*
PF	*Pennsylvania Freeman*

Introduction

1. [Smith], "Address of the Anti-Slavery Convention of the State of New-York, Held in Peterboro', January 19th, 1842, to the Slaves in the U. States of America"; [Garrison], "Address to the Slaves of the United States"; Garnet, *Walker's Appeal, with a Brief Sketch of His Life. . . . And also Garnet's Address to the Slaves of the United States of America*, 89-96 (cited hereafter as Garnet, *Walker's Appeal and Garnet's Address*).

2. *Liberator*, Jan. 1, 1831 (1st quotation); Sanborn, ed., *Life*

and Letters of John Brown, 620 (2nd quotation). There are several anthologies of abolitionist writings: Mason Lowance, ed., *Against Slavery: An Abolitionist Reader*; William H. Pease and Jane H. Pease, eds., *The Antislavery Argument*; Louis Ruchames, ed., *The Abolitionists: A Collection of Their Writings*.

3. Dillon, *Slavery Attacked*, 208-16; Quarles, *Black Abolitionists*, 227; Ripley, et al., eds., *Black Abolitionist Papers*, 3:407-9; Pease and Pease, *They Who Would Be Free*, 250; Stuckey, "A Last Stern Struggle: Henry Highland Garnet and Liberation Theory," 135-38. Pease and Pease regard black abolitionist calls for slave revolt also to have been merely rhetorical.

4. Barnes, *Antislavery Impulse*; Kraditor, *Means and Ends*; Stewart, "The Aims and Impact of Garrisonian Abolitionism," 197-209 (quotation); Perry, *Radical Abolitionism*.

5. Harrold, *American Abolitionists*, 16-20, 107-8; Anthony Benezet to Joseph Phipps, May 28, 1763, Quaker Manuscript Collection; Genovese, *From Rebellion to Revolution*, 82-125; Newman, *Transformation of American Abolitionism*, 16-38 ; Horton and Horton, *In Hope of Liberty*, 55-76; Soderlund, *Quakers and Slavery*; Mullin, *Flight and Rebellion*; Essig, *Bonds of Wickedness*. On emancipation in the North and its results: Litwack, *North of Slavery*; Melish, *Disowning Slavery*; Berlin, *Many Thousands Gone*, 228-55.

6. Walters, *Antislavery Appeal*, 64-65, 72-78, 80, 121-28; Floan, *South in Northern Eyes*, 13-14, 20-33.

7. Newman, *Transformation of American Abolitionism*, 5, 31, 61; Dillon, *Lundy*, 34-169; Blight, "Perceptions of Southern Intransigence and the Rise of Radical Antislavery Thought," 144, 149-50.

8. Fox, *American Colonization Society*, 27-34; Staudenraus, *African Colonization Movement*; Miller, *Search for Black Nationality*, 3-90; Berlin, *Slaves without Masters*, 201.

9. *Freedom's Journal*, May 18, June 8, 1827; Horton and Horton, *In Hope of Liberty*, 196-200; Newman, *Transformation of American Abolitionism*, 97-100. Newman overlooks black support for the ACS.

10. Dillon, *Lundy*, 53-54, 75-78, 106-9, 154-55; Abzug, *Cosmos Crumbling*, 129-62; Horton and Horton, *In Hope of Liberty*, 224-25; Goodman, *Of One Blood*, 23-44; Newman, *Transformation of American Abolitionism*, 86-106; Harrold, *Subversives*, 18-19, 23-24; Hinks, *Walker*, 116-72.

11. Hinks, *Walker*, 269-70; Dillon, *Lundy*, 162, 212; Mayer, *Garrison*, 97-120; Stewart, *Garrison*, 50-55; Stewart, "Peaceful Hopes and Violent Experiences," 294-99; Dillon, *Abolitionists*, 56-64.

12. Dillon, *Slavery Attacked*, 170-71; *Emancipator*, Aug. 19, Nov. 12, 1844; "Declaration of Sentiments of the American Anti-Slavery Society," in *Liberator*, Dec. 14, 1833.

13. This was true of Smith, Garrison, and Garnet, as well as others, prior to 1842 and 1843. Smith: Smith to W. E. Channing, Aug. 17, 1841, Smith to Nathaniel Crenshaw, Dec. 30, 1841, letter book copies, Smith Papers. Garrison: *Liberator*, Sept. 3, 1831; Garrison to President, Anti-Slavery Convention, Jan. 30, 1836, in Merrill and Ruchames, eds., *Letters of William Lloyd Garrison*, 2:32 (hereafter cited as *Garrison Letters*). Garnet: *Emancipator*, Mar. 14, 1842. See also Abzug, "Influence of Garrisonian Abolitionists' Fear of Slave Violence," 15-28; Stewart, "Peaceful Hopes," 293-309; Dillon, *Slavery Attacked*, 206.

14. Abzug, "Influence of Garrisonian Abolitionists' Fear of Slave Violence," 24-26; Stewart, "Peaceful Hopes," 298-303. Stewart explains the feeling of failure among abolitionists by the late 1830s, but does not note the movement toward aggressive tactics by "conservative" abolitionists like Gerrit Smith.

15. Harrold, *American Abolitionists*, 35-38; Bell, *A Survey of the Negro Convention Movement*; Quarles, *Black Abolitionists*, 45-46; Sewell, *Ballots for Freedom*, 24-42, 100-101; Kraditor, *Means and Ends*, 39-140; Merrill and Ruchames, eds., *Garrison Letters*, 3:1, 383-84, 459; M. W. C. in *Liberator*, Sept. 22, 1843 (quotation). See also DeBoer, *Be Jubilant My Feet*; Pease and Pease, *They Who Would Be Free*, 81-82.

16. Garnet, *Walker's Appeal and Garnet's Address*, 95.

17. Until recently historians have believed that abolitionists after 1835 concentrated on converting the North to antislavery. See Wyatt-Brown, "Abolitionists' Postal Campaign of 1835," 227-38.

18. Garnet, *Walker's Appeal and Garnet's Address*, viii.

19. On Smith and his associates, see Frothingham, *Smith*, 38-39; Harlow, *Smith*; Friedman, *Gregarious Saints*, 96-128; Strong, *Perfectionist Politics*; Wiecek, *Sources of Antislavery Constitutionalism*, 249-75; Stauffer, *Black Hearts of Men*; Sernett, *North Star Country*. I believe that Friedman overemphasizes the local perspective of Smith and his associates.

20. On Garrison, see Thomas, *Garrison*; Merrill, *Garrison*; Stewart, *Garrison*; Mayer, *Garrison*.

21. On Garnet, see Ofari, *Garnet*; Schor, *Garnet*; Pasternak, *Garnet*; Pease and Pease, *Bound with Them in Chains*, 162-90; Stuckey, "Garnet," 129-48. None of the three book-length biographies of Garnet are adequate. Schor's and Pasternak's citations are full of errors and are, therefore, not reliable. On Garnet's ties to Smith, see Smith to Garnet, June 10, 1843, letter book copy, Garnet to Smith, Sept. 19, 1845, Smith Papers.

22. Smith to Oliver Johnson, Feb. 2, 1842, letter book copy, Smith Papers.

23. On republican ideology, see Shallope, "Toward a Republican Synthesis," 49-80; Rodgers, "Republicanism," 11-38; Wilenz, *Chants Democratic*, 61-103; Huston, *Securing the Fruits of Labor*.

24. Sellers, *Market Revolution*; Dawley, *Class and Community*; Johnson, *A Shop Keeper's Millennium*, 37-61; Kerber, "Paradox of Women's Citizenship in the Early Republic," 349-78; Cott, *Bonds of Womanhood*; Pessen, *Riches, Class, and Power before the Civil War*.

25. Roediger, *Wages of Whiteness*; Horton and Horton, *In Hope of Liberty*, 166-67; Young, *Antebellum Black Activists*, 175-76; Yarborough, "Race, Violence, and Manhood," 167-70.

26. Stanton, *Leopard's Spots*; Fredrickson, *Black Image in the White Mind*, 1-164; Gould, *Mismeasure of Man*; Roediger, *Wages of Whiteness*.

27. Strong, *Perfectionist Politics*, 4-5 and passim.

28. R. J. Young notes that when antebellum "African Americans talked about assuming a manly bearing or taking a manly stand they didn't mean a 'human' stand or a 'humanly' bearing. They meant speaking and acting in ways that society prescribed for males." This was true for antebellum whites as well. See Young, *Antebellum Black Activists*, 175.

29. Richards, *"Gentlemen of Property and Standing,"* 34-64; Grimsted, *American Mobbing*, 3-64.

30. Brown, "Missouri Crisis, Slavery, and the Politics of Jacksonianism," 52-72; Richards, *Slave Power*, 1-133; Fehrenbacher, *Slaveholding Republic*; Garnet, *Walker's Appeal and Garnet's Address*, 91 (quotation).

31. Fredrickson, *Black Image in the White Mind*, 97-129; Matthews, "Abolitionists on Slavery," 178-79; Blassingame, et al., eds., *Douglass Papers, Series One*, 1:21 (quotation).

Chapter One. Ambiguous Manifestos

1. On the influence of Christian perfectionism on this outlook, see Strong, *Perfectionist Politics*, 71.

2. Harrold, *Abolitionists and the South*, 68, and "Romanticizing Slave Revolt," 89-90.

3. Mabee, *Black Freedom*, 47-48, 55-56, 7-72; Walters, *Antislavery Appeal*, 29-30; Friedman, *Gregarious Saints*, 206; Stauffer, *Black Hearts of Men*, 262-65. Robert H. Abzug was the first historian to emphasize how abolitionists used the threat of slave revolt. See Abzug, "Influence of Garrisonian Abolitionists' Fear of Slave Violence," 15-28.

4. Smith later indicated that, while he believed slaves had a moral right to revolt, he also believed it was inexpedient for them to exercise the right. See Smith to William Lloyd Garrison, n.d., in *Liberator*, Mar. 4, 1842.

5. *NASS*, Feb. 24, 1842.

6. *Emancipator*, Feb. 17, 1842. I have found no indication that Smith attended the meeting.

7. *Liberator*, Feb. 11, 1842.

8. See Garrison to Editor of the *Boston Courier*, Mar. 11, 1837, in Merrill and Ruchames, eds., *Garrison Letters*, 2:224; H[enry] C. Wright to Brother, n.d., in *Liberator*, Sept. 13, 1839.

9. Wiecek, *Sources of Antislavery Constitutionalism*, 236-48; *Liberator*, Feb. 4, 1842; MASS, *Tenth Annual Report*, 10.

10. Smith to Garnet, June 10, 1843, Garnet to Smith, Sept. 19, 1845, Smith Papers. See also Pasternak, *Garnet*, 4, 38-39; Swift, *Black Prophets of Justice*, 136.

11. *Emancipator*, Mar. 4, 1842.

12. See, for example, Pasternak, *Garnet*, 46-47; Aptheker, "Militant Abolitionism," 457-58; Shiffrin, "Rhetoric of Black Violence in the Antebellum Period: Henry Highland Garnet," 45-56; Stuckey, "Garnet," 135-40; Quarles, *Black Abolitionists*, 226; Rael, *Black Identity and Black Protest*, 273.

13. Pease and Pease, *They Who Would Be Free*, 239; *Minutes of the National Convention of Colored Citizens*, 12-24; Garnet to Maria W. Chapman, Nov. 17, 1843, in *Liberator*, Dec. 8, 1843; Garnet, *Memorial Discourse*.

14. An allusion to the war against Mexico (1846-1848) could not have been in the 1843 version and is in both the 1848 and 1865

versions. See Garnet, *Walker's Appeal and Garnet's Address*, 94, and *Memorial Discourse*, 49. At the point where the "INEXPEDIENT" passage had been, the 1865 version updates the slave population from three million to four million, indicating that a deletion has taken place rather than reliance on a lost 1843 version.

15. *Emancipator*, Mar. 4, 1842.

16. *Minutes of the National Convention of Colored Citizens, Held at Buffalo*, 17; E. A. Marsh to [editor], Aug. 24, 1843, in *Liberator*, Sept. 8, 1843.

17. Because it is in part premised on the United States invasion of Mexico that began in 1846, it is possible, if not likely, that this passage was not in the original 1843 address.

18. Garnet quotes the *New York Evangelist*, July 27, 1843. Garnet was not the first to suggest that slaves strike. Gerrit Smith received a letter during the fall of 1842 suggesting that slaves cease to work. See Alice Eliza Hamilton to Smith, Sept. 22, 1842, Smith Papers.

19. Fredrickson, *Black Image in the White Mind*, 71-129; Bay, *White Image in the Black Mind*, 38-74; Takaki, "Black Child-Savage in Antebellum America," 27-44.

Chapter Two. Circumstances

1. Jones, *Mutiny on the* Amistad; Jones, "Case of the *Creole* Slave Revolt," 29-33; *Emancipator*, Jan. 20, 1842 (quotation).

2. Seward, *Autobiography*, 428-29, 437-38, 463-65, 528-31; Finkelman, "Protection of Black Rights in Seward's New York," 211-28; *PF*, Nov. 28, 1839, Feb. 13, 1840; *Globe*, Feb. 17, 1842; Harrold, *Subversives*, 71-72.

3. *Emancipator*, Mar. 31, 1842.

4. *Emancipator*, Jan. 20 (1st quotation), Mar. 4, 31, 1842; *NYE*, May 12, 1843; Torrey to Alden, Mar. 19, 1842, in *Emancipator*, Mar. 31, 1842 (2nd quotation). Torrey kept abolitionists informed concerning these events with a series of letters that appeared in the *NYE* between Mar. 10 and Ap. 25, 1842.

5. Anthony Benezet to Joseph Phipps, May 28, 1763, Quaker Manuscript Collection; Woolman, "Considerations on the Keeping of Negroes," 324-27; *Liberator*, Sept. 3, 1831 (1st quotation); Grimke, *Appeal to the Christian Women of the South*, 24 (2nd quotation); *Emancipator*, Sept. 19, 1839 (3rd quotation). See also *Herald of Freedom*, quoted in *Liberator*, Sept. 13, 1839.

6. Garrison to the Editor of the *Boston Courier*, Mar. 18, 1837, in Merrill and Ruchames, eds., *Garrison Letters*, 2:234-38.

7. *Emancipator*, June 7, 1838 (lst quotation); *Liberator*, Mar. 11, 1837 (2nd quotation). See also Whittier, *Conflict with Slavery*, 73; Milo D. Codding to [editors], n.d., in *NASS*, Mar. 14, 1842.

8. *AP*, Mar. 30, 1843.

9. Ibid., June 15, 1843.

10. Marsh, *Writings and Speeches of Alvan Stewart*, 193 (1st quotation); *Liberator*, Feb. 4, 1842 (2nd-3rd quotations). Recent books on antebellum black masculinity include: Harper, *Are We Not Men?*, and Sale, *Slumbering Volcano*.

11. *Colored American*, May 30, 1840; Hunt, *Haiti's Influence on Antebellum America*, 153-55; *Emancipator*, Feb. 17, 1842; O. L. to Editor, n.d., in *Liberator*, Sept. 17, 1831 (quotation).

12. Aptheker, ed., *"One Continual Cry,"* 75, 79.

13. W. G., "Addressing the Colored People," *Emancipator*, Oct. 20, 1835 (1st quotation); A Kentuckian to [editor], June 8, 1839, in *Colored American*, July 30, 1839; *Emancipator*, Nov. 28, 1839 (2nd quotation).

14. Garrison, *Address Delivered before the Free People of Color*; Grimke, *Appeal to the Christian Women of the South* and *An Appeal to the Women of the Nominally Free States*; [Jay], *Address to the Non-Slaveholders of the South* and in *AP*, Mar. 2-Ap. 6, 1843.

15. Johnson to [Editor], Jan. 22, 1841[2], in *NASS*, Feb. 10, 1842. Among other things he notes about Smithfield, Alan Kraut points out that twenty-two African Americans lived there during the 1840s. None of the black men among them had the right to vote. See Kraut, "Liberty Men," 312-21. John Stauffer maintains that Smith "transformed Peterboro and Madison County into a multiracial community" but provides no figures and is imprecise concerning dates. See Stauffer, *Black Hearts of Men*, 63, 127 (quotation), 130.

16. Strong, *Perfectionist Politics*, esp. 66-90; Wellman, *Grassroots Reform in the Burned-Over District*, 129-60; 193-214: Kraut, "Liberty Men," 13-18; Harrold, *Abolitionists and the South*, 74-75, 80-81, 91-92. On the early electoral success of the Liberty party, see Sewell, *Ballots for Freedom*, 110.

17. Johnson to [Editor], Jan. 22, 1841[2], in *NASS*, Feb. 10, 1842. An article in the *Daily Albany Argus* based on material from the *Friend of Man* (Utica) supports Johnson's numbers. See *Argus*,

Jan. 28, 1842. Elizabeth Cady Stanton describes a trip in a "stage sleigh" in New York at about this time. See Stanton, *Eighty Years and More*, 110.

18. R. N. to Editor, Jan. 21, 1842, in *NYDT*, Jan. 25, 1842. Portions of Johnson's report and this one are very similar, which suggests that one of the dispatches is in part derived from the other.

19. Johnson, *Garrison*, 208-10; Kraut, "Liberty Men," 320.

20. Johnson to [Editor], Jan. 22, 1841[2], in *NASS*, Feb. 10, 1842; *AP*, Sept. 24, 1845.

21. Ibid.

22. *Liberator*, June 9, 1843; Strong, *Perfectionist Politics*, 59.

23. Quarles, *Black Abolitionists*, 193-94; *Christian World* (quotations) and *Herkimer Journal*, in *Liberator*, June 16, 1843. Henry Mayer provides a detailed account of the Latimer case and contends that it directly influenced Garrison's decision to address the slaves. See Mayer, *Garrison*, 317-20.

24. Stanton, *Eighty Years and More*, 131 (1st quotation); *Herkimer Journal* (2nd quotation) and *Christian World* (4th quotation), in *Liberator*, June 16, 1843; Mayer, *Garrison*, 321, 328-29; MASS, *Eleventh Annual Report*, 97 (3rd quotation); Eaklor, *American Antislavery Songs*, 276, 324 (remaining quotations). The convention concluded by singing "From All that Dwell Below the Skies." See *Liberator*, June 9, 1843.

25. *Liberator*, June 2 (quotation), 9, 16, 1843; *NASS*, June 8, 1843.

26. Stanton, *Eighty Years and More*, 130-31. The first quoted phrase is also used in the *Herkimer Journal*, June 7, 1843, quoted in *Liberator*, June 16, 1843.

27. *Herkimer Journal*, June 7, 1843, quoted in *Liberator*, June 16, 1843 (1st quotation); "Address of the Board of Managers of the Massachusetts Anti-Slavery Society" (2nd quotation) in *Liberator*, June 16, 1843; *NASS*, June 22, 1843.

28. *Minutes of the National Convention of Colored Citizens*, 10, 12, 24.

29. *AP*, June 8, 1843, reported that not many of Buffalo's citizens "are known as active anti-slavery men." See also Graf, "Abolition and Anti-Slavery in Buffalo and Erie County," 1-3; Farrison, "William Wells Brown in Buffalo," 300-303. There were no more than seven hundred African Americans living in Buffalo in 1843. That is the number given in the convention's *Minutes*, but a recent history of black people in the city estimates that their number was

about five hundred in 1860. See *Minutes of the National Convention of Colored Citizens*, 37; and Williams, *Strangers in the Land of Paradise*, 11.

30. Brown to Torrey, July 21, 1843, in *AP*, Aug. 22, 1843; William W. Brown to Editor, Sept. 26, 1843, in *NASS*, Oct. 5, 1843; Farrison, "William Wells Brown in Buffalo," 307; Remond to Esteemed Friend, Aug. 12, 1843, in *Liberator*, Sept. 11, 1843, and to Esteemed Friend, Aug. 30, 1843, in *Liberator*, Sept. 22, 1843; J. W. Alden to Joshua Leavitt, Aug. 29, 1843, in *Emancipator*, Aug. 31, 1843. John Quincy Adams also visited Buffalo that July. See *Buffalo Daily Mercantile Courier*, July 27, 1843, quoted in *Daily Albany Argus*, July 29, 1843. The *AP* ran announcements for the black national convention and the Liberty national convention simultaneously on Aug. 3, 1843.

31. Alden to Leavitt, Aug. 29, 1843, in *Emancipator*, Aug. 31, 1843; *AP*, Sept. 9, 1843; [?] to Editors, Sept. 4, 1843, in *NYE*, Sept. 7, 1843. Regarding the lack of rail links, see Goldman, *High Hopes*, 89; Graf, "Abolition and Anti-Slavery in Buffalo and Erie County," 39-40. Alden reported that it took him twenty-seven hours to travel from Albany to Buffalo.

32. Mabee, *Black Freedom*, 57-59; *Liberator*, Aug. 4, 1843; *NASS*, Sept. 7, 1843. A meeting in Boston failed to pass resolutions against sending delegates to the convention, but of the five delegates it appointed, only Douglass and Remond attended. A meeting in New Bedford refused to send delegates. For an enlightening discussion of the tensions within the black national convention movement, see Pease and Pease, "Negro Conventions and the Problem of Black Leadership," 29-44.

33. Remond to Esteemed Friend, Aug. 12, 1843, in *Liberator*, Sept. 11, 1843. Gregory P. Lampe indicates that Douglass and Remond were the only delegates from Massachusetts, and he is backed up by the *Minutes of the National Convention of Colored Citizens*. But James Oliver Horton and Lois E. Horton contend that William C. Nell and John T. Hilton also represented that state. The low turnout in Buffalo was not exceptional for black national conventions. Those held during the early 1830s had been small affairs. Prior to the Buffalo meeting, the largest had been in Philadelphia in 1833 when sixty-two participated. See Lampe, *Douglass*, 182; Horton and Horton, *In Hope of Liberty*, 208, 319n.

34. *Minutes of the National Convention of Colored Citizens*, 4, 7; E. A. Marsh [to editor], Aug. 24, 1843, in *Liberator*, Sept. 8, 1843; Remond to

Esteemed Friend, Aug. 30, 1843, in *Liberator*, Sept. 22, 1843; Aptheker, *Documentary History of the Negro People*, 226; Quarles, *Black Abolitionists*, 226-27; *Liberator*, Aug. 4, 1843 (quotation). Quarles provides no source for his remark concerning whites in the audience. Aptheker states that there were "over sixty" delegates. Lampe indicates that there were seventy-three. I have found no basis for these numbers.

35. *Minutes of the National Convention of Colored Citizens*, 4 (1st quotation), 26; Douglass, *Life and Times of Frederick Douglass*, 195 (2nd-3rd quotations); Farrison, "William Wells Brown in Buffalo," 307. Farrison establishes that the building Douglass describes was the same building in which the National Convention of Colored Citizens met. There were two black churches in Buffalo in 1843—an AME and a Baptist. It may be that their buildings were too small to house even a small convention. See *Minutes*, 37, and Williams, *Strangers in the Land*, 11-12.

36. *Commercial Advertiser*, quoted in *Emancipator*, Oct. 12, 1843 (1st and 3rd quotations); Quarles, *Black Abolitionists*, 226 (2nd quotation); Mabee, *Black Freedom*, 60. At least two fugitive slaves served as delegates at the Buffalo convention, but the convention *Minutes* does not indicate that they acted in conjunction with Garnet's Address. See *Minutes of the National Convention of Colored Citizens*, 15.

37. *Commercial Advertiser*, quoted in *Emancipator*, Oct. 12, 1843 (1st-6th quotation); A[mos] G. B[eman], to Editor, Mar. 8, 1863, in *Weekly Anglo-African*, Mar. 14, 1863 (7th quotation).

38. On antebellum oratory, see Browne, *Angelina Grimke*, 111; Smith, *Dominion of Voice*, 92, 102-11; Bacon, *Humblest May Stand Forth*. Garnet: Amos A. Beman to Editor, Mar. 6, 1863, *Weekly Anglo-African*, Mar. 14, 1863. Smith: Henry B. Stanton, *Random Recollections*, 65. Garrison: Thomas, *The Liberator*, 310.

Chapter Three. Proceedings

1. Black national conventions always attracted men who represented contrasting points of view. See Pease and Pease, "Negro Conventions and the Problem of Black Leadership," 29-44.

2. "Minutes of the New York State Liberty Party Convention, January 19 and 20, 1842" [1].

3. Sorin, *New York Abolitionists*, 47-52, 57-61, 94-96; Sewell, *Ballots for Freedom*, 49-51; Wiecek, *Sources of Antislavery Constitutionalism*, 254-57; Friedman, *Gregarious Saints*, 98; Sernett, *Green*;

Stewart, *Holy Warriors*, 95; *Liberator*, Feb. 25, 1842; Strong, *Perfectionist Politics*, 206 n. 44.

4. Stewart, *Holy Warriors*, 101, 117; Rice, "Stanton," 248-49, 262-65, 271-81, 286-310.

5. *Emancipator*, Mar. 10, 1842; "Minutes of the New York State Liberty Party Convention" [3].

6. *Emancipator*, Mar. 10, 1842.

7. Friedman, *Gregarious Saints*, 100-102; Johnson, *Garrison*, 209-10; *Emancipator*, Feb. 11, 1842 (1st quotation); Kraut, "Liberty Men," 69; Oliver Johnson to [editor], Jan. 22, 1841, in *NASS*, Feb. 10, 1842 (2nd-3rd quotations); "Minutes of the New York State Liberty Party Convention" [5] (4th quotation). Smith had served as the New York Liberty gubernatorial candidate in 1840.

8. "Minutes of the New York State Liberty Party Convention" [6].

9. "Minutes of the New York State Liberty Party Convention" does not indicate the positions the debaters took. My interpretation is based on the order in which the men spoke, on their predilections and associations, and, in Goodell's case, on his deep commitment to peaceful means. On Goodell, see Perkal, "Goodell," 135-38, 257-60, and Quarles, *Black Abolitionists*, 242.

10. "Minutes of the New York State Liberty Party Convention" [8 (1st quotation)-9]; *Emancipator*, Feb. 11, 1842 (2nd quotation).

11. Yacovone, *May*; Stewart, *Phillips*; *Dictionary of American Biography*, S.V. Quincy, Edmund; Ward, "Remond"; Pease and Pease, *Bound with Them in Chains*, 28-59, 73, 191-217, 276-307; McFeely, *Douglass*, 84–106.

12. *Herkimer Journal*, June 7, 1843, quoted in *Liberator*, June 16, 1843.

13. *Liberator*, June 16, 1843.

14. Ibid.

15. Ibid., June 2, 1843.

16. *Liberator*, June 16, Aug 4, 1843; Alvan Stewart to *Liberty Press*, n.d., in *Emancipator*, July 13, 1843; *AP*, July 20, 1843; *Liberty Press*, Aug. 22, Oct. 31, 1843.

17. Williams, *Strangers in the Land*, 15; Quarles, *Black Abolitionists*, 68. Later Davis migrated to Canada and worked with the American Baptist Free Missions Society. See *Provincial Freeman*, Sept. 29, Dec. 1, 1855.

18. Quarles, *Black Abolitionists*, 239; Work, "Ray," 361-71; Oates, *Brown*, 243-44.

19. *Colored American*, Aug. 25, 1838, Nov. 20, 1841; *North Star*, Sept. 15, 1848.

20. Farrison, *Brown*; Hunter, *Loguen*.

21. *Minutes of the National Convention of Colored Citizens*, 4-7.

22. Ibid., 7-8; E. A. Marsh to [Editor], Aug. 24, 1843, in *Liberator*, Sept. 8, 1843.

23. *Minutes of the National Convention of Colored Citizens*, 10-12. Garnet probably also perplexed the twelve delegates who refused to vote on the church issue. As chair of the business committee, he determined which resolutions would be brought to a vote. A few days earlier Remond had complained, without much accuracy, that the Liberty Party was unwilling to denounce churches. See Remond to Esteemed Friend, Aug. 12, 1843, in *Liberator*, Sept. 1, 1843.

24. *Minutes of the National Convention of Colored Citizens*, 7-8, 16 (quotation), 21-22, 24-25; Marsh to [Editor], Aug. 24, 1843, in *Liberator*, Sept. 8, 1843.

25. *Minutes of the National Convention of Colored Citizens*, 12-13 (1st-6th quotations); Marsh to [Editor], Aug. 24, 1843, in *Liberator*, Sept. 8, 1843 (7th quotation). On Garnet's relationship with Ray, see Swift, *Black Prophets of Justice*, 113-45.

26. *Minutes of the National Convention of Colored Citizens*, 13 (1st and 2nd quotations); Marsh to [Editor], Aug. 24, 1843, in *Liberator*, Sept. 8, 1843 (3rd quotation).

27. *Minutes of the National Convention of Colored Citizens*, 17. Marsh wrote similarly that the Address "came back about the same thing."

28. Ibid., 18.

29. Ibid., 18-19. All three delegates from Buffalo voted nay.

30. Ibid., 23.

31. Ibid., 24. Marsh suggests that Beman and Ray were in favor of the Address, which considering the outcome does not make sense. For another extended analysis of the proceedings, see Swift, *Black Prophets of Justice*, 135-38.

32. See, for example, Swift, *Black Prophets of Justice*, 138-39.

Chapter Four. Goals and Reactions

1. Dumond, *Antislavery*, 197-227; MASS, *Fifth Annual Report*, v. William W. Freehling provides a less than flattering ac-

count of Birney's dealings with mob pressure. See Freehling, *Road to Disunion*, 113-16.

2. *Emancipator*, May 18, 1833 (1st quotation); Theodore Weld to James G. Birney, Dec. 11, 1834, in Dumond, ed., *Letters of James G. Birney* (hereafter cited as *Birney Letters*), 1:155 (2nd quotation); *Anti-Slavery Reporter*, Ap. 1835 (3rd quotation); Hart, *Slavery and Abolition*, 202-3 (4th quotation).

3. On antislavery propaganda in the South, see *Emancipator*, May 18, 1833, Oct. 1835. On the need to change the North, see Theodore Weld to James G. Birney, Feb. 11, 1834, in Dumond, ed., *Birney Letters*, 1:155; *Anti-Slavery Reporter*, Ap. 1835, 46-47; *PF*, June 20, 1839. On danger, see Garrison and Garrison, *Garrison*, 1:507 (quotation).

4. Hart, *Slavery and Abolition*, 206, 232, 234, 315; Wyatt-Brown, "Abolitionists' Postal Campaign of 1835," 238; Freehling, *Road to Disunion*, 383; Fogel, *Without Consent or Contract*, 265, 269; Stewart, *Holy Warriors*, 88, 93; Dillon, *Abolitionists*, 40; Mabee, *Black Freedom*, 28.

5. AASS, *Second Annual Report*, 46; *Emancipator*, July 8, 1846, Dec. 15, 1847; *Radical Abolitionist* 2 (Feb. 1857): 63; *Oberlin Evangelist*, Aug. 18, 1858.

6. *NASS*, Feb. 24, 1842; *Philanthropist*, Mar. 30, 1842; *NYE*, Nov. 19, 1836; Tappan, et al., "To the Public," Sept. 3, 1835, in *Emancipator*, Oct. 1835; Garrison to editor of the *Boston Courier*, [Mar. 18, 1837], in Merrill and Ruchames, eds., *Garrison Letters*, 2:241; *Minutes of the National Convention of Colored Citizens*, 13; A. E. Marsh to [Editor], Aug. 24, 1843, in *Liberator*, Sept. 8, 1843; *Liberator*, Mar. 13, 1858 (quotation).

7. *Liberator*, Feb. 11, 1842 (1st-3rd quotations), June 16, 1843 (4th quotation); Schor, *Garnet*, 31; Pasternak, *Garnet*, 21-22; Blassingame, et al., eds., *Douglass Papers, Series One*, 1:21-22.

8. Wyatt-Brown, "Abolitionists' Postal Campaign of 1835," 229; Browne, *Angelina Grimke*, 63, 72, 80-81; Smith, *Letter to . . . Rev. James Smylie*; *Correspondence between the Hon. F. H. Elmore . . . and J. G. Birney*; *Emancipator*, Feb. 15, 1838; Ohio Anti-Slavery Society, *Report of the 3rd Anniversary*, 16; *Friend of Man*, Oct. 17, 1838; Dillon, *Slavery Attacked*, 189; Harrold, *Abolitionists and the South*, 96, 140-43; Gerrit Smith to Nathaniel Crenshaw, Dec. 30, 1841, Smith to W. E. Channing, Aug. 17, 1841, letter book copies, Smith Papers; Samuel M. Janney to J. M. McKim, Dec. 1, 1843,

Antislavery Papers; John G. Fee to E. C. Allen, June 25, 1844, Chase Papers; David Gamble to Dear Sir, Oct. 28, 1847, John G. Fee to Lewis Tappan, Dec. 27, 1848, American Missionary Association Archives; *National Era*, Jan. 7, 1847.

9. Hinks, *Walker*, 116-71; Grover, *Fugitive's Gibraltar*, 82-93; Dillon, *Slavery Attacked*, 146-47. In 1830 Garrison noted that Walker's *Appeal* was circulating among African Americans in Baltimore. See *Genius of Universal Emancipation*, Jan. 15, 1830.

10. A[bel] B[rown] to G. Smith, Oct. 1, 1843, in *Albany Patriot*, Nov. 21, 1843.

11. On conversations with slaves, see Harrold, *Subversives*, 64-92; Its First Public Advocate to Gamaliel Bailey, Mar. 16, 1842, in *Philanthropist*, Ap. 13, 1842; Nelson to [Editor], n.d. and to Friend, June 20, 1842, in *American and Foreign Anti-Slavery Reporter*, Sept. 1, 1842. On escapees returning south, see Harrold, "Romanticizing Slave Revolt," 90-91; A[bel] B[rown] to G. Smith, Oct. 1, 1843, in *AP*, Nov. 21, 1843; *PF*, Nov. 28, 1839. On masters' charges, see Aidt-Guy, "Persistent Maryland," 68-69; Berlin, *Slaves without Masters*, 95; *PF*, Oct. 21, 1847; Harrold, *Abolitionists and the South*, 153-56.

12. Dillon, *Slavery Attacked*, 182-83.

13. Marsh to [Editor], Aug. 24, 1843, in *Liberator*, Sept. 8, 1843 (1st quotation); *Emancipator*, Mar. 4, 1842 (2nd quotation); Blassingame, et al., eds., *Douglass Papers*, 1:21-22 (3rd quotation).

14. Garnet, *Walker's Appeal and Garnet's Address*, 89 (1st quotation); *Liberator*, June 30, 1843 (2nd quotation).

15. *Observer*, Feb. 19, 26, Mar. 5, 1842; *NYE*, Mar. 10, 1842; R. N. to [Greeley], Jan. 21, 1842, in *NYDT*, Jan. 25, 1842 (1st quotation); Weld to Weld, Jan. 30, 1842, in Barnes and Dumond, eds., *Weld-Grimke Letters*, 2:907 (2nd quotation); *Emancipator*, Feb. 24, 1842; *NYE*, Feb. 24, 1842 (3rd-4th quotations). Weld mistakenly believed that Alvan Stewart had written the Address to the Slaves.

16. Blanchard and Rice, *Debate on Slavery*, 286-87.

17. A minority of delegates at Peterboro had, of course, raised the earliest opposition to Smith's advice that slaves expropriate all they needed to escape. See chapter 2.

18. Smith to Oliver Johnson, Feb. 2, 1843, letter book copy, Alice Eliza Hamilton to Smith, Sept. 22, 1842, Smith Papers; Davis, *Leavitt*, 214-15; *Liberty Press*, quoted in *Emancipator*, June 1, 1843 (1st quotation); *Emancipator*, Feb. 11 (2nd quotation), 24 (3rd quo-

tation), 1842. See also Its First Public Advocate to Gamaliel Bailey, Mar. 16, 1842, in *Philanthropist*, Ap. 13, 1842.

19. Tappan to Smith, Feb. 7 (quotations), 25, 1842, Smith Papers. What little is known about Johnson is provided in Theodore Fiske Savage, *The Presbyterian Church in New York City* (New York: Presbytery of New York, 1949), 161; and Samuel D. Alexander, *The Presbytery of New York, 1738-1888* (New York: Randolph, 1888), 108. I thank Professor Hugh Davis of Southern Connecticut State University for directing me to these books.

20. *NYE*, Feb. 24 (1st-5th quotations), Mar. 10 (6th-7th quotations), 1842.

21. See also ibid., Mar. 10, Ap. 21, 28, 1842.

22. Ibid., Feb. 24, 1842 (1st-2nd quotations), July 27, 1843 (3rd quotation).

23. Ibid., Mar. 10 (1st-6th quotations), Ap. 21 (7th-10th quotations), 1842.

24. [Smith], *Address of the Peterboro State Convention to the Slaves and Its Vindication*, 17 (quotation); Wyatt-Brown, *Tappan*, 24-27; Mayer, *Garrison*, 219-20; Friedman, *Gregarious Saints*, 22, 46. On Channing and the abolitionists, see Mendelshon, *Channing*, 223-77.

25. Channing, *Works of William E. Channing*, 6:317, 419.

26. Ibid., 419 (1st quotation), 319 (2nd-6th quotations).

27. Ibid., 319 (1st-2nd quotations), 320, 321 (4th quotation), 322 (3rd quotation), 325.

28. Ibid., 321 (1st and 5th quotations), 325 (3rd, 4th, and 6th quotations), 326 (2nd quotation).

29. *Philanthropist*, Oct. 13, 1841, Feb. 9, Ap. 6, 1842.

30. Ibid., Feb. 9, 1842 (1st quotation); Chase to Thaddeus Stevens, Ap. 8, 1842, Stevens Papers; Brisbane to Bailey, n.d., in *Philanthropist*, Mar. 30, 1842 (2nd-3rd quotations).

31. *Philanthropist*, Feb. 9, 1842.

32. Johnson to [editor], Jan. 22, 1841[2], in *NASS*, Feb. 10, 1842 (1st quotation); Johnson to [Lydia Maria Child], Feb. 17, 1842, in *NASS*, Mar. 3, 1842 (2nd quotation). Joseph C. Hathaway joined Johnson in defense of Smith's Address at East Bloomfield. Later Hathaway became a radical political abolitionist.

33. *Liberator*, Feb. 1, 1843.

34. Executive Committee of the AASS to Fellow Citizens, Jan. 25, 1842, in *NASS*, Jan. 27, 1842. For a different perspective

on Child's reaction to the Williamsburg resolutions and Smith's address, see Karcher, *Child*, 281-83.

35. *NASS*, Feb. 24, 1842.

36. Ibid.

37. *NASS*, June 8, 1843; *Practical Christian*, quoted in *Liberator*, June 30, 1843; Benjamin Wymam to Garrison, June 15, 1843, in *Liberator*, June 23, 1843; *AP*, June 15, 1843 (quotation); Janney to J. Miller McKim, Dec. 1, 1843, Antislavery Papers; Mayer, *Garrison*, 320.

38. *Philanthropist*, June 14, 1843. See also *Spirit of Liberty*, June 24, 1843.

39. *NASS*, June 8, 1843 (1st quotation); *Tribune*, quoted in *NASS*, June 22, 1843 (2nd-4th quotations); *Practical Christian*, quoted in *Liberator*, June 30, 1843 (5th-9th quotations). See also MASS, *Twelfth Annual Report*, 32-33.

40. *Liberator*, June 23, 1843. On Portsmouth, see Grover, *Fugitive's Gibraltar*, 239, 241-42. David Lee Child declared that "the absorbing topic of discussion [at the New England Anti-Slavery Convention] was the position of the church and clergy, in relation to all projects of reform" and this became a theme of the Hundred Conventions that summer. See *NASS*, June 8, 1843.

41. Torrey, who must have seen copies of Douglass's and Remond's lost speeches, wrote that they "more than hinted at the possibility of a bloody end to slavery." See *AP*, June 15, 1843. On disunion, see Kraditor, *Means and Ends*, 196-201; MASS, *Twelfth Annual Report*, 81-86; Karcher, *Child*, 283-85.

42. *Herald of Freedom*, quoted in *Liberator*, Nov. 27, 1840; *NASS*, Feb. 24, 1842; Foster to Garrison, Aug. 22, 1851, Garrison Papers.

43. *Western New Yorker*, Oct. 18, Nov. 8, 1843, as quoted in Strong, *Perfectionist Politics*, 288 n. 22.

44. J. W. Alden to Joshua Leavitt, Aug. 29, 1843, in *Emancipator*, Aug. 31, 1843; [?] to Editors, Sept. 4, 1843, in *NYE*, Sept. 7, 1843 (1st quotation); *Emancipator*, Sept. 14, 1843 (2nd-3rd quotations). One report claims that there were 5,000 at an evening session and at the following morning session there were 2,500 men and 500 women. See *AP*, Sept. 5, 1843.

45. Merrill and Ruchames, eds., *Garrison Letters*, 3:197-227.

46. Remond to Esteemed Friend, Aug. 30, 1843, in *Liberator*, Sept. 22, 1843. At about the same time the *NASS* published a let-

ter from William Wells Brown pointing out that Garnet had falsely claimed that only Douglass and Remond had opposed the convention's endorsement of the Liberty Party. See Brown to Editor, Sept. 26, 1843, in *NASS*, Oct. 5, 1843.

47. Marsh to [editor], Aug. 24, 1843, in *Liberator*, Sept. 8, 1843.

48. *Liberator*, Sept. 22, 1843.

49. Garnet to Chapman, Nov. 17, 1843, in *Emancipator*, Nov. 30, 1843, in *Liberator*, Dec. 8, 1843.

50. On the Free Soil Party, see Blue, *Free Soilers*.

Chapter Five. Abolitionists and Slaves

1. Mullin, *Flight and Rebellion*, 111-15; Berlin, *Slaves without Masters*, 17-18; Drake, *Quakers and Slavery*, 74-75, 96, 119.

2. Rankin, "Letter on Slavery, #3," *Liberator*, Sept. 8, 1832; *Journal of Commerce*, quoted in *Emancipator*, July 13, 1833; *Emancipator*, July 29, Aug. 5, Nov. 4, 1834, May 5, 1836; *Reflector*, quoted in *Emancipator*, Nov. 14, 1839.

3. *Emancipator*, Mar. 17, 1842 (1st-2nd quotations), May 6 (3rd quotation), Ap. 8 (4th quotation), June 17 (5th quotation), 1846. Leavitt expressed surprise that the conservative *Observer* published the letter. In 1847 Leavitt noted that there were no laws against distributing Bibles to slaves in Delaware, Maryland, Virginia, Kentucky, Tennessee, and Missouri. See *AP*, June 16, 1847. On slave literacy, see Cornelius, *"When I Can Read My Title Clear."*

4. *Emancipator*, Ap. 8, May 6, June 17, 1846, Feb. 10, 1847; *American Missionary* 1 (June 1847): 58-59; Johnson, "American Missionary Association," 447-49; Harrold, *Abolitionists and the South*, 98-99. See also McKivigan, "Gospel Will Burst the Bonds of the Slave," 62-64, 77.

5. Nicholson, *Wesleyan Methodism in the South*, 8-52; Matlack, *History of American Slavery and Methodism*, esp. 358-62; *AP*, Dec. 29, 1847 (quotation); *American Missionary* 2 (Ap. 1848): 46-47, 3 (Nov. 1848): 7, 3 (July 1849): 76-77; AMA, *Second Annual Report* (1848), 76-77; AFASS, *Ninth Annual Report* (1849), 6-10.

6. McBride to Luther Lee, Aug. 2, 1851, in *True Wesleyan*, Aug. 16, 1851 (quotation); Harrold, *Abolitionists and the South*, 87-88, 98-99, 101; Johnson, "Abolitionist Missionary Activities in North Carolina," 295-320.

7. AMA, *Second Annual Report* (1848), 22-23; *American Missionary* 3 (Nov. 1848): 7; Fee to George Whipple, Mar. 8, 1849, AMA Archives; AMA, *Third Annual Report* (1849), 30 (1st quotation); AMA, *Fourth Annual Report* (1850), 38 (2nd quotation); AMA, *Sixth Annual Report* (1851), 44-46; AMA, *Seventh Annual Report* (1852), 60; AMA, *Thirteenth Annual Report* (1859), 58-61. See also Sears, *Kentucky Abolitionists in the Midst of Slavery.*

8. Harrold, *Abolitionists and the South*, 98-99.

9. Henry Bibb to Editors, May 21, 1847, in *Emancipator,* June 2, 1847; *NS,* Jan. 14, 1848 (1st-2nd quotations), June 8 (3rd quotation), 25, 1849.

10. AASS resolution quoted in Bibb to Editors, May 21, 1847, in *Emancipator,* June 2, 1847 (1st quotation); *NS,* Jan. 14, 1848 (2nd quotation). Douglass conceded that slaves who read the Bible would become "restless in their chains" (see *NS,* June 1, 1849). After he became a radical political abolitionist in 1851, Douglass derided the Garrisonian point of view by publishing extreme forms of it. Among them was a British Garrisonian's rejection of building schools for African Americans so long as slavery existed. See *Frederick Douglass' Paper,* Mar. 31, Ap. 7, 1854.

11. *Liberator,* June 1, 1849; Garnet to Douglass, June 10, [1849] (1st quotation) and Douglass's reply, in *NS,* June 25, 1849 (2nd quotation); McKivigan, "Gospel Will Burst the Bonds of the Slave," 63-64. By the mid-1850s, Garrisonians were praising antislavery missionaries. See Harrold, *Abolitionists and the South*, 104.

12. Fladeland, "Compensated Emancipation," 169-86.

13. Some of these Quakers were northern-born residents of Maryland. Others were from Pennsylvania. See Soderlund, *Quakers and Slavery*, 178; Graham, *Baltimore*, 63; Whitman, "Slavery, Manumission, and Free Black Workers in Early National Baltimore," 170-71; Torrey, *Portraiture of Domestic Slavery*, 76-77; Gara, *Liberty Line*, 71; Berlin, *Slaves without Masters*, 157. Richard S. Newman provides information on the Pennsylvania Abolition Society. See Newman, *Transformation of American Abolitionism*, 16-59.

14. Garrison and Garrison, *Garrison*, 1:151, 175-218. On continued purchases of freedom, see W[illiam] S[lade] to Editor of the *Emancipator,* Feb. 18, 1839, in *PF,* Mar. 14, 1839; David A. Hall to Julia Butler and her children, deed of manumission, Sept. 11, 1840, Slave Manumissions, 3:277.

15. *American Citizen,* Jan. 19, 1841; Sturge, *Visit to the United*

States, 114-16, Appendix K; Gerrit Smith to William Ellery Channing, Aug. 17, 1841, letter book copy, Smith Papers. Later in Kentucky, abolitionist John G. Fee found himself in a similar situation and reacted similarly. See Fee to Lewis Tappan, June 10, 1847, AMA Archives.

16. Smith to Gates, Mar. 19, 1842, letter book copy, Smith Papers (1st quotation); Smith to Myrtilla Miner, Jan. 10, 1848, Miner Papers (2nd quotation); Smith to Samuel Worthington, July 15, Aug. 25, 1841 (3rd quotation), Smith and Ann C. Smith to Samuel and Harriet Russell, Oct. 1, 1841, Smith to Nathaniel Crenshaw, Dec. 30, 1841, letter book copies, Smith Papers.

17. Fairbank, *Fairbank*, 26-34; Coleman, *Slavery Times in Kentucky*, 131-34.

18. [Chaplin to *AP*], Feb. 3, [1845], in Feb. 12, 1845; Chaplin to Charles A. Wheaton, Dec. 30, 1845, in *AP*, Jan. 7, 1847 (quotation; this is also in *Pennsylvania Freeman*, Jan. 22, 1846 and *Emancipator*, Jan. 28, 1846); W. L. C. to Gerrit Smith and Charles A. Wheaton, Feb. 15, 1848, in *AP*, Feb. 23, 1848; *AP*, Mar. 22, 1848. See also John Henry to Pat, Jan. 12, 1846, in *AP*, Jan. 21, 1846; W. L. C. [to *AP*], [Feb. 14, 1846], in *AP*, Feb. 25, 1846; W. L. C. to Charles A. Wheaton, Feb. 25, 1846, in *AP*, Mar. 4, 1846; Chaplin to Gerrit Smith, June 28, 1846, Smith Papers; J. B. W. [Jacob Bigelow] to Chaplin, Sept. 1846, in *AP*, Sept. 30, 1846; J. B. W. to [*Boston Daily Whig*], July 13, 1847, in *AP*, July 28, 1847.

19. *NE*, July 22, Aug. 12, Dec. 30, 1847; Abelard Guthrie to Arthur Tappan, Dec. 12, 22, 1847, Jan. 13, 1848, AMA Archives; E[zra] L. S[tevens] to Editor, Nov. 7, 1849, in *Ashtabula Sentinel*, Nov. 17, 1849.

20. Giddings to [Laura Waters Giddings], Jan. 23, 1848, Giddings Papers (1st quotation); E[zra] L. S[tevens] to [*Daily True Democrat* (Cleveland)], Jan. 24, 1848, in *True Democrat*, Feb. 1, 1848; Stevens to Editor, Nov. 7, 1849, in *Ashtabula Sentinel*, Nov. 17, 1849. W. L. C. to Gerrit Smith and Charles A. Wheaton, Feb. 15, 1848, in *AP*, Feb. 23, 1848 (2nd quotation).

21. *PF*, Jan. 16, 1845; *Ram's Horn*, quoted in *PF*, Dec. 6, 1849. Some nonabolitionist antislavery northerners also opposed purchasing freedom. See *New York Tribune*, quoted in *Frederick Douglass' Paper*, July 16, 1852.

22. *Liberator*, Jan. 8, 29, 1847; Increase Smith to Sir, Jan. 9, 1847, in *Liberator*, Jan. 15, 1847; *PF*, Jan. 28, 1847 (quotation); Henry

C. Wright to Frederick Douglass, Dec. 12, 1846, in *Liberator,* Jan. 29, 1847; *NS,* July 13, 1849.

23. *AP,* Dec. 16, 1848 (1st-5th quotations); Smith to Sarah Pugh, Ap. 14, 1847, in *AP,* Ap. 14, 1847 (6th-8th quotations); W. L. C. to Pat, n.d., in *AP,* Mar. 22, 1848 (9th quotation); *Anti-Slavery Reporter* 1, 3rd series (May 1, 1853): 114 (10th quotation). On Smith's emphasis on the primacy of emotion, see Stauffer, *Black Hearts of Men,* 17-18, 108.

24. Mullin, *Flight and Rebellion,* 113-15; Grover, *Fugitive's Gibraltar,* 67-93; Berlin, *Many Thousands Gone,* 282-83; Schwartz, *Migrants against Slavery,* 24-25; Celcelski, "Shores of Freedom," 174-206.

25. *PF,* Sept. 1, 1841; Smith, "Address to the Slaves," in *Liberator,* Feb. 11, 1842; Garrison, "Address to the Slaves," in *AP,* June 22, 1843; *NE,* Aug. 22, 1850; Dillon, *Slavery Attacked,* 206.

26. *Philanthropist,* Mar. 27, 1838; Gamaliel Bailey to James G. Birney, Oct. 28, 1838, in Dumond, ed., *Birney Letters,* 1:475-76; Volpe, *Forlorn Hope of Freedom,* 27-28; Finkelman, "Protection of Black Rights," 211-28; Seward, *Seward 1801 to 1872,* 1:428-29, 437-38, 463-65, 528-31; Harrold, *Abolitionists and the South,* 68; Harrold, "Romanticizing Slave Revolt," 89-107.

27. Harrold, *Subversives,* 64-93, 116-47; Brown, *Memoir,* 86-88. A young black man who was a friend of Gerrit Smith may also have gone south from New York to help slaves escape during the late 1830s. See Wellman, "James Watkins Seward."

28. *AP,* July 3, 1844; *Liberator,* July 26, 1844; Fairbank, *Fairbank,* 45-50; G. D. Jewett to [?], Nov. 4, 1844, in *Liberator,* Nov. 29, 1844; Mabee, *Black Freedom,* 282-83; Walker, *Trial and Imprisonment; Warren Liberty Herald,* Mar. 20, 1845; Harrold, *Abolitionists and the South,* 75.

29. Smallwood, *Narrative of Thomas Smallwood,* 18-39; William L. Chaplin to Gerrit Smith, Nov. 2, 11, 1848, Smith Papers. According to Smallwood, Torrey led slaves to Troy in August 1842.

30. Harrold, *Subversives,* 64-93; Wilson, *History of the Rise and Fall of the Slave Power,* 2:80.

31. Harrold, *Subversives,* 94-115, 127-29, 146-47, 154-55.

32. Chaplin to J. C. Jackson, Jan. 1, 1845, in *AP,* Jan. 8, 1845; *AP,* May 24, 1848; *NE,* Oct. 10, 1850.

33. *Liberator,* Aug. 9, 30, 1844; Blassingame, et al., eds., *Douglass Papers,* 1:116-17, 308-9, 2:118-20; *NS,* May 5, 1848.

34. *Liberator,* Aug. 9, Sept. 6, 1844, May 19, 1848; *PF,* Sept. 5, 1850; MASS, *Thirteenth Annual Report* (1845), 39-40, *Fourteenth Annual Report* (1846), 53-54, *Sixteenth Annual Report* (1848), 28 (quotation), *Seventeenth Annual Report* (1849), 41-42.

35. *Herald of Freedom,* quoted in *Liberator,* Nov. 27, 1840 (1st-2nd quotations); *NASS,* Feb. 24, 1842 (3rd quotation). Child noted that even if Smith's Address to the Slaves "should induce ten thousand slaves a year to run off," seventy thousand would be born during that period. Therefore, she calculated, increased escapes would have no impact beyond raising the market value of the slaves who remained.

36. *NASS,* Dec. 26, 1844 (quotations); *NS,* June 8, 1849. See also Abigail Kelley Foster to Garrison, Aug. 22, 1851, Garrison Papers.

37. Tappan to John W. Alden, July 8, 1844, letter book copy, Tappan Papers (1st-2nd quotations); Tappan to Gerrit Smith, Sept. 16, 1844, Smith Papers; Tappan to John Scoble, Nov. 9, 1844, in Abel and Klingberg, eds., *Side-Light on Anglo-American Relations,* 193-94; *NE,* May 25, 1848 (3rd quotation), Oct. 10, 1850.

38. *Boston Morning Chronicle,* quoted in *Cincinnati Weekly Herald and Philanthropist,* Ap. 23, 1845 (quotation); *Congressional Globe,* 30th Cong., 1 sess. (Ap. 20, 1848), 649-56.

39. *Philanthropist,* Oct. 13, 1841 (1st quotation); Torrey to Smith, Aug. 3, 1844, Smith Papers; *NE,* Ap. 20, 1848 (2nd-3rd quotations); Oct. 10, 1850; *Proceedings of the National Liberty Convention,* 45.

40. *Proceedings of the National Liberty Convention,* 47 (1st quotation), 8 (2nd quotation), 46 (3rd quotation). See also *AP,* May 24, 1848; *NE,* Aug. 15, Oct. 10 (4th quotation), 1850.

41. See, for example, Karcher, *Child,* 282-83.

42. Harrold, *Bailey,* 112-13; Davis, *Leavitt,* 221-25; Tappan to John W. Alden, July 8, 1844, letter book copy, Tappan Papers; Wyatt-Brown, *Tappan,* 281.

43. Kraditor, *Means and Ends,* 182-85; Harrold, *Bailey,* 149, 152-53; Sewell, *Ballots for Freedom,* 285-88, 339-42.

Chapter Six. Convergence

1. Garnet to Secretary, American Home Missionary Society (AHMS), July 25, 1843, Garnet to Lewis Tappan, Oct. 2, 1843,

AMA Archives; Pasternak, *Garnet*, 41-42, 67-79; Mabee, *Black Freedom*, 391 n. 26. Garnet's motive for working for the AHMS was financial.

2. [William C. Nell], "The Colored Convention," *NS*, Dec. 3, 1847 (1st quotation); *Proceedings of the National Convention of Colored People and Their Friends*, 14-15, [31] (2nd quotation).

3. *NS*, May 5, 1848; Garnet, *Walker's Appeal and Garnet's Address*, viii.

4. Garnet, ibid., vi.

5. Shortly after the *Pearl* sailed, black Garrisonian William C. Nell praised the underground railroad work of Charles T. Torrey, Isaac T. Hopper, and David Ruggles. See *NS*, Ap. 14, 1848; "Report of the Proceedings," 14, in Bell, ed., *Minutes and Proceedings of the National Negro Conventions*.

6. *Minutes and Addresses of the State Convention of the Colored Citizens of Ohio*, 18. Whether or not the delegates adopted this resolution is not clear. See also Quarles, *Black Abolitionists*, 227-28, 290 n. 10. During the summer of 1849, the *Ram's Horn*, a black weekly published in New York City, paraphrased Garnet's call for slaves to strike. See Aptheker, ed., *Documentary History of the Negro People*, 1:290-91.

7. *Liberator*, May 19, 1848; *PF*, Dec. 6, 1849.

8. *NS*, June 23, 1848; *Proceedings of the National Liberty Convention*, 10-13.

9. *NS*, July 27, 1849 (1st-2nd quotations); [Garnet to Douglass] Aug. 31, [1849], in *NS*, Sept. 7, 1849 (succeeding quotations).

10. Bruce, *Violence and Culture in the Antebellum South*, 158-59; Levine, *Martin Delany, Frederick Douglass, and the Politics of Representative Identity*, 28 (1st quotation); *Liberator*, June 9, 1848 (2nd quotation).

11. "Great Anti-Colonization Mass Meeting of the Coloured Citizens of the State of New York," Ap. 22, 1849, in *NASS*, May 3, 1849.

12. Ellis Grey Loring to William Lloyd Garrison, June 28, 1847, in *Liberator*, July 9, 1847 (quotation); Pease and Pease, *They Who Would Be Free*, 237.

13. On the Free Soil Party and abolitionists, see *Radical Abolitionist*, 1 (Oct. 1855): 17-20; AFASS, [Ninth] *Annual Report* (1850), 11, 154-55; Wyatt-Brown, *Tappan*, 280-81; McKivigan, *War against Proslavery Religion*, 157-58. On the confluence of Garrisonians and

radical political abolitionists during the 1850s, see MASS, *Eighteenth Annual Report* (1850), 40-42; Gerrit Smith to William Lloyd Garrison, May 6, 1852, letter book copy, Smith Papers; Garrison to Samuel Joseph May, Sept. 23, 1853, Oct. 26, 1855, in Merrill and Ruchames, eds., *Garrison Letters*, 4: 256, 349; *Frederick Douglass' Paper*, May 13, 1852; *NASS*, Sept. 19, 1857.

14. *Liberator*, Sept. 20, 1850; Stewart, *Holy Warriors*, 157.

15. Pease and Pease portray the new fugitive slave law as influencing the Cazenovia Convention. They also contend that violent rhetoric, but not violence itself, increased among black and white abolitionists. See Pease and Pease, *They Who Would Be Free*, 239-40, 247-48, 250.

16. Sewell, *Ballots for Freedom*, 285-89; Humphries, "'Agitate! Agitate! Agitate!,'" 9, 14; John Thomas to Smith, Aug. 2, 1850, Smith Papers.

17. On Smith's feminist views, see Stauffer, *Black Hearts of Men*, 208-18.

18. Smith to May, Aug. 4, 1850, Smith to Beriah Green, Aug. 11, 1850, Smith to William L. Chaplin, Aug. 11, 1850, letter book copies, Smith Papers; Harrold, *Subversives*, 99-101; *Utica Daily Gazette*, Aug. 22, 1850.

19. See *NE*, Aug. 15, Oct. 10, 1850.

20. Harrold, *Subversives*, 146-47, 156; *New York Daily Tribune*, Aug. 24, 26 (quotation), 1850; *Liberator*, Sept. 20, 1850.

21. *Utica Daily Gazette*, Aug. 22, 24, 1850; George W. Clark to Editors, Aug. 25, 1850, in *NYDT*, Aug. 30, 1850; *NS*, Sept. 5, 1850. Hugh C. Humphries, who has thoroughly studied the convention, dismisses a local paper's estimate that the crowd was much smaller. See Humphries, "'Agitate! Agitate! Agitate!,'" 19.

22. Hunter, *Loguen*, 151-57, 165-69; Mathews to [Editor], n.d., in *American Baptist*, Aug. 29, 1850 (quotation); Harrold, *Abolitionists and the South*, 88, 97, 99; *NS*, Sept. 5, 1850; Humphries, "'Agitate! Agitate! Agitate!,'" 18-19.

23. *NS*, Sept. 5, 1850; Humphries, "'Agitate! Agitate! Agitate!,'" 45 (1st-2nd quotations); Clark to Editor, Aug. 24, 1850, in *NYDT*, Aug. 30, 1850 (3rd quotation); [Clark], *Free Soil Minstrel*, 104-6 (4th quotation).

24. *New Englander*, quoted in *Liberator*, Sept. 27, 1850.

25. *Utica Daily Gazette*, Aug. 22, 1850; James C. Jackson, "Circular from the Chaplin fund Committee," Aug. 22, 1850, in *NS*, Sept.

5, 1850; *NYDT,* Aug. 23, 24, 1850; *Madison County Whig,* Aug. 28, 1850, quoted in Humphries, "'Agitate! Agitate! Agitate!,'" 27-28 (quotations); Julia Griffiths to Mrs. Howitt, n.d., in *NS,* Sept. 5, 1850.

26. *NYDT,* Aug. 23, 25, 1850. On women in the Liberty Party, see Jeffrey, *Great Silent Army,* 164-65, 168-69.

27. Ibid, Aug. 23, 1850; *NS,* Sept. 5, 1850 (quotation).

28. *NYDT,* Aug. 24, 1850; *Utica Daily Gazette,* Aug. 24, 1850.

29. *NS,* Sept. 5, 1850; *Madison County Whig,* Aug. 28, 1850 (quotation), quoted in Humphries, "'Agitate! Agitate! Agitate!,'" 29.

30. Ambiguity emerges immediately after these passages concerning slave revolt and northern black assistance in it. The letter declares, "We tell you these things not to encourage, or justify, your resort to physical force" (see p. 192).

31. On enforcement of the Fugitive Slave Law, see Campbell, *Slave Catchers,* 110-85.

32. *Madison County Whig,* Aug. 28, 1850 (1st quotation), quoted in Humphries, "'Agitate! Agitate! Agitate!,'" 21; Mathews to Mr. Walker, n.d., in *American Baptist,* Aug. 29, 1850 (2nd quotation). Mathews went on to say, "I will not, however, disguise the fact that a portion of the Convention are not peace men."

33. *NYDT,* Aug. 23, 1850 (1st quotation); *Madison County Whig,* Aug. 28, 1850 (2nd quotation), quoted in Humphries, "'Agitate! Agitate! Agitate!,'" 22.

34. Friedman, *Gregarious Saints,* 196-224; *NASS,* Aug. 29, Sept. 5, 1850; *Liberator,* Sept. 13, 1850; *PF,* Aug. 29, 1850. See also Silas Cornell to Gerrit Smith, Sept. 2, 1850, Smith Papers.

35. *Buffalo Morning Express,* Aug. 28, 1850, quoted in Humphries, "'Agitate! Agitate! Agitate!,'" 31 (1st quotation); *Utica Daily Gazette,* Aug. 26, 1850; *New York Observer,* quoted in *Liberator,* Sept. 20, 1850 (2nd quotation); *NYDT,* Aug. 26, 1850 (3rd quotation). Garrison placed the *Observer* article in his "Refuge of Oppression" column, which he dedicated to proslavery articles.

36. *Liberator,* Aug. 30, 1850; Humphries, "'Agitate! Agitate! Agitate!,'" 36. A similar account of Yulee's remarks, published in the *NE,* Oct. 10, 1850, describes him as using the Cazenovia Convention as evidence that a new fugitive slave law would have no effect. The newspapers Humphries cites are the *Southern Press* (Washington) and the *Columbus* [Georgia] *Times.*

37. "Mr. J. C. Hathaway's account of his visit to Wm. L. Chaplin," in *American Baptist,* Aug. 29, 1850.

38. On the ties of John Brown to Gerrit Smith and the radical political abolitionists, see Stauffer, *Black Hearts of Men*, 1-44, 134-81.

39. On the enforcement of and resistance to the Fugitive Slave Law of 1850, see Brandt, *Town that Started the Civil War*; Campbell, *Slave Catchers*, 110-69, 199-207; Grimsted, *American Mobbing*, 33-84; Slaughter, *Bloody Dawn*. On the law's role in refocusing abolitionists on the North, see *Frederick Douglass' Paper*, June 20, 1851, Dec. 25, 1851, Jan. 8, 1852.

Conclusion

1. *Liberator*, Feb. 13, 1857 (1st quotation), Aug. 13, 1858 (2nd quotation); *NASS*, Aug. 7, 1858.

2. *Frederick Douglass' Paper*, Nov. 5, 1852.

3. Thompson, "Tubman," 1-21; Campbell, *Slave Catchers*, 148-69; Grimsted, *American Mobbing*, 33-84; Brandt, *Town that Started the Civil War*; Sernett, *North Star Country*, 162-94; Stewart, *Holy Warriors*, 157-58.

4. Boyer, *Brown*, 436-37.

5. James McCune Smith claimed in 1865 that Brown published Garnet's Address, but there is no contemporary verification. Several historians credit Smith's claim, but Brown biographer Stephen Oates writes, "maybe this is true and maybe it is not." See Garnet, *Memorial Discourse*, 52; Oates, *Brown*, 61; Boyer, *Brown*, 78, 436-37 (quotation); Aptheker, *To Be Free*, 204; Schor, *Garnet*, 60-61.

6. Boyer, *Brown*, 359, 366. Oates indicates that they met, but does not say when. See Oates, *Brown*, 61. David E. Swift emphasizes the impact Garnet may have had on Brown. See Swift, *Black Prophets of Justice*, 137.

7. Stauffer, *Black Hearts of Men*, 196-72; Douglass, *Autobiographies*, 715-19.

8. Redpath, *Roving Editor*, 46, 119 (1st-2nd quotations), 121, 122n, xv (3rd quotation), xxiv–xxv, 86 (4th quotation).

9. Oates, *Brown*, 224-52; Dillon, *Slavery Attacked*, 232-37; Boyer, *Brown*, 8.

10. James M. McPherson, "Who Freed the Slaves," 1-2.

11. Davis and Mintz, eds., *The Boisterous Sea of Liberty*, 520-22.

12. *Douglass Monthly* (Mar. 1863): 802.

13. Dillon, *Slavery Attacked*, 243-48; Friedman, *Gregarious Saints*, 220; Swift, *Black Prophets of Justice*, 139.

14. Kraditor, *Means and Ends*, 141-43, 157-68. Alan M. Kraut summarizes the disdain expressed by historians for the Liberty Party. See Kraut, "Partisanship and Principles," 72-73. The best account of abolitionist isolation is Friedman, *Gregarious Saints*.

15. Dillon, *Slavery Attacked*, 201-42; DeBoer, *Be Jubilant My Feet*; Goodman, *Of One Blood*; McKivigan, "Frederick Douglass-Gerrit Smith Friendship"; Stauffer, *Black Hearts of Men*.

BIBLIOGRAPHY

Manuscripts

American Missionary Association Archives. Amistad Research Center. Tulane University. New Orleans.
Antislavery Papers. Cornell University Library. Ithaca, N.Y.
Chase, Salmon P., Papers. Library of Congress.
Garrison, William Lloyd, Papers. Boston Public Library.
Giddings, Joshua R., Papers. Ohio Historical Society. Columbus, Ohio.
Miner, Myrtilla, Papers. Library of Congress.
"Minutes of the New York State Liberty Party Convention, January 19 and 20, 1842." New York Historical Society. New York.
Quaker Manuscript Collection. Haverford College. Haverford, Pa.
Slave Manumissions. Record Group 21. National Archives.
Smith, Gerrit, Papers. Syracuse University. Syracuse, N.Y.
Stevens, Thaddeus, Papers. Library of Congress.
Tappan, Lewis, Papers. Library of Congress.

Newspapers and Periodicals

Albany Patriot (Albany, N.Y.), 1843–1848.
American and Foreign Anti-Slavery Reporter (New York), 1 Sept. 1842.
American Baptist (Utica, N.Y.), 29 Aug. 1850.
American Citizen (Rochester, N.Y.), 19 Jan. 1841.
American Missionary (New York), 1848–1849.
Anti-Slavery Reporter (London), 1835, 1853.
Ashtabula Sentinel (Jefferson, Ohio), 17 Nov. 1849.
Cincinnati Weekly Herald and Philanthropist, 23 Ap. 1845.

Colored American (New York), 1838–1840.
Daily Albany Argus (Albany, N.Y.), 1842–1843.
Douglass Monthly (Rochester, N.Y.), Mar. 1863.
Emancipator (New York and Boston), 1833–1848.
Frederick Douglass' Paper (Rochester, N.Y.), 1852.
Freedom's Journal (New York), 1827.
Friend of Man (Utica, N.Y.), 17 Oct. 1838.
Genius of Universal Emancipation (Baltimore), 1830.
Globe (Washington, D.C.), 17 Feb. 1842.
Liberator (Boston), 1831–1857.
Liberty Press (Utica, N.Y.), 1843.
National Anti-Slavery Standard (New York), 1840–1858.
National Era (Washington, D.C.), 1847–1850.
New York Daily Tribune, 1842–1850.
New York Evangelist, 1836–1843.
New York Observer, 1842.
North Star (Rochester, N.Y.), 1847–1850.
Oberlin Evangelist (Oberlin, Ohio), 18 Aug. 1858.
Pennsylvania Freeman (Philadelphia), 1839–1850.
Philanthropist (Cincinnati), 1838–1842.
Provincial Freeman (Toronto), 1855.
Radical Abolitionist (New York), 1855–1857.
Spirit of Liberty (Pittsburgh), 24 June 1843.
True Democrat (Cleveland), 1 Feb. 1848.
True Wesleyan (New York), 16 Aug. 1851.
Utica Daily Gazette (Utica, N.Y.), 1850.
Warren Liberty Herald (Warren, Ohio), 20 Mar. 1845.
Weekly Anglo-African (New York), 14 Mar. 1863.

Other Published Primary Sources

Abel, Annie H., and Frank J. Klingberg, eds. *A Side-Light on Anglo-American Relations, 1839–1850; Furnished by the Correspondence of Lewis Tappan and Others with the British and Foreign Anti-Slavery Society*. Lancaster, Pa.: Association for the Study of Negro Life and History, 1927.

American and Foreign Anti-Slavery Society. *Annual Reports*. New York: AFASS, 1849–1850.

American Anti-Slavery Society. *Second Annual Report*. New York: AASS, 1835.

American Missionary Association. *Annual Reports*. New York: AMA, 1848–1859.

Aptheker, Herbert, ed. *A Documentary History of the Negro People in the United States*. 5th ed. 2 vols. New York: Citadel, 1968.

———. *"One Continual Cry": David Walker's Appeal to the Colored Citizens of the World*. New York: Humanities, 1965.

———. *To Be Free: Pioneering Studies in Afro-American History*. New York: Citadel, 1991.

Barnes, Gilbert H., and Dwight L. Dumond, eds. *The Letters of Theodore Dwight Weld, Angelina Grimke Weld, and Sarah Grimke, 1822–1844*. 2 vols. 1934. Reprint, Gloucester, Ma.: Peter Smith, 1965.

Bell, Howard M. *Minutes and Proceedings of the National Negro Conventions, 1830–1864*. New York: Arno, 1969.

Blanchard, J., and N. L. Rice. *A Debate on Slavery Held in the City of Cincinnati, on the First, Second, Third, and Sixth of October, 1845*. 1846. Reprint, New York: Negro Universities Press, 1969.

Blassingame, John W., et al., eds. *The Frederick Douglass Papers, Series One*. 4 vols. New Haven: Yale University Press, 1979–86.

Brown, C. S. *Memoir of Rev. Abel Brown by His Companion*. Worcester, Ma.: C. S. Brown, 1849.

Channing, William Ellery. *The Works of William E. Channing, D.D.* 13th ed. 6 vols. New York: C. S. Francis, 1854.

[Clark, George W.] *The Free Soil Minstrel*. New York: Martyn and Ely, 1848.

Congressional Globe, 30th Cong., 1st sess. 20 Ap. 1848, 649-56.

Correspondence between the Hon. F. H. Elmore, One of the South Carolina Delegates in Congress, and J. G. Birney, One of the Secretaries of the American Anti-Slavery Society. New York: American Anti-Slavery Society, 1838.

Davis, David Bryon, and Steven Mintz, eds. *The Boisterous Sea of Liberty: A Documentary History of America from Discovery through the Civil War*. New York: Oxford University Press, 1998.

Douglass, Frederick. *Autobiographies: Narrative of the Life of Frederick Douglass, An American Slave, My Bondage and My Freedom, Life and Times of Frederick Douglass*. New York: Library of America, 1994.

———. *Life and Times of Frederick Douglass, Written by Himself*. Rev. ed. Boston: DeWolfe, Fisk, 1892.

Dumond, Dwight L., ed. *The Letters of James G. Birney.* 2 vols. New York: Appleton-Century, 1938.

Eaklor, Vicki L., ed. *American Antislavery Songs: A Collection and Analysis.* New York: Greenwood, 1988.

Fairbank, Calvin. *Rev. Calvin Fairbank during Slavery Times.* 1890. Reprint, New York: Negro Universities Press, 1969.

Garnet, Henry Highland. *Memorial Discourse, by Rev. Henry Highland Garnet, Delivered in the Hall of the House of Representatives, Washington City, D.C. on Sabbath, February 12, 1865, with an Introduction by James McCune Smith.* Philadelphia: Joseph M. Wilson, 1865.

———. *Walker's Appeal, with a Brief Sketch of His Life by Henry Highland Garnet. And also Garnet's Address to the Slaves of the United States of America.* New York: [Garnet], 1848.

Garrison, William Lloyd. *Address Delivered before the Free People of Color, in Philadelphia, New-York, and Other Cities, during the Month of June, 1831.* 3rd ed. Boston: Stephen Foster, 1831.

———. "Address to the Slaves of the United States." *Liberator,* 2 June 1843; *Albany Patriot,* 22 June 1843.

Grimke, Angelina. *An Appeal to the Christian Women of the South.* New York: American Anti-Slavery Society, 1836.

———. *An Appeal to the Women of the Nominally Free States, Issued by an Anti-Slavery Convention of American Women.* New York: Dorr, 1837.

[Jay, William]. *Address to the Non-Slaveholders of the South, on the Social and Political Evils of Slavery.* New York: S. W. Benedict, 1843.

Lowance, Mason, ed. *Against Slavery: An Abolitionist Reader.* New York: Penguin, 2000.

Marsh, Luther Rawson. *The Writings and Speeches of Alvan Stewart on Slavery.* 1860. Reprint, New York: Negro Universities Press, 1969.

Massachusetts Anti-Slavery Society. *Annual Reports.* 1835–1856. Reprint, Westport, Ct.: Negro Universities Press, 1970.

Merrill, Walter M., and Louis Ruchames, eds. *The Letters of William Lloyd Garrison.* 4 vols. Cambridge, Ma.: Harvard University Press, 1971–1975.

Minutes and Addresses of the State Convention of the Colored Citizens of Ohio, Convened at Columbus, January 10, 11, 12, and 13, 1849. Oberlin, Ohio: privately printed, 1849.

Minutes of the National Convention of Colored Citizens, Held at Buffalo, on the 15th, 16th, 17th, 18th and 19th of August, 1843. New York: Pieroy and Reed Printers, 1843.

Ohio Anti-Slavery Society. *Report of the 3rd Anniversary.* Cincinnati: OASS, 1838.

Pease, William, and Jane Pease, eds. *The Antislavery Argument.* Indianapolis: Bobbs-Merrill, 1965.

Proceedings of the National Convention of Colored People and Their Friends, Held in Troy, N.Y. on the 6th, 7th, 8th, and 9th October, 1847. Troy, N.Y.: privately printed, 1847.

Proceedings of the National Liberty Convention, Held at Buffalo, N.Y., June 14th and 15th, 1848. Utica: S. W. Green, 1848.

Redpath, James. *The Roving Editor, or Talks with Slaves in the Southern States.* Edited by John R. McKivigan. University Park: Pennsylvania State University Press, 1996.

Ripley, C. Peter, et al., eds. *The Black Abolitionist Papers.* 5 vols. Chapel Hill: University of North Carolina Press, 1985–1992.

Ruchames, Louis, ed. *The Abolitionists: A Collection of Their Writings.* New York: G. P. Putnam's, 1960.

Sanborn, Franklin B., ed. *The Life and Letters of John Brown, Liberator of Kansas, and Martyr of Virginia.* 1885. Reprint, New York: Negro Universities Press, 1969.

Smallwood, Thomas. *A Narrative of Thomas Smallwood (Colored Man).* Toronto: James Stephens, 1851.

Smith, Gerrit. "Address of the Anti-Slavery Convention of the State of New-York, Held in Peterboro', January 19th, 1842, to the Slaves in the U. States of America." *Liberator,* 11 Feb. 1842.

———. *Address of the Peterboro State Convention to the Slaves and Its Vindication.* Cazenovia, N.Y.: R. L. Myrick Printer, 1842.

———. *Letter of Gerrit Smith to Rev. James Smylie of the State of Mississippi.* New York: American Anti-Slavery Society, 1837.

Stanton, Elizabeth Cady. *Eighty Years and More (1815–1897) Reminiscences.* 1898. Reprint, New York: Source Book Press, 1970.

Stanton, Henry B. *Random Recollections.* 3rd ed. New York: Harper and Brothers, 1887.

Sturge, Joseph A. *A Visit to the United States in 1841.* London: Hamilton, 1842.

Torrey, Jesse, Jr. *Portraiture of Domestic Slavery in the U.S.* 2nd ed. Ballston, Pa.: Torrey, 1818.

Walker, Jonathan. *Trial and Imprisonment of Jonathan Walker.* 2nd ed. 1848. Reprint, New York: Negro Universities Press, 1970.

Whittier, John G. *The Conflict with Slavery, Politics, and Reform: The Inner Life.* New York: Houghton Mifflin, 1889.

Woolman, John. "Considerations on the Keeping of Negroes." In *Works of John Woolman.* Philadelphia: Joseph Crukshank, 1774.

Secondary Sources

Abzug, Robert H. *Cosmos Crumbling: American Reform and the Religious Imagination.* New York: Oxford University Press, 1994.

———. "The Influence of Garrisonian Abolitionists' Fear of Slave Violence and the Antislavery Argument, 1829–1840." *Journal of Negro History* 55 (Jan. 1970): 15-28.

Aidt-Guy, Anita Louise. "Persistent Maryland: Antislavery Activity between 1850 and 1864." Ph.D. diss., Georgetown University, 1994.

Aptheker, Herbert. "Militant Abolitionism." *Journal of Negro History* 26 (Oct. 1941): 438-84.

Bacon, Jacqueline. *The Humblest May Stand Forth: Rhetoric, Empowerment, and Abolition.* Columbia: University of South Carolina Press, 2002.

Barnes, Gilbert H. *The Antislavery Impulse.* 1933. Reprint, Gloucester, Ma.: Peter Smith, 1973.

Bay, Mia. *The White Image in the Black Mind: African-American Ideas about White People, 1830–1925.* New York: Oxford University Press, 2000.

Bell, Howard Holman. *A Survey of the Negro Convention Movement, 1830–1861.* New York: Arno, 1969.

Berlin, Ira. *Many Thousands Gone: The First Two Centuries of Slavery in North America.* Cambridge, Ma.: Harvard University Press, 1998.

———. *Slaves without Masters: The Free Negro in the Antebellum South.* New York: Random House, 1974.

Blight, David W. "Perceptions of Southern Intransigence and the Rise of Radical Antislavery Thought, 1816–1830." *Journal of the Early Republic* 3 (Summer 1983): 139-63.

Blue, Frederick J. *The Free Soilers: Third Party Politics, 1848–1850.* Urbana: University of Illinois Press, 1973.

Boyer, Richard O. *The Legend of John Brown: A Biography and a History.* New York: Knopf, 1973.

Brandt, Nat. *The Town that Started the Civil War.* Syracuse, N.Y.: Syracuse University Press, 1990.

Brown, Richard H. "The Missouri Crisis, Slavery, and the Politics of Jacksonianism." *South Atlantic Quarterly* 65 (Winter 1966): 52-72.

Browne, Stephen H. *Angelina Grimke: Rhetoric, Identity, and the Radical Imagination.* East Lansing: Michigan State University Press, 1999.

Bruce, Dixon D., Jr. *Violence and Culture in the Antebellum South.* Austin: University of Texas Press, 1979.

Campbell, Stanley W. *The Slave Catchers: Enforcement of the Fugitive Slave Law, 1850–1860.* Chapel Hill: University of North Carolina Press, 1968.

Celcelski, David S. "The Shores of Freedom: The Maritime Underground Railroad in North Carolina, 1800–1861." *North Carolina Historical Review* 71 (Ap. 1994): 174-206.

Coleman, J. Winston. *Slavery Times in Kentucky.* Chapel Hill: University of North Carolina Press, 1940.

Cornelius, Janet Duitsman. *"When I Can Read My Title Clear": Literacy, Slavery, and Religion in the Antebellum South.* Columbia: University of South Carolina Press, 1991.

Cott, Nancy E. *The Bonds of Womanhood: "Women's Sphere" in New England, 1780–1835.* New Haven: Yale University Press, 1977.

Davis, Hugh. *Joshua Leavitt: Evangelical Abolitionist.* Baton Rouge: Louisiana State University Press, 1990.

Dawley, Alan. *Class and Community: The Industrial Revolution in Lynn.* Cambridge, Ma.: Harvard University Press, 1976.

DeBoer, Clara Merritt. *Be Jubilant My Feet: African American Abolitionists in the American Missionary Association, 1839–1868.* New York: Garland, 1994.

Dillon, Merton L. *Abolitionists: The Growth of a Dissenting Minority.* New York: Norton, 1974.

———. *Benjamin Lundy and the Struggle for Negro Freedom.* Urbana: University of Illinois Press, 1966.

———. *Slavery Attacked: Southern Slaves and Their Allies, 1619–1865.* Baton Rouge: Louisiana State University Press, 1990.

Drake, Thomas E. *Quakers and Slavery in America.* New Haven: Yale University Press, 1950.

Dumond, Dwight L. *Antislavery: The Crusade for Freedom in America.* Ann Arbor: University of Michigan Press, 1961.

Essig, James D. *The Bonds of Wickedness: American Evangelicals against Slavery, 1770–1808*. Philadelphia: Temple University Press, 1982.

Farrison, William. *William Wells Brown: Author and Reformer.* Chicago: University of Chicago Press, 1969.

———. "William Wells Brown in Buffalo." *Journal of Negro History* 39 (Oct. 1954): 298-314.

Fehrenbacher, Don E. *The Slaveholding Republic: An Account of the United States' Government's Relations to Slavery*. Edited by Ward M. McAfee. New York: Oxford University Press, 2001.

Finkelman, Paul. "The Protection of Black Rights in Seward's New York." *Civil War History* 34 (Sept. 1988): 211-28.

Fladeland, Betty L. "Compensated Emancipation: A Rejected Alternative." *Journal of Southern History* 42 (Feb. 1976): 169-86.

Floan, Howard R. *The South in Northern Eyes, 1831–1861*. Austin: University of Texas Press, 1958.

Fogel, Robert W. *Without Consent or Contract: The Rise and Fall of American Slavery*. New York: Norton, 1989.

Fox, Early Lee. *The American Colonization Society, 1817–1840*. Baltimore: Johns Hopkins Press, 1919.

Fredrickson, George M. *The Black Image in the White Mind: The Debate on Afro-American Character and Destiny, 1817–1914*. New York: Harper and Row, 1971.

Freehling, William W. *The Road to Disunion: Secessionists at Bay, 1776–1854*. New York: Oxford University Press, 1990.

Friedman, Lawrence J. *Gregarious Saints: Self and Community in American Abolitionism, 1830–1870*. New York: Cambridge University Press, 1982.

Frothingham, Octavius Brooks. *Gerrit Smith: A Biography*. 1878. Reprint, Negro Universities Press, 1969.

Gara, Larry. *The Liberty Line: The Legend of the Underground Railroad*. Lexington: University of Kentucky Press, 1961.

Garrison, Wendell Phillips, and Francis Jackson Garrison. *William Lloyd Garrison, 1805–1899: The Story of His Life Told by His Children*. 4 vols. New York: Century, 1885–89.

Genovese, Eugene D. *From Rebellion to Revolution: Afro-American Slave Revolts in the Making of the Modern World*. Baton Rouge: Louisiana State University Press, 1979.

Goldman, Mark. *High Hopes: The Rise and Decline of Buffalo, New York*. Albany: State University of New York Press, 1983.

Goodman, Paul. *Of One Blood: Abolitionism and the Origins of Racial Equality.* Berkeley: University of California Press, 1998.

Gould, Stephen Jay. *The Mismeasure of Man.* New York: Norton, 1981.

Graf, Hildegarde F. "Abolition and Anti-Slavery in Buffalo and Erie County." Master's thesis, University of Buffalo, 1939.

Graham, Leroy. *Baltimore: Nineteenth Century Black Capital.* Washington: University Press of America, 1982.

Grimsted, David. *American Mobbing, 1828–1861: Toward Civil War.* New York: Oxford University Press, 1998.

Grover, Kathryn. *The Fugitive's Gibraltar: Escaping Slaves and Abolitionism in New Bedford, Massachusetts.* Amherst: University of Massachusetts Press, 2001.

Harlow, Ralph V. *Gerrit Smith: Philanthropist and Reformer.* New York: Holt, 1939.

Harper, Phillip Brian. *Are We Not Men?: Masculine Anxiety and the Problem of African-American Identity.* New York: Oxford University Press, 1996.

Harrold, Stanley. *The Abolitionists and the South, 1831–1865.* Lexington: University Press of Kentucky, 1995.

———. *American Abolitionists.* Harlow, U.K.: Longman, 2001.

———. *Gamaliel Bailey and Antislavery Union.* Kent, Oh.: Kent State University Press, 1986.

———. "Romanticizing Slave Revolt: Madison Washington, the *Creole* Mutiny, and Abolitionist Celebration of Violent Means." In *Antislavery Violence: Sectional, Racial, and Cultural Conflict in Antebellum America*, edited by John R. McKivigan and Stanley Harrold, 108-27. Knoxville: University of Tennessee Press, 1999.

———. *Subversives: Antislavery Community in Washington, D.C., 1828–1865.* Baton Rouge: Louisiana State University Press, 2003.

Hart, Albert Bushnell. *Slavery and Abolition, 1831–1841.* 1906. Reprint, New York: New American Library, 1969.

Hinks, Peter P. *Awaken My Afflicted Brethren: David Walker and the Problem of Antebellum Slave Resistance.* University Park: Pennsylvania State University Press, 1997.

Horton, James Oliver, and Lois E. Horton. "The Affirmation of Manhood: Black Garrisonians in Antebellum Boston." In *Courage and Conscience: Black and White Abolitionists in Boston,* edited by Donald M. Jacobs, 127-54. Bloomington: Indiana University Press, 1993.

———. *In Hope of Liberty: Culture, Community and Protest among Northern Free Blacks, 1700–1860.* New York: Oxford University Press, 1997.

Humphries, Hugh C. "'Agitate! Agitate! Agitate!': The Great Fugitive Slave Law Convention and Its Rare Daguerreotype." *Madison County Heritage* 19 (1994): 3-64.

Hunt, Alfred N. *Haiti's Influence on Antebellum America: Slumbering Volcano in the Caribbean.* Baton Rouge: Louisiana State University Press, 1988.

Hunter, Carol M. *To Set the Captive Free: Reverend Jermain Wesley Loguen and the Struggle for Freedom in Central New York, 1835–1872.* New York: Garland, 1989.

Huston, James L. *Securing the Fruits of Labor: The American Concept of Wealth Distribution, 1765–1900.* Baton Rouge: Louisiana State University Press, 1998.

Jeffrey, Julie Roy. *The Great Silent Army of Abolitionism: Ordinary Women in the Antislavery Movement.* Chapel Hill: University of North Carolina Press, 1998.

Johnson, Clifton H. "Abolitionist Missionary Activities in North Carolina." *North Carolina Historical Review* 40 (July 1863): 295-320.

———. "The American Missionary Association, 1846–1861: A Study of Christian Abolitionism." Ph.D. diss., University of North Carolina, 1958.

Johnson, Oliver. *William Lloyd Garrison and His Times: Or Sketches of the Anti-Slavery Movement in America.* 1881. Reprint, Miami: Mnemosyne, 1969.

Johnson, Paul. *A Shop Keeper's Millennium: Society and Revivals in Rochester, New York, 1815–1837.* New York: Hill and Wang, 1978.

Jones, Howard. *Mutiny on the* Amistad: *The Saga of a Slave Revolt and Its Impact on American Abolition, Law, and Diplomacy.* New York: Oxford University Press, 1987.

———. "The Peculiar Institution and National Honor: The Case of the *Creole* Slave Revolt." *Civil War History* 21 (Mar. 1975): 28-50.

Karcher, Carolyn L. *The First Woman of the Republic: A Cultural Biography of Lydia Maria Child.* Durham, N.C.: Duke University Press, 1994.

Kerber, Linda K. "The Paradox of Women's Citizenship in the Early Republic: The Case of *Martin vs. Massachusetts*, 1805." *American Historical Review* 97 (Ap. 1992): 349-78.

Kraditor, Eileen. *Means and Ends in American Abolitionism: Garrison and His Critics on Strategy and Tactics.* New York: Random House, 1967.

Kraut, Alan. "The Liberty Men of New York: Political Abolitionism in New York State, 1840–1848." Ph.D. diss., Cornell University, 1975.

———. "Partisanship and Principles: The Liberty Party in Antebellum Political Culture." In *Crusaders and Compromisers: Essays on the Relationship of the Antislavery Struggle to the Antebellum Party System*, edited by Alan Kraut, 45-70. Westport, Ct.: Greenwood, 1983.

Lampe, Gregory P. *Frederick Douglass: Freedom's Voice, 1818–1845.* East Lansing: Michigan State University Press, 1998.

Levine, Robert S. *Martin Delany, Frederick Douglass, and the Politics of Representative Identity.* Chapel Hill: University of North Carolina Press, 1997.

Litwack, Leon. *North of Slavery: The Negro in the Free States, 1790–1860.* Chicago: University of Chicago Press, 1960.

Mabee, Carlton. *Black Freedom: The Nonviolent Abolitionists from 1830 through the Civil War.* London: Macmillan, 1970.

Matlack, Lucius C. *History of American Slavery and Methodism, from 1810 to 1849, and History of the Wesleyan Connection of America.* New York: Privately printed, 1849.

Matthews, Donald G. "The Abolitionists on Slavery: The Critique Behind the Social Movement." *Journal of Southern History* 33 (May 1967): 163-82.

Mayer, Henry. *All on Fire: William Lloyd Garrison and the Abolition of Slavery.* New York: St. Martin's Griffin, 1998.

McFeely, William S. *Frederick Douglass.* New York: Simon and Schuster, 1991.

McKivigan, John R. "The Frederick Douglass–Gerrit Smith Friendship and Political Abolitionism in the 1850s." In *Frederick Douglass: New Literary and Historical Essays*, edited by Eric Sundquist, 205-32. New York: Cambridge University Press, 1996.

———. "The Gospel Will Burst the Bonds of the Slave: The Abolitionist Bible for Slaves Campaign." *Negro History Bulletin* 45 (July–Sept. 1982): 62-64, 77.

————. "James Redpath, John Brown, and the Abolitionist Advocacy of Slave Insurrection." *Civil War History* 34 (Dec. 1991): 293-313.

————. *The War against Proslavery Religion: Abolition and the Northern Churches, 1830–1865.* Ithaca, N.Y.: Cornell University Press, 1984.

McPherson, James M. "Who Freed the Slaves." *Proceedings of the American Philosophical Society* 139 (Mar. 1995): 1-10.

Melish, Joanne Pope. *Disowning Slavery: Gradual Emancipation and "Race" in New England, 1780–1860.* Ithaca, N.Y.: Cornell University Press, 1998.

Mendelshon, Jack. *Channing, the Reluctant Radical: A Biography.* Boston: Little, Brown, 1971.

Merrill, Walter. *Against Wind and Tide: A Biography of William Lloyd Garrison.* Cambridge, Ma.: Harvard University Press, 1963.

Miller, Floyd J. *The Search for Black Nationality: Black Colonization and Emigration, 1778–1863.* Urbana: University of Illinois Press, 1975.

Mullin, Gerald W. *Flight and Rebellion: Slave Resistance in Eighteenth-Century Virginia.* New York: Oxford University Press, 1972.

Newman, Richard. *The Transformation of American Abolitionism: Fighting Slavery in the Early Republic.* Chapel Hill: University of North Carolina Press, 2002.

Nicholson, Roy S. *Wesleyan Methodism in the South.* Syracuse, N.Y.: Wesleyan Methodist Publishing, 1933.

Oates, Stephen B. *To Purge this Land with Blood: A Biography of John Brown.* 2nd ed. Amherst: University of Massachusetts Press, 1948.

Ofari, Earl. *"Let Your Motto Be Resistance": The Life and Thought of Henry Highland Garnet.* Boston: Beacon, 1972.

Pasternak, Martin B. *Rise Now and Fly to Arms: The Life of Henry Highland Garnet.* New York: Garland, 1995.

Pease, Jane H., and William H. Pease. *Bound with Them in Chains: A Biographical History of the Antislavery Movement.* Westport, Ct.: Greenwood, 1972.

————. "Negro Conventions and the Problem of Black Leadership." *Journal of Black Studies* 2 (Sept. 1971): 29-44

————. *They Who Would Be Free: Blacks' Search for Freedom, 1830–1861.* New York: Athenaeum, 1974.

Perkal, M. Leon. "William Goodell: A Life in Reform." Ph.D. diss., City University of New York, 1972.

Perry, Lewis. *Radical Abolitionism: Anarchy and the Government of God in Antislavery Thought.* 2nd ed. Knoxville: University of Tennessee Press, 1995.

Pessen, Edward. *Riches, Class, and Power before the Civil War.* Lexington, Ma.: Heath, 1973.

Quarles, Benjamin. *Black Abolitionists.* New York: Oxford University Press, 1969.

Rael, Patrick. *Black Identity and Black Protest in the Antebellum North.* Chapel Hill: University of North Carolina Press, 2002.

Rice, Arthur R. "Henry B. Stanton as a Political Abolitionist." Ed.D. dissertation, Columbia University, 1968.

Richards, Leonard L. *"Gentlemen of Property and Standing": Anti-Abolitionist Mobs in Jacksonian America.* New York: Oxford University Press, 1970.

———. *The Slave Power: The Free North and Southern Domination, 1780–1860.* Baton Rouge: Louisiana State University Press, 2000.

Rodgers, Daniel T. "Republicanism: The Career of a Concept." *Journal of American History* 79 (June 1992): 11-38

Roediger, David R. *The Wages of Whiteness: Race and the Making of the American Working Class.* New York: Verso, 1973.

Sale, Maggie Montesinos. *The Slumbering Volcano: American Slave Ship Revolts and the Production of Rebellious Masculinity.* Durham, N.C.: Duke University Press, 1997.

Schor, Joel. *Henry Highland Garnet: A Voice of Black Radicalism in the Nineteenth Century.* Westport, Ct.: Greenwood, 1977.

Schwartz, Philip J. *Migrants against Slavery: Virginia and the Nation.* Charlottesville: University Press of Virginia, 2001.

Sears, Richard. *Kentucky Abolitionists in the Midst of Slavery, 1854–1864: Exiles for Freedom.* Lewiston, N.Y.: Mellon, 1993.

Sellers, Charles. *The Market Revolution: Jacksonian America, 1815–1846.* New York: Oxford University Press, 1991.

Sernett, Milton C. *Abolition's Axe: Beriah Green, Oneida Institute, and the Black Freedom Struggle.* Syracuse, N.Y.: Syracuse University Press, 1986.

———. *North Star Country: Upstate New York in the Crusade for African American Freedom.* Syracuse, N.Y.: Syracuse University Press, 2002.

Seward, Frederick W. *William Henry Seward, 1801–1872.* 3 vols. New York: Derby and Miller, 1891.

————. *William H. Seward: An Autobiography from 1801 to 1834 with a Memoir of His Life and Selections from His Letters from 1831 to 1846.* New York: D. Appleton, 1877.

Sewell, Richard H. *Ballots for Freedom: Antislavery Politics in the United States, 1837–1860.* New York: Oxford University Press, 1976.

Shallope, Robert E. "Toward a Republican Synthesis: The Emergence of an Understanding of Republicanism in American History." *William and Mary Quarterly* 29 (Jan. 1972): 49–80.

Shiffrin, Steven H. "The Rhetoric of Black Violence in the Antebellum Period: Henry Highland Garnet." *Journal of Black Studies* 2 (Sept. 1971): 45–56.

Slaughter, Thomas. *Bloody Dawn: The Christiana Riot and Racial Violence in the Antebellum North.* New York: Oxford University Press, 1991.

Smith, Kimberly K. *The Dominion of Voice: Riot, Reason, and Romance in Antebellum Politics.* Lawrence: University Press of Kansas, 1999.

Soderlund, Jean R. *Quakers and Slavery: A Divided Spirit.* Princeton, N.J.: Princeton University Press, 1985.

Sorin, Gerald. *New York Abolitionists: A Case Study of Political Radicalism.* Westport, Ct.: Greenwood, 1971.

Stanton, William Ragan. *The Leopard's Spots: Scientific Attitudes toward Race in America, 1815–59.* Chicago: University of Chicago Press, 1960.

Staudenraus, Philip J. *The African Colonization Movement.* New York: Columbia University Press, 1961.

Stauffer, John. *The Black Hearts of Men: Radical Abolitionists and the Transformation of Race.* Cambridge, Ma.: Harvard University Press, 2002.

Stewart, James Brewer. "The Aims and Impact of Garrisonian Abolitionism, 1840-1860." *Civil War History* 15 (Sept. 1969): 197-209.

————. *Holy Warriors: The Abolitionists and American Slavery.* 2nd ed. New York: Hill and Wang, 1997.

————. "Peaceful Hopes and Violent Experiences: The Origins of Radial and Reforming Abolitionism, 1831–1837." *Civil War History* 17 (Dec. 1971): 294-99.

————. *Wendell Phillips: Liberty's Hero.* Baton Rouge: Louisiana State University Press, 1986.

————. *William Lloyd Garrison and the Challenge of Emancipation.* Arlington Heights: Harlan Davidson, 1992.

Strong, Douglas M. *Perfectionist Politics: Abolitionism and the Religious Tensions of American Democracy.* Syracuse, N.Y.: Syracuse University Press, 1999.

Stuckey, Sterling. "A Last Stern Struggle: Henry Highland Garnet and Liberation Theory." In *Black Leaders of the Nineteenth Century*, edited by Leon Litwack and August Meier, 129-48. Urbana: University of Illinois Press, 1988.

Swift, David E. *Black Prophets of Justice: Activist Clergy before the Civil War.* Baton Rouge: Louisiana State University Press, 1989.

Takaki, Ronald. "The Black Child-Savage in Antebellum America." In *The Great Fear: Race in the Mind of America*, edited by Gary B. Nash and Richard Weiss, 27-44. New York: Rienhart and Winston, 1970.

Thomas, John L. *The Liberator, William Lloyd Garrison: A Biography.* Boston: Little, Brown, 1963.

Thompson, Priscilla. "Harriet Tubman, Thomas Garrett, and the Underground Railroad." *Delaware History* 22 (Sept. 1986): 1-21.

Volpe, Vernon L. *Forlorn Hope of Freedom: The Liberty Party in the Old Northwest, 1838–1848.* Kent, Ohio: Kent State University Press, 1990.

Walters, Ronald G. *The Antislavery Appeal: American Abolitionism after 1830.* Baltimore: Johns Hopkins University Press, 1976.

Ward, William E. "Charles Lenox Remond: Black Abolitionist, 1838–1873." Ph.D. diss., Clark University, 1977.

Wellman, Judith. *Grassroots Reform in the Burned-Over District of Upstate New York.* New York: Garland, 2000.

————. "James Watkins Seward: Common Criminal or Hero of the Freedom Trail?" Paper presented at the annual meeting of the Organization of American Historians/National Council of Public History, Washington, D.C., April 2002.

Whitman, Torrey Stephen. "Slavery, Manumission, and Free Black Workers in Early National Baltimore." Ph.D. diss., Johns Hopkins University, 1993.

Wiecek, William M. *The Sources of Antislavery Constitutionalism in America, 1760–1848.* Ithaca, N.Y.: Cornell University Press, 1977.

Wilenz, Sean. *Chants Democratic: New York City and the Rise of the American Working Class, 1788–1850.* New York: Oxford University Press, 1984.

Williams, Lillian Serece. *Strangers in the Land of Paradise: The Creation of an African American Community, Buffalo, New York, 1900–1940.* Bloomington: Indiana University Press, 1999.

Wilson, Henry. *History of the Rise and Fall of the Slave Power in America.* 3 vols. Boston: J. R. Osgood, 1872–77.

Work, Monroe N. "Life of Charles B. Ray." *Journal of Negro History* 4 (Oct. 1919): 361-71.

Wyatt-Brown, Bertram. "The Abolitionists' Postal Campaign of 1835." *Journal of Negro History* 50 (Oct. 1965): 227-38.

———. *Lewis Tappan and the Evangelical War against Slavery.* Cleveland: Case-Western Reserve University Press, 1969.

Yacovone, Donald. *Samuel Joseph May and the Dilemmas of the Liberal Persuasion, 1797–1871.* Philadelphia: Temple University Press, 1991.

Yarborough, Richard. "Race, Violence, and Manhood: The Masculine Ideal in Frederick Douglass's 'The Heroic Slave.'" In *Frederick Douglass: New Literary and Historical Essays,* edited by Eric Sundquist, 166-88. New York: Cambridge University Press, 1996.

Young, R. J. *Antebellum Black Activists: Race, Gender, Self.* New York: Garland, 1996.

INDEX

DATE DUE